Anti-Racism — An Assault on Education and Value

Anti-Racism — An Assault on Education and Value

Edited by
Frank Palmer

The Sherwood Press

All rights reserved. No part of this publication may be reproduced or transmitted in any form or by any means, including photocopying and recording, without the written permission of the copyright holder, application for which should be addressed to the Publishers. Such written permission must also be obtained before any part of this publication is stored in a retrieval system of any nature.

First published 1986

© The Sherwood Press Ltd 1986

The Sherwood Press Ltd, 88 Tylney Road, London E7 0LY

ISBN 0 907671 26 8

Printed and bound by Redwood Burn,
Trowbridge, Wiltshire

Contents

Notes on the Contributors   vii
Editor's Acknowledgements   xiii
Introduction   *Frank Palmer*   1

SECTION 1   EDUCATION OR REVOLUTION?

1. Clarifying the Concepts   *Anthony Flew*   15
2. 'Anti-Racism'—Revolution not Education   *John Marks*   32
3. Anti-Racist Rhetoric   *Ray Honeyford*   43

SECTION 2   THE MATERIALS OF PROPAGANDA

4. History, Race and Propaganda   *Tom Hastie*   61
5. From 'Auschwitz—Yesterday's Racism' to GCHQ   *Caroline Cox*   74
6. Racial Mischief: The Case of Dr Sivanandan   *David Dale*   82

SECTION 3   FREEDOM, LANGUAGE AND CENSORSHIP

7. Language, Race and Colour   *Linda Hall*   97
8. Reading and Discrimination: 'Anti-Racism' in English Studies   *A. C. Capey*   106
9. Here be Witches! 'Anti-Racism' and the Making of a New Inquisition   *David J. Levy*   117

SECTION 4 CULTURE AND VALUE

10 The Myth of Cultural Relativism *Roger Scruton* 127
11 Swann and the Spirit of the Age *Simon Pearce* 136
12 Moral Understanding and the Ethics of Indignation
    Frank Palmer 149
13 Pentecostalists and the 'Black Movement'
    Roy Kerridge 169
14 Preference and Prejudice:
    The Mythology of British Racism *Dennis J. O'Keeffe* 185

Index 197

Notes on the Contributors

Arthur C. Capey taught for nine years in independent schools, for nine in Colleges of Education and the University of Sheffield, and for nine as principal lecturer in English at Elizabeth Gaskell College, Manchester. He is now retired. He wrote the chapter on post-war English fiction in *Literature and Environment* (edited by Fred Inglis, Chatto and Windus, 1971), and 'The Language of Enlightenment' in *The Black Rainbow* (edited by Peter Abbs, Heinemann, 1975); and he assisted Frank Whitehead in the preparation of the Schools Council report on children's reading habits *Children and their Books* (Macmillan, 1977). He has also contributed to *The Gadfly*, *Universities Quarterly*, *The Use of English* and other periodicals.

Caroline Cox was formerly Director of the Nursing Education Research Unit, Chelsea College, University of London and Head of the Sociology Department at the Polytechnic of North London. She qualified as a nurse at the London Hospital and later studied part-time at the Central London Polytechnic, gaining a BSc (Sociology) and an MSc (Economics) from London University. She has been co-director of a DES research project in higher education and has been a tutor with the Open University. Her publications include *People in Polytechnics* (SRHE, 1976) (Co-author), *A Sociology of Medical Practice* (Collier-Macmillan, 1975) (co-editor) and *A Guide to Sociology for Nurses, Midwives and Health Visitors* (Butterworths, 1983). She is co-author, with John Marks, of numerous publications on education, including *Student Representation in Polytechnics* (Universities Quarterly, Spring 1975); *Real Concern* (Centre for

Policy Studies, 1980); with Keith Jacka, *Rape of Reason—the Corruption of the Polytechnic of North London* (Churchill Press, 1976), and *Marxism, Knowledge and the Academies* (in Black Paper, 1977, Temple Smith); *Education and Freedom—the Roots of Diversity* (NCES, 1980) and *Standards in English Schools* (NCES, 1983). They are also co-editors of *The Right to Learn—Purpose, Professionalism and Accountability in State Education* (Centre for Policy Studies, 1982). She was created a Life Peer in 1982. She has three children, all of whom attended a comprehensive school.

David Dale is a social worker with Westminster City Council and has worked in several inner-city areas, including Brixton and Notting Hill Gate. He gained his BSc in Social Sciences at Middlesex Polytechnic in 1982 and has just completed post-graduate studies at the London School of Economics. He has published articles in *The Times Educational Supplement, The Times Higher Education Supplement, The Salisbury Review* and various social work journals. He will shortly be publishing work on trans-racial adoption.

Antony Flew is Emeritus Professor of Philosophy, University of Reading and, currently, Distinguished Research Fellow, Social Philosophy and Policy Center, Bowling Green, Ohio. Also Founder-member of the Council of the Freedom Association and of the Education Group of the Centre for Policy Studies and Vice-President of the Rationalist Press Association. His books include *Hume's Philosophy of Belief, An Introduction to Western Philosophy, Crime or Disease?, A Rational Animal, Sociology, Equality and Education, The Politics of Procrustes, Darwinian Evolution* and *Thinking about Social Thinking*.

Linda Hall went to one of the first co-educational comprehensive schools in London. From there she went on to London University, where she gained her BA and a PhD in English Language and Literature. She has taught in schools both in Britain and in France and in both comprehensive and grammar schools. She is at present a Senior Lecturer in English at Bulmershe College of Higher Education. She has long been, on and off, an active member of the Labour Party and was secretary of the Labour Club during her undergraduate years at King's College. She is a Labour nominee on the board of governors of two local schools. She has had articles on educational matters published in *The Times Educational Supplement, Junior Education*, the *Daily Telegraph, The Times Higher Education Supplement* and *Women's Studies International Forum*. She is married to Tom Hastie.

Tom Hastie left his native Dundee in 1938 to enter the Civil Service in London. During the war he was an RAF sergeant and after a course of teacher training at Wandsworth Emergency Training College he joined ILEA in 1950. He taught for five years in a primary school in Walworth, South London, before moving to Dunraven Comprehensive School, where he became Head of History. In 1970 he was appointed the founder-Warden of the ILEA's History and Social Sciences Teachers' Centre, taking early retirement in 1980. During his career he was a scheduled speaker at several teachers' conferences, was honorary secretary of the London Teachers' Association for eight years and has been a frequent contributor to *The Times Educational Supplement* and the national press. He is a long-standing member of the Labour Party and is married to Linda Hall.

Ray Honeyford completed his teacher training with three distinctions and a commendation. Later, he took a Master's degree after research into the spoken language of teachers and working-class parents. He is also an MA in educational psychology, and a member of the British Psychological Society. He is a Fellow of the College of Preceptors. He has worked for many years in inner-city secondary modern and comprehensive schools, and, for the past six years, has been head of a multi-racial school in Bradford. He was for four years a part-time tutor in educational psychology with the Open University. He has published articles in the following journals: *The Teacher, The British Journal of Communication Disorders, The Use of English, The Times Educational Supplement,* the *Guardian, The Times, The Salisbury Review*, and is the author of *Starting Teaching* (Croom Helm). Ray Honeyford was recently compelled to leave his position as headmaster of Drummond Middle School, Bradford, as a result of pressures of the kind described in this book.

Roy Kerridge is a journalist. His publications include three novels published by Brymill Press: *Beside the Seaside, The Store's Outing* and *Druid's Madonna*. His non-fiction books are *Real Wicked Guy* (Blackwell, 1983), his autobiography *The Lone Conformist* (Chatto and Windus, 1984) and his latest book, *Bizarre Britain* (Blackwell, 1985). He has also written articles for *The Spectator, Daily Telegraph, The Mail On Sunday, The Sun, The Salisbury Review, New Agenda, Country Music, English Dance and Song, Prag, Musical Traditions* and *The Free Nation*.

David J. Levy is a senior lecturer in sociology at Middlesex Polytechnic. He was educated at Stowe School, Christchurch College, Oxford, and the London School of Economics. He has published widely in journals in the UK, in the United States, in France and in West Germany. He is the author of *Realism: an Essay in Interpretation and Social Reality* (1981), *Political Order: an Essay in Philosophical Anthropology* (forthcoming: Louisiana State University Press, 1987). He is currently writing a book entitled *Hermeneutics and the Restoration of Social Theory*.

John Marks is a Senior Lecturer in the School of Applied Physics at the Polytechnic of North London and is currently responsible for a course 'Science and the Making of the Modern World' taken by all science students at the Polytechnic. He took a BA (Natural Science), a Post-graduate Certificate in Education at Cambridge University and a PhD (Nuclear Physics) at London University. He has taught at a direct grant School and has been a university lecturer at London University and in Sweden. He has also been a tutor with the Open University since its inception. His publications include *Relativity* (Geoffrey Chapman, 1972) and *Science and the Making of the Modern World* (Heinemann Educational, 1983). He is also co-author, with Caroline Cox, of numerous publications on education (see note on Caroline Cox). He has three children, two of whom are currently attending a comprehensive school of which he is an elected parent-governor.

Dennis J. O'Keeffe is a Senior Lecturer in the Sociology of Education at the Polytechnic of North London and a member of the Advisory Council of the Social Affairs Unit. He taught English for six years in secondary modern schools, was Head of Economics at Ealing Grammar School from 1967 to 1973 and has taught part-time at the London University Institute of Education for many years. He has published widely in the social sciences, politics and education. *The Sociology of Human Capital* is in press with Routledge and Kegan Paul and he is the editor of *The Wayward Curriculum*, which was published by the Social Affairs Unit in 1986.

Frank Palmer completed his teacher training in 1967 with distinctions in the theory and practice of Education and began his career as a teacher of English in a secondary modern school in Northampton. In 1969 he moved to a comprehensive school in Hounslow as a teacher of English with special responsibility for Philosophy in 6th Form General Studies. He later studied for a BA in Philosophy at Birkbeck College, London University, and graduated in 1974 with First Class Honours. Having undertaken full-time post-graduate research at King's College London, and, having worked for a time as a temporary part-time tutor in Philosophy at the Polytechnic of North London, he re-entered teaching in 1978 to teach English in comprehensive schools in Hounslow. In 1984 he resigned his post of Deputy Head of English and Librarian in a Hillingdon comprehensive school and now writes full-time. He has published articles in The *Times Educational Supplement, The Use of English* and *The Salisbury Review* and is a contributor to *The Wayward Curriculum* edited by Dennis O'Keeffe (The Social Affairs Unit, 1986). He is a member of the Royal Institute of Philosophy.

Simon Pearce is Deputy Chairman of the Conservative Monday Club's Immigration and Race Relations Committee and author of its paper *Education and the Multi-Racial Society* (1985). He was educated at multi-racial schools in East London and at York University. He now works in local government.

Roger Scruton is Professor of Aesthetics at Birkbeck College, London, and editor of *The Salisbury Review*. He has published widely in philosophy, criticism and political theory, and his books include: *Art and Imagination* (1974), *The Aesthetics of Architecture* (1979), *The Meaning of Conservatism* (1980), *A Dictionary of Political Thought* (1982), *A Short History of Modern Philosophy*

From Descartes To Wittgenstein (1984) and *Sexual Desire* (1986). He is also co-author (with Caroline Cox) of *Peace Studies: A Critical Survey* (1984), co-author (with Angela Ellis-Jones and Dennis O'Keeffe) of *Education and Indoctrination: An Attempt at Definition and a Review of Social and Political Implications* (1985), and author of *World Studies: Education or Indoctrination?* (1986).

Editor's Acknowledgements

I should like to express my gratitude to, among others, John Marks for his advice and help with the compiling of this volume and to Joanna North for her help with typing and for other kinds of practical assistance. I am also greatly indebted to Roger Scruton in a number of ways. Not only was the idea for this book his own, but he has been, and remains, a source of inspiration and support.

Introduction

Frank Palmer

'Power is in tearing human minds to pieces and putting them together again in new shapes of your own choosing' (George Orwell, *Nineteen Eighty-Four*).

No reasonable or decent person could condone racial discrimination or racial victimisation. Yet the word 'racism'—now so often indiscriminately invoked—has acquired such power to mesmerise the intellect and to animate the sentiments that calm discussion of the complex issues connoted by it is now almost impossible. Even the *wish* to be calm may be taken as symptomatic of the 'racism' that needs to be 'torn out by the roots'. As a result of political agitation in the late 1960s and in the 1970s more and more LEAs and local government departments are allowing themselves to be dominated by a doctrine which is mandatory—or, to use a more modish expression, 'non-negotiable'. The premises of this doctrine cannot be questioned but must be reinforced through 'Racism Awareness' courses administered to teachers and, in some LEAs, to administrative and ancillary workers. Reading, Newcastle, Coventry, Birmingham, ILEA, Brent and Bradford are only a few of the LEAs in which such courses now operate.

'Racism-awareness', of course, implies that there must exist widespread racism to be aware *of.* Not the kind of 'racism' we could detect for ourselves but that which is 'hidden' from all but the enlightened or re-educated eye. As the anti-racist/multiculturalist advocate Jon Nixon puts it: we must 'deconstruct the obvious'.[1] What, of course, is *not* 'obvious' is that Britain is a deeply racist society which is riddled with 'unintentional', 'unconscious' or 'institutionalised' racism. Yet the presumption that we do live in a racist society lies at the heart of 'anti-racist' programmes for education—the purpose of which consists in changing the nature (or the 'structures') of society and the attitudes of its citizens. Schools, in short, are to become agents of social change. And, presumably, our perception that this might be unwise, educationally short-sighted or even immoral is one of the many perceptions to be 'deconstructed'.

With the publication of the Swann Report in March 1985 it is likely that the unquestioning acceptance of the premises upon which 'anti-racism' is based will become a criterion not only of a teacher's fitness to teach but of the successful completion of teacher training. The implications of this for education and for the nature of life in British society are far-reaching and profoundly disturbing. The content of school subjects, I believe, will become more and more politicised, less and less educational, more and more judged by the criteria of 'relevance'. At the extreme, schools could be transformed from centres of learning into instruments of political revolution—ideological power-stations calculated to promote a cynical, if not openly hostile, outlook on British society and all major British institutions, including the forces of law and order. Such an outlook, thriving upon a failure to distinguish education from indoctrination, could easily encourage civil strife and racial discord. While this consequence may not be unwelcome to those activists who seek a charter for revolution in the guise of 'anti-racism', it is unlikely that 'anti-racist' doctrines would enjoy their fashionable pre-eminence if the nest of fallacies, contentious propositions and misguided sentiments from which they spring were more widely understood.

Perhaps no-one is more dangerous to the enterprise of peaceful accommodation than the person who says 'he who is not with us is against us!', and who proceeds thereupon to divide humanity into two exclusive groups of friend and enemy. This moral tendency—which has on several occasions during our century built itself into dangerous mass movements—is a threat to tolerance, to free opinion and to the democratic process. And it is surely no exaggeration to find it once again displayed in the language of those who divide the world into exclusive camps of 'racist' and 'anti-racist' and who—in their more extreme moments—describe all members of the first camp as 'white' and all members of the second as 'black'. To say the least, it can hardly be the effect of such language to generate harmonious relations between the races. We should be better served by distinguishing 'racist' from 'non-racist' and by recognising the many shades of attitude and opinion that might be covered by that second label. The writers in this book are non-racists: they neither share nor condone the view that people of some other race are for that reason inferior. Indeed, it is in the nature of their non-racist outlook that they find themselves opposed to the divisive intolerance of the anti-racists.

It is, then, not a contention of this book that 'racism' is excusable. Nor is it a contention that all those who take themselves to be opposed to 'racism' are involved in a political conspiracy. What is suggested is that teachers, trainee teachers, parents and citizens of this country have the right to question the intellectual, moral and educational status of 'anti-racist' policies, and the right to expect rational answers rather than slogans, catch-phrases and personal vilification. If education is centrally concerned with the acquisition of knowledge and the opening of the mind, it can hardly be facilitated by training programmes which proscribe free thought and intellectual enquiry. In February 1985 an ILEA school governor revealed that candidates for first appointments or for promotion were, during interview, virtually obliged to 'mouth the accepted platitudes [about "multiculturalism" and mixed-ability teaching] as if they were the Nicene Creed'.[2] The writer, who likened this intellectual ethos to the dogmatism of the medieval church, went on to demonstrate that a further requirement of interviewees was a willingness on their part to underplay the value of academic as opposed to 'social' development—an outlook I have also discovered from working as a teacher in Greater London. Even more disturbing, evidence has come to light that in the summer of 1985 a headteacher of an Inner London comprehensive school received, from an ILEA inspector, a report on a prospective candidate for a Scale 1 post which gave no real information about his academic qualifications, his enthusiasm for his main subject, his capacity to relate to classes or to individual children, his thoroughness of preparation and so on, but effectively confined itself to the comment that he was sound on ILEA's anti-sexist/racist strategies.[3] It would not be unreasonable to infer from this that the inspector considered allegiance to 'anti-sexism/racism' to be more important than the other qualifications a teacher should have, and—even more disturbing—that reservations about such policies amount to *dis*qualification.

Any reader not yet disturbed by this evidence should consider a third example. Writing in the *Times Educational Supplement* on 6

December 1985 Anne Sofer revealed that candidates being interviewed in a left-wing authority need, as a survival technique, a willingness to avoid the male pronoun and a willingness to parrot the received wisdom of 'racism-awareness'. She went as far as saying that allegiance to the 'multicultural'/'anti-racist' curriculum is not enough: the term 'anti-racist' should precede 'multicultural'. Moreover, so powerful is the idol of egalitarianism that candidates must never use the word 'gifted' to describe pupils of exceptional ability, since in such authorities the very idea that some pupils stride nearer to excellence than others is 'unacceptably elitist'. Since Ms Sofer has sat in on a large number of appointment panels, and since she is the SDP member of the GLC/ILEA for St Pancras North, her testimony can neither be dismissed on the grounds of inexperience nor on the grounds that it is 'right-wing-inspired'. Indeed, if the *TES* is to be believed (and nobody could accuse the *TES* of a 'right-wing' bias) the situation is far worse than Ms Sofer indicated, and 'anti-racism' is at the forefront of a campaign to take possession of our schools in the name of a political movement.[4]

It places an intolerable restriction on teachers if they are not considered sufficiently professional to state, or even *hold*, reasoned opinions on educational policies—let alone policies which are highly contentious. Also it would be foolish to conclude from the paucity of opposition that the majority of teachers are in agreement with, or have no reservations about, 'anti-racist' proposals. Tendentious accusations of being 'negative' and 'inflexible' are enough to deter nearly any teacher from questioning the educational validity of school or borough policies. Such scepticism is reserved for the heroic or the foolhardy. It is not without significance that one of the intended contributors to this volume—Mr Jonathan Savery, a teacher in the county of Avon—has felt it necessary to withdraw in the light of pressure brought to bear upon him for publishing an article which questioned the methods of 'anti-racism'. It has been reported that the calls to have Mr Savery dismissed have come from a group of people who work at Bristol's Horfield Multi-Cultural Centre. A Mr Charanjit Singh is reported as saying: 'They should simply read the article and sack him.'[5] What is, of course, conspicuously absent from this demand is the phrase 'decide whether to ...'. A number of contributors to this book have been approached by HMIs and LEA advisors who share our deep concern about the educational soundness of 'anti-racist' education but fear the consequences of saying so in public. As one headteacher has remarked: 'The race lobby is now so powerful that decent people cannot voice decent thoughts.'[6]

The contributors to this volume are drawn from different political persuasions, different academic specialisms and different walks of life. However, they have shared concern for intellectual honesty and, to use Tom Hastie's words, 'for a sound and balanced education for *all* our children, both black and white'. Such concerns are not to be promoted by shallow and confused thinking, nor by highly presumptuous and racially inflammatory pronouncements on the 'white psyche'. The object of Section 1, *Education or Revolution? Defining the Terms*, is to examine the way that words such as 'racist' and 'black' are used in various policy documents and in 'anti-racist' discourse. A common theme emerging from this section is that such words are frequently misused and subject to misleading equivocations. As a result, the old meaning of the word 'racism' which lay behind the spirit of the 1976 Race Relations Act has given way to a new, politicised meaning which, if uncritically received, licenses racist practices such as 'positive discrimination' and misleadingly encourages the view that human relationships have, as their background, an inevitable polarisation between black and white. Antony Flew's essay, 'Clarifying the Concepts', examines the confusions and linguistic sleights of hand in ILEA and Berkshire documents and identifies the following undefended—perhaps indefensible—presuppositions common to their arguments:

(1) That individuals are inert, infinitely plastic and moulded by (hypostatised) 'institutions'.
(2) That equality of opportunity is to be equated with equality of outcome.
(3) That no culture can be superior or inferior to any other *in any respect*.

Professor Flew's arguments are further supported by John Marks's essay, ' "Anti-racism"—Revolution Not Education', which argues that questions of race and ethnic difference need to be approached with caution and sensitivity. Vague and equivocal definitions of 'racism' are responsible for fudging the issues in such a way that an honest concern for empirical evidence in investigating the factors involved in educational or socio-economic achievement is circumvented by crude, single-cause explanations. Dr Marks concludes that the concept of 'institutionalised racism' is thus little more than a weapon for attacking British society and for producing political agitation. Its object is both anti-educational and conducive to the heightening of racial tensions (as can be seen, indeed, in the inflammatory writings of Professor Chris Mullard).

'Anti-racist Rhetoric', by Ray Honeyford, considers three key words from the basic vocabulary of the race relations industry: 'access', 'black' and 'racism'. 'Access', Mr Honeyford argues, is a misleading metaphor, wedded to the solecism known as 'social justice'; misleading because it suggests that the 'under-performance' of any ethnic group can be automatically attributed to a *denial* of 'access'. When the term 'black' is used to cover all non-whites not only does this suggest that all minority groups are equally worse off but also collapses important distinctions between different cultural backgrounds. Used in such a programme, the word 'racist' is little more than a sophistical device, a mechanism for instilling irrational and unproductive guilt into the white majority—and is therefore not conducive to harmonious race relations.

Twenty years ago any attempt to politicise the content of school subjects would neither have gone unnoticed nor unchecked. There was some measure of agreement that education is an end in itself and one of the greatest goods. This view of education is now often regarded as a form of mystical incantation. The term 'relevance' acts as a password. Upon its more radical utterance the canons of scholarship are thrown to the winds and more 'useful' materials are ushered in: materials which sometimes encourage, or even insist upon, politically 'loaded' ways of perceiving the world. The teaching of English often lends itself to such exploitation. One might have thought that it is more difficult to get away with bias in the teaching of history, but the second section, *The Materials of Propaganda*, is a salutary reminder that, in the hands of the most committed, 'anti-racism' is considered so important a cause that a concern for truth and evidence, where inconvenient, must take second place. 'History, Race and Propaganda', by Tom Hastie, is a thorough examination of a booklet (of anonymous authorship) published by the Institute of Race Relations and entitled *How Racism Came to Britain*. This booklet, printed in cartoon format and widely available for schools, is, in its presentation of half-truths and, at times, serious distortions of

British history, not only an assault upon the techniques being developed in history teaching to make pupils aware of the risk of bias but is racially hostile in its stereotyping of British whites. It is worth adding that Ronald Butt, in commenting on the same booklet, has pointed out that those who take the law into their own hands 'in the light of police indifference' are praised and that 'this torrent of hate and provocation ends with an invitation: "It's your move next, what's it to be?". . .'.[7]

The same booklet is also briefly examined by Caroline Cox, in her essay 'From "Auschwitz—Yesterday's Racism" to GCHQ'. The main body of her essay, however, is devoted to a critical examination of a teaching pack on 'Auschwitz' produced by the Learning Resources Branch of ILEA. An examination of these and other materials available suggests that the effect of such propaganda may be to increase social tension between groups. David Dale's 'Racial Mischief: The Case of Doctor Sivanandan' is a critique of the views of the Director of the Institute of Race Relations under whose auspices *How Racism Came to Britain* was produced, and an examination of two other pamphlets from the same source, issued specifically for schools and urging teachers and pupils to question the basic assumptions and values of Britain. Given the evidence David Dale provides it is not difficult to interpret what 'question' means here, and what 'answers' are to be encouraged. David Dale argues that Sivanandan's views, however well-intentioned, may in the long term prove detrimental to education in the UK.

The alternative face of propaganda is unwarranted or unjust censorship. Three types are discussed in Section 3, *Freedom, Language and Censorship*. The first concerns the attempt to persuade teachers and pupils that English-speaking white people cannot escape 'unconscious racism' because they speak a language which is itself racist—the evidence for this being that many uses of the word 'black' have 'negative' or 'unfortunate' connotations. 'Language, Race and Colour' by Linda Hall is an incisive rebuttal of the idea that such 'unfortunate connotations' have anything to do with black *people*. Dr Hall provides a thorough and scholarly investigation of the etymology of the 'offending' words. Again the voice of Orwell seems apposite: 'In the end we shall make thoughtcrime literally impossible, because there will be no words in which to express it.'

It is the same voice that warned: 'There will be no art, no literature, no science.' This brings me to the second type of censorship: relieving the library shelves of their 'racist material'—a practice already in process in London and other areas. This may look harmless enough to those who find themselves unable, or unwilling, to share Orwell's perspicacity. Harmless, that is, until it is realised that the criteria being used for deeming literature 'racist' are, to say the *very* least, dubious. For there seems to be no way of distinguishing what *is* racially offensive from what 'anti-racists' *find* offensive. Literary merit is no longer of concern; the criteria are undeniably political. Not only the innocuous works of Enid Blyton, but great works of literature by Jane Austen and even Shakespeare may be deemed suspect. The matter is now so out of hand that the Bishop of Stepney has recently spoken out against 'the throwing away of literature' (including *Alice in Wonderland*).[8] Given that the Chairwoman of the National Committee on Racism in Children's Books (who must be an avid reader) estimates that 95 per cent of these books in the UK contain racial bias,[9] so far, it seems, we have got off lightly. Arthur Capey's 'Reading and Discrimination: "Anti-Racism" in English Studies' presents a lucidly argued case that this form of censorship is ill-conceived and culturally debilitating. He argues that The Children's Rights Workshop—a body devoted to the expulsion of 'racist and sexist images' from children's books—has an inadequate grasp of the nature of literature and the nature of literary criticism, an argument he illustrates by contesting the bowdlerisation of *Huckleberry Finn*.

The final essay in this section, 'Here Be Witches! "Anti-Racism" and the Making of a New Inquisition' by David J. Levy, is concerned with an even more invidious attack on human freedom: the silencing of opposing voices by means of vilification—or, to use his own evocative phrase, by 'ritual condemnation'. The example given is that of the sociology section of the British Association for the Advancement of Science conference in August 1985, which devoted its energies to a personal attack on Ray Honeyford, Roger Scruton and others who have contested 'anti-racism' in *The Salisbury Review* and who were not invited to attend the conference in order to give a reply. David Levy's argument is that this kind of personal vendetta cannot be understood in isolation from a largely Marxist-inspired ideology that is less concerned with the promotion of racial harmony than with the promotion of the kind of social unrest upon which political revolution feeds. At the risk of overdoing Orwell, perhaps a brief reminder of the 'Two Minutes' Hate' is germane here.

The final section, *Culture and Value*, is an attempt to widen the debate by considering the cultural, moral and spiritual values that are threatened by 'anti-racism'. Roger Scruton's 'The Myth of Cultural Relativism' presents the argument that our society is not 'multicultural' in *all* respects; that any educational philosophy which does not recognise the need to facilitate the acceptance of children into a shared social order and a common culture is one which consigns them to a meaningless existence, cut off from their surroundings. The idea that cultures can be 'chosen' is absurd and *a fortiori* cannot be supported by the thesis of cultural relativism which, if true, vitiates the grounds upon which such a 'choice' could be made. Moreover, cultural relativism would require the truth of *moral* relativism—a thesis no-one accepts in his dealings with other persons. The conclusion is that teachers in Britain have a duty to transmit British culture, which is, in any case, not hostile or impervious to other cultures but 'open' and 'growing'.

This in itself provides grounds for questioning the proposals of the Swann Report, but Simon Pearce's 'Swann and the Spirit of the Age' goes further, maintaining that it is a manifestly unjust document, which systematically damages the rights of the indigenous population and is less concerned with education than with social engineering; it is 'anti-democratic' and 'incipiently totalitarian' and, far from being concerned with the promotion of tolerance, is more concerned with the removal of 'structures' in British society which permit disagreement with the Swann Committee's opinions. A particularly interesting dimension to Simon Pearce's argument is that the anti-establishment sentiments expressed in the Swann Report are best understood against the background of 'the spirit of the age' in which the fruits of relativism—uncertainty, moral scepticism, loss of spiritual values—have turned nihilism into a surrogate religion whose commandments must be obeyed.

'Moral Understanding and the Ethics of Indignation' is concerned with the status of 'anti-racism' as a *moral* argument. A frequent reply to criticism of 'anti-racist' excesses is that extremists should be ignored, but nevertheless education should 'do' something about 'racism' (in the non-politicised sense of the word). My response to this is that even if 'racism' is treated as a defect in human nature, 'anti-racism' entails an impoverished conception of morality and of the moral agent. The final section of my essay argues that 'anti-racist' education is misconceived and trades upon the further misconception that traditional education has no significant purchase upon moral development. Roy Kerridge's sparkling and informative essay, 'Pentecostalists and the "Black Movement" ', is a further example of the way that spiritual values not only have no part to play in 'anti-racism' but are undermined by it. He reveals the ways in which Marxist-inspired promulgations of 'Race-awareness' attempt to subvert devout West Indian churchgoers and create mischief in schools and social service departments. The final essay by Dennis O'Keeffe, 'Preference and Prejudice: The Mythology of British Racism', is a wide-ranging piece which places many other issues raised by this book in a broader perspective. His diagnosis of the spirit behind 'anti-racism' takes account of the decline of religious faith, and maintains that the gap has been filled with a quest for righteousness in the shape of indignation and intolerance—a form of neo-Marxism fired by despair and hatred. Even if Britain were deeply racist, he points out, it would not follow that the best way of dealing with it would be to extend the powers of the state. But, he argues, the view that Britain is deeply racist is sustained against a failure to distinguish preference from prejudice and against a propensity to exaggerate the amount of prejudice which actually exists. Other aspects of his essay deal with the inconsistencies in the 'anti-racists' ' position, not least the moral contradictions.

It would be grossly unfair not to acknowledge that a number of 'anti-racists' and advocates of 'multicultural education' are well-meaning. However, it is hoped that this book will raise questions that are long overdue, and promote open and honest discussions which hitherto may have been prevented by fear of public denunciations and disciplinary proceedings. Suppression of intellectual enquiry is not a healthy foundation for any educational policy, or for living in a society that wishes to remain a liberal democracy.

Notes

1. *A Teacher's Guide to Multicultural Education*, Blackwell, 1985, p.34.

2. 'The New Inquisition', *Times Educational Supplement*, 15 February 1985.
3. Although the story was reported in the *Daily Telegraph*, 3 October 1985, it was mistakenly stated that the candidate's main subject was mathematics. In fact it was a different subject.
4. See Hilary Wilce, 'The Ultra-Left Tightens Grip on Schools', a *TES* report, *Times Educational Supplement*, 10 January 1986, and the sober editorial in that issue.
5. *Daily Mail*, 26 November 1985. See also *The Guardian* (same date).
6. *Daily Telegraph*, 12 June 1984.
7. *The Times*, 25 July 1985.
8. *The Times*, 28 November 1985.
9. *Asian Herald*, 12 November 1984.

SECTION 1

Education or Revolution?
Defining the Terms

1

Clarifying the Concepts

Antony Flew

> I want to be a man on the same basis and level as any white citizen—I want to be as free as the whitest citizen. I want to exercise, and in full, the same rights as the white American. I want to be eligible for employment exclusively on the basis of my skills and employability, and for housing solely on my capacity to pay. I want to have the same privileges, the same treatment in public places as every other person (Dr Ralph Bunche, the first black American to serve as, among many other things, US permanent representative at the UN).

1

The Commission for Racial Equality (CRE), as it likes to tell us in its advertisements, 'was set up by the Race Relations Act 1976 with the duties of working towards the elimination of discrimination and promoting equality of opportunity and good relations between different racial groups generally'. These are indeed admirable objectives, which no person of goodwill could fail to share. Certainly, racism is an outrage; if but only if, that is, the word 'racism' is, as it should be, construed as meaning the advantaging or disadvantaging of individuals for no other or better reason than that they happen to be members of this racial group rather than that.

The purpose of that Act, like the purpose of all the 1964 Civil Rights legislation in the USA, was to answer a cry for justice, a cry such as that eloquently raised in our epigraph from Dr Ralph Bunche. This cry was, in the most straightforward and traditional understanding, an appeal for justice. It was an insistence that he, and, of course, all others, should as a matter of absolute right be accorded their own several and individual deserts and entitlements. In particular, he was demanding that he should be appointed, or not appointed, to any position for which he might choose to apply strictly and solely on the basis of his own individual merits, or lack of them; and to be neither disadvantaged in any such contests by negative discrimination against members of the racial group to which he happened to belong, nor advantaged by any positive discrimination in favour of that same racial group.[1]

It is also very much to the point to emphasise from the beginning that the equality which justice always demands is: not a substantial equality of outcome, either for individuals or for sets,[2] but rather a formal equality of treatment for all relevantly like cases. To say that this sort of equality is formal is not to say that it is empty, inessential or unimportant: quite the reverse. The point is that, to be rules at all, the rules of justice, like every other sort of rule, must be applied equally to all relevantly like cases. Another point—and this time very substantial indeed—is that there is nothing, or almost nothing, to which differences in skin colour are properly relevant. However it would be absurd to confuse this formal equality of treatment, which is indeed a first essential, with the imposition of an equality of outcome, which would in many cases be flatly incompatible with the most manifest mandates of justice. What, for instance, should we think of what called itself a system of criminal justice yet demanded that convicted criminals be treated in all respects like everybody else?

Racism, therefore, in this clear and only proper understanding, is manifestly evil, because manifestly unjust. However, although the implications of deliberate and undeniable wickedness continue to be intended, the term is nowadays frequently abused in order to demoralize and disarm opposition to policies and privileges which are themselves, in the sense explained in the previous paragraphs, racist. It was indeed wryly typical of the present condition of what we cannot but call the race relations industry, that the former Bradford headmaster, Ray Honeyford, was denounced as a racist for publishing an article in which he complained that (majority) Asian, unlike (minority) white parents, are being allowed to withdraw children from legally compulsory education for long periods.

When, therefore, Penguin Education commissioned a collection of essays on *Race, Culture and Intelligence*[3] one might—had one been unfamiliar with previous output under that particular imprint—have expected that the editors would indeed 'have attempted to step back from the debate itself and look at the concepts which underlie it'. But in fact the book is so far from containing the 'close examination of the key ideas' promised in its Foreword that no-one, from beginning to end, can spare a moment from execrating reactionaries and racists in order to spell out what it is to be a racist, and why it is wrong.

2

Suppose now that we turn to some more recent documents. The first is *Education for Equality* (EE). This was distributed to all teachers in LEA schools by the Advisory Committee for Multicultural Education, a sub-committee of Berkshire Education Committee, at that time Conservative-controlled. Although written by a newly appointed race relations official, and described by him in my wife's presence as 'a Marxist document', this and three successors issued in the name of the Director of Education were all, apparently, accepted without reservation. Four further documents were issued by the Inner London Education Authority (ILEA), all to all teachers in its employ. Whereas Berkshire was concerned explicitly with race alone, all four ILEA documents share the significantly extended title *Race, Sex and Class*. Their subtitles follow: (1) *Achievement in Schools* (AS); (2) *Multi-ethnic Education in Schools* (MEES); (3) *A Policy for Equality: Race*; and (4) *Anti-Racist Statement and Guidelines*. We are nowhere told either that or why (3) and (4) contain nothing not previously included as, respectively, Appendix A and Appendix B of (2). The most astonishing thing about that Appendix A itself is that it is almost all, word for word, the same as Berkshire's EE. So, since it was in fact issued one term earlier, I shall concentrate on that.

EE begins by distinguishing what, trendily, it calls three 'perspectives', dismissing the first two in favour of the third. These first two are 'A perspective emphasising mainly Integration' and 'A perspective emphasising mainly Diversity' (pp. 5–6 and 6–7). It is difficult to see any force at all in the author's objections to these two approaches, until we realise that it is in terms of a quite different conception of racism that he is faulting them both as either positively racist or else inadequately anti-racist.

It is also clear that he is a faithful client of the confusion between race and culture, a confusion which itself both has been and remains a perennial source of—in the old and true sense—racism.[4] For there neither is nor could be any 'black [or white, or brown] cultural identtity' (p.6): there are only cultures which just happen to be common to a set of people all or most of whom are black, or white or brown. Or, if blackness or whiteness or brownness is in fact made so much of by those who share that culture that those of alien race are not admissible, then that racially exclusive culture is indeed most categorically to be condemned as being—always in the old and proper sense—racist. If this were true of our own so much condemned British culture, which it plainly is not, then 'Integration' would be not so much an unacceptable option as no option at all.

The third and for Berkshire today the only permissible option is 'A perspective emphasising primarily Equality' (pp.8–12). This is said to have 'developed in the 1970s', but it 'has so far received less official attention' (p.8). How very true that is can be seen when we study the two key redefinitions: the first of 'black'; and the second of 'racism'.

(a) The employment of the term 'black' even by the Commission for Racial Equality is loose and confusing. Sometimes they refer only to blacks, sometimes to all non-whites and sometimes their intentions are obscure or indeterminate. But official Berkshire proposes so to redefine the word as to include, unequivocally, '*both* Afro-Caribbean *and* Asian people' (p.3: emphasis original), while simultaneously extending 'Afro-Caribbean' to cover all and only those previously rated black. These manoeuvres might appear merely perverse, or a cheap concession to the vulgar, or both. Concession to the vulgar they may also be, but the prime purpose is as straightforwardly intelligible as it is both obscurantist and sinister.

That purpose is so to collapse distinctions between different groups of non-white immigrants that it becomes possible to maintain that any relatively poor economic or educational performance by any such groups is mainly, perhaps wholly, attributable to white racism. By thus concealing relevant differences between different non-white groups, this bit of Marxist analysis suggests: both that they are all and always victims of (exclusively white) racism; and that there is nothing which they themselves can do to better their victim conditions. There is nothing, that is, which they can do apart from supporting the right left-wing political campaigns. 'The term "black", ' we are told, 'emphasises the common experience which both Afro-Caribbean and Asian people have of being victims of racism, and their common determination to oppose racism' (p.3).

It is, however, impossible to emphasise too strongly the import-

Clarifying the Concepts

ance of NOT thinking of all immigrants, or even of all non-white immigrants, as one homogeneous mass. For there is already a good deal of evidence to show that, especially in the second generation, Asians are reaching higher levels of achievement than blacks; and hence evidence to suggest that white racism cannot be the sole factor accounting for black failures; at least not unless we insist, in the teeth of the evidence, that what white racism there is is exclusively or mainly anti-black.

Consider, for instance, a finding of the National Child Development Study (NCDS) or the National Children's Bureau (NCB). The NCDS has, it seems, discovered that whereas in the first generation all immigrants—West Indian, Asian, and Irish too—live on average in above averagely overcrowded conditions; and whereas with *both* the West Indian *and* the Irish a considerable disparity persists into the second generation; with the Asians the disparity has, in the second generation, disappeared completely.[5]

As a further indication both of the motivation behind, and of the vested interests in, this seemingly perverse and arbitrary redefinition of 'black' let us turn again to the *1982 Annual Report* of the CRE. In the body of the text the Commission asserts that 'ethnic minorities have taken more than their fair share' of youth unemployment; supporting this with the statement that 'In June 1982, the Commission published a survey of inner city youth unemployment . . . which indicated that 59% of young people of West Indian origin were unemployed, as compared with 41% of their white peers' (p.9).

It is clear that the CRE believes, or at any rate would like the rest of us to believe, that this certainly 'potentially explosive' disparity is due to white racism, to discrimination against non-whites as such; and, therefore, that it falls within the CRE's statutory terms of reference. Yet on the very same page they present in diagram form fuller and slightly different figures. These show: that their wholesale claim extended to all 'ethnic minorities' is simply false; that their suggested explanation of this 59 per cent to 41 per cent disparity, in terms of white discrimination against all non-whites, must be mistaken; and, hence, that the cherished corollary conclusion, that to destroy it is their own peculiar and appointed business falls to the ground. For the diagram reveals other disparities in inner-city juvenile unemployment. Its figures are: (not 41 but) 42 per cent for

Whites, 59 per cent for Afro-Caribbeans; and 40 per cent—a little less, that is, than for Whites—for Asians.

There are two morals which we should draw from this sort of evidence: the first primary; and the second consequential. The primary moral is that we should now look for most of the explanation of underachievement in any underachieving immigrant group: not in white, or even in non-white, racism; but in cultural differences, in the broadest sense, between those groups and others. Suppose, for instance that it is the case that in British schools 43 per cent of the children from West Indian families have only one parent, as against 5 per cent of those from Asian and 20 per cent of those from all families.[6] Then that fact alone might be sufficient to explain most of the present scholastic underachievement of our British Afro-Caribbeans.

Anyone sincerely concerned, not just to plug a political or private interest line but actually to solve some of the theoretical and policy problems in this area, should read the works of Thomas Sowell—above all his superb *Ethnic America*.[7] Sowell is a Columbia- and Chicago-trained black economist, whose family moved during his boyhood from the Deep South to Harlem. His books are full of fascinating evidence of often quite spectacular differences in educational, economic and political achievement as between different, always immigrant, minority groups. Members of such culturally different groups may be in practice indistinguishable by even the most determined racial bigot. In the USA, for example, Afro-Caribbeans from the formerly British islands have a record in every area of achievement superior to that of native-born American blacks. (In the face of the UK's very different experience of Afro-Caribbean immigrants this surely constitutes the juiciest of juicy problems for any genuinely curious and unprejudiced investigative sociologists to get their teeth into!)

The second and consequential moral is that we badly need research focusing on cultural differences rather than racial similarities. For if only our researchers—in this encouraged and supported by formidable vested interests in race relations—were not so obsessed with race and racism, we might have evidence also of significant differences in performance between those coming from different parts of the Caribbean. It was, after all, non-racial differences between inhabitants of the different islands which killed the project of a West Indies Federation.⁸ Again, it was cultural rather than racial differences which led to the division of the Indian sub-continent into first two, then three, not always friendly nation states.

(b) The second obnoxious redefinition offered by *Education for Equality* is one which will, if adopted, license the transformation of the CRE and its local subsidiaries into instruments of revolution; and that a revolution not in education only. Under the italicised heading, '*The central and pervasive influence of racism*' the crucial clauses run: 'There are certain routine practices, customs and procedures in our society whose consequence is that black people have poorer jobs, health, housing and life-chances than do the white majority . . . These practices and customs are maintained by relations and structures of power, and are justified by centuries-old beliefs and attitudes which hold that black people are essentially inferior to white people— biologically, or culturally, or both. "Racism" is a shorthand term for this combination of discriminatory practices; unequal relations and structures of power, and negative beliefs and attitudes' (p.9).

Look now at the implications of thus pouring new wine into old bottles. Given this redefinition of 'racism', and given too that, whatever the word is to be used to mean, racism has to be eschewed and abominated, then we are going sooner or later to be asked to condemn and abandon any and every institution or practice the actual effects of which are that the racial distribution in any social group is substantially different from that in the population as a whole. If there are n per cent of blacks and m per cent of browns in the population as a whole, then there will have to be n per cent of blacks and m per cent of browns in every profession, class, team, area or what have you. Anything, but anything, which stands in the way of this proposed ideal is to be denounced and execrated. It has to be, by definition, racist.

Now no-one denies that in Britain, as no doubt in every other multi-racial society too, some racial groups are in various ways underachieving and others—if we may for one moment genuflect towards Procrustean meanness and malignancy—overachieving.⁹ Certainly in the USA blacks are heavily overrepresented in professional basketball, while Jews have been about nine times overrepresented among America's Nobel Prizewinners (27 per cent to 3 per cent). So if we accept the new definition, or anything like it, we shall be required to put down any such overrepresentation, as well as the necessarily consequent underrepresentations, to 'institutionlised racism'. And this we will be required to do notwithstanding that we know perfectly well that these overrepresentations actually result from entirely honest and racially colour-blind attempts to appoint the strongest candidates. (In a business as savagely competitive as professional basketball no-one could afford to indulge any racial preferences, even if they had them.)

These and further implications of this or similar redefinitions ought to have made an Education Committee one of the last rather than the first to concede. It, above all others, should have noticed the ruinous consequences: not only for the maintenance of any racially unbiased standards of achievement in anything; but also for the untrammelled pursuit of factual truth.

The second sinister and potentially obscurantist thing here is the introduction of references to actual or alleged matters of fact—to 'negative beliefs', as Berkshire tactfully puts it. For this is to demand, irrespective of any evidence which might be turned up to the contrary, that everyone must renounce certain disapproved propositions about average or universal differences and similarities as between races and racial groups; differences and similarities, that is, either in respect of biology or in respect of culture. To concede such a demand to the often Marxist militants of race relations is to open the door to purges: not only of libraries and of textbooks and of curricula; but also of people. It is not ten years since many a campus in the USA was ringing with calls to 'Sack' and even to 'Kill Jensen'—Jensen being a psychologist who dared to publish evidence suggesting that there may be genetically determined average differences between different races and racial groups in respect of other than their racial defining characteristics.[10]

A third altogether unacceptable implication of any such redefinition, although this consequence too is clearly intended by our redefiners, is that the offence of racism now becomes, by definition, one which can be committed only by whites, and against victims who can only be (Berkshire) blacks; that is, either Afro-Caribbean or Asian. Yet tens of thousands of our British Asians—the refugees from Uganda under the monstrous rule of Amin—have the bitterest and most intimate reason to know that this cherished but malign implication is utterly false.

The practical upshot of Section 2(b) is, therefore, that we need to do two things: first, to make as plain as we can the enormous differences between what we must insist to be the old and true sense of 'racism' and this new neo-Marxist monstrosity; and, second, to urge that LEAs and everyone else should refuse to accept any such unacceptably tendentious redefinition. We would further suggest that the CRE must be directed, on pain of dissolution: first to formulate its own redefinition, consistent with the spirit of the 1976 Act; and then to demand that all its agents and subsidiaries stick to that appointed brief. It is also overtime to appoint to that commission a few members fully seized of the erroneousness of all the errors to be examined in Section 3 below.

We have to speak here of the spirit of the 1976 Act, or of the spirit behind it, because in places the parliamentary draftspersons made rather a mess of the letter. The trouble was that they never succeeded in sorting out the relations and lack of relations between race and culture. One well-remembered consequence was the at least temporarily successful prosecution of a municipal bus company, which refused to sanction any turban variant of its uniform cap. Certainly no-one who has ever served alongside Sikhs in the armed forces of the Crown will have the slightest patience with such wooden bumbledom. Yet equally certainly Sikhism is a religion, and hence a matter of culture, not of race.

3

At this third and last stage of our journey it may be helpful to detach ourselves a little from hotly controversial current documents. We proceed therefore to a short, systematic, sharp review of a constellation of fallacies and falsehoods, all of which are somewhere committed or asserted, presupposed or implied, in both the Berkshire and the ILEA documents; as well as in the other literature of the 'perspective emphasising primarily Equality ... developed in the 1970s'.

(a) The first fundamental false assumption is that of environmental omnipotence. Society or the social system, usually hypostatised as agents capable of planning and intention, are taken to mould and confine individuals and groups—as if human beings were originally inert, uniform and infinitely malleable. This assumption is, of course, contrary to all our experience both as and of those diverse and peculiar creatures which we are. In particular, and most relevantly, it conflicts with all such evidence as is deployed by Sowell. This evidence shows enormous differences in subsequent performance as between different immigrant groups, immigrant groups often coming from vastly different cultural traditions, yet all starting—to employ the tendentious contemporary cant—more or less equally deprived and equally disadvantaged. What distinguished these groups, even as they were all living in similar and similarly wretched material conditions, was differences between—in the broadest sense—their cultures. It was these differences and not any decisions by Capitalism, or any other sort of hypostatised collective Society or System, which resulted in their individual members being and becoming either more or less able and inclined to see and to take opportunities.

This false general assumption of environmental omnipotence is sometimes linked with a particular fallacy of equivocation. Some educationists find it seductive. These two errors together were the main stock-in-trade of Bernard Coard's *How the West Indian child is made educationally sub-normal in the British School System* (New Beacon, London, 1971). This book has a dual topical interest: both because it is now one of those most strongly recommended by ILEA; and because its author, who used to be a London teacher, later became Deputy Prime Minister of Grenada. The particular present fallacy confounds casual with criterial senses of 'make': we move invalidly from observing that, given certain criteria, these lads and lasses are made, or rated as, ESN; to the grotesque conclusion that it is employing those criteria which makes, or causes, them to be as they are; i.e., educationally sub-normal. Hence, presumably, all that we have to do in order to raise the level of their educational achievement is to jettison these criteria.

(b) Next, there are the confusions between opportunity and outcome, and about what it means to say that all contestants had a fair and equal chance of success in some competition. Again and again evidence shows members of one social or racial set doing better, on average, than members of another social or racial set. These differences in outcome are then confidently construed as by themselves sufficient to demonstrate corresponding differences in opportunity. Yet we have here a valid argument only when we are in a position to supply a further premise stating that, in whatever may be the relevant respects, the members of all the sets compared were equally able, equally eager and equally well qualified. And this we almost never are.

Suppose that we really do want to discover where there is and is not equal opportunity, and where there is and is not actual racial discrimination in selection. Then we shall have to look at the actual selection procedures, rather than at the eventual outcomes of those procedures. What we shall certainly not do is immediately to infer: from the observation that, compared with its representation in the population as a whole, this or that social or racial set is in this or that area over- or underrepresented; the categorical conclusions that this or that social or racial set owes its over- or underrepresentation to some form of positive or negative discrimination—and, furthermore, that this is one more scandal to set at the door of Racist White British Society and its (partly) Capitalist Social System.

We have already seen several examples of this fallacious argument applied to racial sets. Several more, applied now to social sets also, are supplied by the ILEA documents. For instance: the first speaks of 'the history of our education system, with elementary schools for the children of the poor and public or endowed grammar schools for the well off, and with well-documented evidence of the scholarship bias in the days of the eleven plus' (p.9). But this 'well-documented evidence' of higher success rates in the higher social classes is by itself simply not evidence of any corresponding bias or distortion in the examination system.

There is another similar, associated fallacy. It consists in inferring that, if the contestants in any competition are all treated fairly by the organisers, and thus have equal opportunities of success, then the success of any one such contestant must be equiprobable with the success of any other. To accept this argument we should have to allow that any competition in which it is most probable that the best competitor will win must, for that reason alone, be put down as being unfairly conducted. Such arguments, though perennially popular, belong not to this world but to Wonderland.

(c) A third outstanding star in this constellation of fallacies and falsehoods is the contention that no language and no culture either is or could be superior or inferior to any other. All, it is assumed or even asserted, are equally good. Or else—presumably because this rephrasing makes it less clear both what is being said and that it is either false or irrelevant—they are said to be equally (sneer) 'good' or equally *valid*.

In the irrelevant interpretation these claims amount to no more than maintaining that all languages, and all cultures, are equally parts of the proper subject matter of linguistic science, or of social science; and perhaps also that all scientists ought in their working hours to be impartial and detached. But such sound and sensible claims about the need for scientists of different sorts to attend—at least collectively—to the whole of their respective fields are often either confounded with, or mistaken for, warrants to place equal instrumental or non-instrumental values on all the objects to be studied.

This requires explanation. To value something non-instrumentally is to value it as good in itself, irrespective of any possible further consequences of having it, whereas to value something instrumentally is to value it as a means to the achieving of some other and further end or ends. To maintain that anything is non-instrumentally valuable is indeed to make a value judgement; which is, no doubt, an inherently contentious move. For it is to say that, regardless of consequences, whatever it is which is thus non-instrumentally valued *ought* to be preferred. But to maintain that something is instrumentally valuable, adding the needed indication of the presumptively good end or ends to which it is alleged in fact to be a means, is to make a purely (would-be) factual and unequivocally true or false assertion. For it is to say, only and precisely, that what is thus instrumentally valuable in fact just *is* an effective means of achieving a presumptively good objective; and all this quite regardless of whether you or I or anyone else either wants or ought to want that particular objective.

The purpose of that brief and, I hope, not too technical excursus into the philosophy of value is to begin to bring out the full outrageousness of the contention that no language and no culture may be said to be in any respect, or with regard to any possible objective, either superior or inferior to any other. A ban on the investigation of all such questions of instrumental efficiency, or on the publication of the findings, must constitute an intolerable restriction upon the freedom of inquiry, or of speech and writing. Yet exactly this is what is demanded when 'negative views' are embargoed, and everyone is required to allow that all cultures and all forms of linguistic expression are equally 'good' or equally *valid*.

Here we need a distinction between two senses of 'culture'. In the more traditional understanding only some of the (higher) activities of any people or group count as cultural, while some people or some group could conceivably be wholly lacking in any (higher) culture at all. The list of particular activities rated as in this sense cultural varies from one language-user to another. But it will always include, surely, music, art and literature? Granted some list on these lines, then at least those miserable and unfortunate Ik—Colin Turnbull's *The Mountain People* (Cape, London, 1973)—must be said to lack all culture, in this (higher) sense. But in the second—that of the anthropologists and other social scientists—even the Ik must have a culture. For now a culture is a matter of every kind of preference, disposition, social practice and what have you; and not only those involved in activities which are, in the first sense, specifically cultural.

Whatever we may want to say about culture in the first sense, where attributions of value will normally be non-instrumental, we cannot but concede that cultures in the second sense may, in certain respects and with reference to certain ends, be superior or inferior one to another. Take first the case of languages. Whatever might be said about the attribution of such non-instrumental values as euphony or elegance, it would be—it is—simply silly to insist that every language is equally good for every possible practical purpose. (Silliness is compounded into academic pretentiousness when this insistence is then supported by appeals to the apparent findings of uncited research.[11]

Waiving all questions about complexity or redundancy, it is sufficient to indicate how ill advised it must be to attempt to employ a language lacking a vocabulary for discussing what you want to discuss. Of course, it is true that, had the history of these islands been very different, we might all be speaking and writing a language other than English, or some other dialect might have achieved the status of Standard English. In that event we might have found that language, or that dialect, in every way as serviceable as English or Standard English. Nevertheless none of this speculative historical linguistics has the slightest tendency to show, as things in fact have been and now are, that it is not imperative for anyone proposing to make their home and their career in the United Kingdom to master English, and Standard English, rather than Urdu or Creole. If we were all proposing to live our lives in Japan and to be Japanese then the imperatives would be different, yet no less imperative: Japanese it would have to be, and Standard Japanese at that.

With appropriate alterations the same applies to cultures. One culture may be well, even perfectly, adapted to the requirements of one form of life. The better that original adaptation, the more likely it is that some features of that culture will constitute handicaps to achievement in another and in many ways very different social environment. Other features may perhaps turn out to constitute positive advantages. For examples of cultural features of both kinds we can again turn to the writings of Thomas Sowell. Here and elsewhere it is impossible to emphasise too strongly the need to emancipate ourselves from blinkering obsessions with race and racism, and to draw deep on the accumulated experience of a country which has in the last hundred and fifty years accepted and assimilated the largest and most various immigration in the entire history of the world.

(d) The final case for treatment in this constellation of errors and confusions is the assumption that, in order to legitimate a repudiation of racism, it is necessary to maintain: both that no culture is either superior or inferior to any other; and that no race or racial group differs in any substantial way in respect of any physiological or physiologically based characteristics from any other. The exception (although it is remarkable how rarely this obvious exception is remembered) must be their racial defining characteristics. (That contrast between races and racial groups is introduced to allow for possible differences and distinctions between the whole race and one or more of its subsets.)

To feel a need to substantiate these two contentions must, surely, be a burden to any realistic and open-minded person. For we have already seen that the first, in any relevant understanding, is false. And, given that no-one is so rash as to dispute the genetic determination of the racial and hence biological defining characteristics, we can have little reason for confidence that there is no significant difference in the distribution of the other genes within the relevant gene pools. We might hope, therefore, that clients of the assumption that these contentions have to be substantiated would be glad to be relieved of it.

We shall, I fear, be disappointed.[12] Nor will those clients be much mollified if it is also pointed out that the possibility of differences between the gene pools of different races and different racial groups constitutes a further reason for rejecting inferences from inequalities of outcome to corresponding inequalities of opportunity. For most of these people are committed to arguments presupposing the far less probable assumption that there are no significant differences between the gene pools of different societies and different social sets (or classes). So let us press on, abandoning all hopes of popularity; pausing only to point out that such differences must result if any genetically different sets happen to achieve different net reproduction rates.

Relief will be found in two directions. First: any relevant genetic differences which may eventually be discovered are going to be differences solely on average. There seems absolutely no reason to anticipate that any genetically determined characteristic of talent or temperament will turn out to be peculiar to members of any particular races or racial groups. Yet the only conceivable grounds for eliminating candidates on the basis of their racial group membership would be knowledge that no members of their particular groups could possess whatever are the relevant kind of talents. Even then, these rejections would of course not really be racist rejections on grounds of racial group membership as such.

Second: the situation could, however, be transformed if we were to accept the new, neo-Marxist conception of racism. For that condemns as racist any disproportionate representation of any racial group anywhere.[13] But, if there are even average differences in the genetic endowments of such groups, then this will most likely result in several over- and underrepresentations. That undermines the practicability of the racial quota ideal of non-racism. This perhaps is a main reason why such Marxist scientists as Professor Steven Rose of the Open University appear to be so committed to the two unbelievable contentions explained earlier in the present subsection.[14]

Notes

1. Regrettably, our 1976 Race Relations Act does seem to open the door, as I am assured that the 1964 American legislation did not, to what has come to be called—in a slimy euphemism—'positive discrimination'. To any genuine and consistent opponent of racism positive discrimination must be as repugnant as negative. The questionable clauses are 35–8 in Part VI. These provide for exceptional exemption from the mandates of Parts I–IV, allowing that it shall not be unlawful to make special provision for special needs 'in regard to their education, training or welfare, or any ancillary benefits'.

In Appendix 4, 'Project Aid Grants approved by the Commission', and in Appendix 5, 'Self Help Fund' (pp.28 and 32), the *1982 Annual Report* lists grants of taxpayers' money to various approved causes: for instance, a 'Festival of Black Independent Film Makers', a 'Black Bookfair 1981' and a 'Society of Black Lawyers'. Presumably this was done under the authority of those 'positive discrimination' clauses in the 1976 Act. To appreciate how obnoxiously racist is this licensed misbehaviour of the CRE, suppose that someone organised a conference of white lawyers and requested a grant-in-aid. Not only would they—quite rightly—be refused. But the CRE would surely—and equally rightly—seek to bring a case under the Act against those daring to organise such a racially exclusive operation.

2. I use the term 'set' in order to avoid the social implications of 'class'. By Cantor's axiom for sets the sole essential feature of a set is that its members have at least one common characteristic, any kind of characteristic.

3. Edited by K. Richardson and D. Spears (Penguin Books, Harmondsworth: 1972), pp.7–8. For a more extensive critique of this disgraceful work, see my *Sociology, Equality and Education* (Macmillan, London, 1976), Chapter 5.

4. This important distinction is well made in, for instance, the 1952 Unesco memorandum on *The Race Concept*. This supplements and corrects the recognised inadequacies of the 1950 Unesco statement. It is a point worth making since Steven Rose, who was commissioned by the National Union of Teachers (NUT) to compose its manifesto on race and racism, makes much of the earlier without noticing the later work. Rose is a member of the Communist Party (Muscovite) as well as Professor of Biology at—surprise, surprise—the Open University. Anyone curious as to why the NUT should have commissioned a Marxist to do this job for it may be referred to Fred Naylor and John Marks, 'The National Union of Teachers—Professional Association or Trade Union or ... ?' in Caroline Cox and John Marks (eds) *The Right to Learn* (Centre for Policy Studies, London, 1982).

5. See K. Fogelman (ed.) *Growing up in Great Britain* (Macmillan, London, 1983).

6. These figures are drawn from an ILEA pre-school survey, mentioned at p.17 of the first document to be considered in Section 4, below.

7. *Ethnic America* (Basic Books, New York, 1983); but compare *Race and Economics* (Longman, New York and London, 1975), *Markets and Minorities* (Basic Books, New York, 1981), *Pink and Brown People* (Hoover Institution Press, Stanford, Ca, 1981), and *The Economics and Politics of Race* (William Morrow, New York, 1983).

8. We shall certainly not get this necessary and interesting research done unless someone is willing to defy intimidation from often Marxist militants fearing the expected findings. A leader in *The Times* (13 March 1985) commenting on the Swann Report put it very delicately: 'Conflict within the committee itself prevented it from pursuing its proposed *factual survey* into the social circumstances of successful and unsuccessful pupils in each major ethnic group' (emphasis supplied).
9. Compare my *The Politics of Procrustes* (Temple Smith, London, 1981), *passim*.
10. Compare, again, the Chapter 5 mentioned in Note 3, above.
11. Compare John Honey *The Language Trap: race, class, and the 'standard English' issue in British Schools* (National Council for Educational Standards, Kenton, Middx, 1983). The Brent Education Committee in its *Book I: Education for a Multicultural Democracy* quotes an official Council policy statement: 'The recognition that all people and cultures are inherently equal must be a constant from which all educational practice will be developed', and the Committee adds in its own account that this 'is not a negotiable principle' (p.7). No-one seems to have noticed that it commits Brent to insist—and in the name of anti-racism and anti-sexism, at that—that male-chauvinist macho cultures and racist cultures are, when compared with sexually egalitarian and non-racist cultures, equally good or 'equally valid' (p.10).
12. See, again, the chapter cited in Note 12, above.
13. Well no, of course, not quite everywhere; not, and very conspicuously not, the heavy overrepresentation of both Great Russians and males in senior political and other Nomenklatura positions in the USSR. See M. Voslensky *Nomenklatura* (The Bodley Head, London, 1985).
14. It is, of course, grotesque to identify the neo-Marxism discussed above with Marx. See, for instance, L. Page *The Marxian Legacy: Race, Nationalities, Colonialism and War* (Freedom Association, London, 1984) or much more fully, N. Weyl *Karl Marx: Racist* (Arlington House, New York, 1979). On this particular count at least Marx himself would have felt more at home with Hitler's National Socialists than with our contemporary neo-Marxists.

2

'Anti-Racism'—Revolution not Education

John Marks

> In various countries around the world, the rise of extremist racial or ethnic political movements within the recent past has progressively undermined and co-opted moderates, and swamped all other political issues under over-riding group antagonism . . .
>
> . . . The rise of extremism in one group has led to counter-extremism in others, and to escalating levels of confrontation in politics, in civil disorders or even outright civil war.[1]
>
> Polarisation by ethnic politics has proven to be easy to achieve . . . but no comparably easy way has been found to de-polarise peoples . . .[2]
>
> . . . all the time I was writing *Black Britain*, I found not solace, comfort, or tolerance, but tension, a disturbing desire to break, smash and riot, to bellow: "Whitey! one day you'll have to pay!"[3]

The first two statements are by the black American economist, Thomas Sowell. They emphasise why it is important to approach questions of race and ethnic differences with caution and sensitivity, with due regard to all the available evidence, and with as much clarity and objectivity as can be mustered.

The third statement is by the black British educationist, Chris Mullard, a leading figure in the self-styled 'anti-racist' movement in Britain. Since writing those words, Chris Mullard became Director of the Race Relations Policy and Practice Unit at the London University Institute of Education, the largest college for the training of teachers in Britain. He has now been appointed Professor in Race and Ethnic Relations at the University of Amsterdam.[4]

The assertions of many 'anti-racists' like Professor Mullard are intellectually so inadequate that they constitute an attack on education rather than a contribution to it. It is also clear that the hidden agenda of the 'anti-racists' includes the adoption of policies, practices and attitudes which increase polarisation, heighten racial tensions and make racial conflict more probable.[5]

Yet 'anti-racist' views now pervade the settled thinking of many teachers and of much of the 'para-educational establishment': that growing body of advisors, administrators, theorists and politicians whose principal activity is to influence what goes on in the classroom.

It is the purpose of this chapter to describe and exemplify the intellectual inadequacies of the 'anti-racists' and to discuss the strategy and tactics of those, many of whom are revolutionary Marxists, who adopt a conflict model of society and attempt to put that model into practice.[6]

Inadequacies of the 'Anti-racist' Position

Definitions of racism

Shifting and imprecise definitions of 'racism' are perhaps the most important sources of confusion and conflict, particularly since an explicit condemnation and abhorrence of 'racism' is currently being required of many in education. Again in the words of Thomas Sowell:

> Racism is a term used to cover so many different kinds of behaviour that it is difficult to pin down a specific meaning. 'Racism' can be used legitimately as a term of moral denunciation of racially discriminatory behaviour, and no confusion results so long as that is understood to be its sole purpose and significance. Confusion and illogic results when this general usage alternates with a more specific designation of racism as a belief in the genetic inferiority of various peoples . . .[7]

This quotation emphasises the desirability of stressing the general usage for the term 'racism' as meaning racially discriminatory behaviour, or more precisely, as the advantaging or disadvantaging of individuals for no better reason than that they are members of one racial group rather than another. It is in this precise sense that the term 'racism' will be used in the rest of this chapter.

The second meaning of 'racism' identified by Sowell is the belief in the genetic superiority or inferiority of various groups—either in general or with respect to specific characteristics. There is no necessary connection between these two distinct meanings of 'racism' for as Sowell puts it:

> The extent to which discriminatory behaviour is related to biological beliefs is an empirical question rather than a foregone conclusion.[7]

Yet these two distinct meanings are almost always run together by the 'anti-racists' and are linked with assertions about 'unequal relations and structures of power' in modern Britain. See, for example, the absolutely identical definitions of 'racism' given by both ILEA and Berkshire Education Committee.[8]

> There are certain routine practices, customs and procedures in our society whose consequence is that black people have poorer jobs, health, housing and life-chances than do the white majority ... These practices and customs are maintained by relations and structures of power, and are justified by centuries-old beliefs and attitudes which hold that black people are inherently inferior to white people—biologically, or culturally, or both. 'Racism' is a shorthand term for this combination of discriminatory practices; unequal relations and structures of power; and negative beliefs and attitudes.

The use of such a confused threefold definition of 'racism'—discrimination + prejudice + power—has two serious consequences. First it makes it almost impossible to argue clearly and rationally about racial questions. Again Sowell puts the point well:

> The question is not about the 'right' or 'best' definition of the word 'racism'. Words are servants, not masters. The real problem is to avoid shifting definitions which play havoc with reasoning.[8]

More specifically this composite definition makes it possible to claim that, in Britain today, only white people are capable of 'racism'. It seems extremely unlikely that the many intelligent 'anti-racists' are unaware of the potential for confusion, conflict and unreason which flow from their chosen definition.

Definitions of 'Black'

Many 'anti-racists' reject distinctions between different ethnic groups except on the basis of a very crude black/white dichotomy, so that, for example, all West Indians and Asians are to be considered together under the category 'Black'.

Professor Mullard supports this approach. For example he has described the term 'West Indian' as 'offensive' on the grounds that

> many of us would prefer to see ourselves as blacks rather than as West Indians, Asians or Africans, for this not only accentuates our common experience in Britain, but it also points to a set of explanations that cannot be presented as ethnically specific.[9]

It is noteworthy that a similarly crude definition, lacking distinctions between different ethnic groups, has been put forward by the Inner London Education Authority (ILEA) in guidelines which it regards as mandatory on teachers. ILEA defines 'black' so as:

> to refer to both Afro-Caribbean and Asian people. The term black emphasises the common experience which both Afro-Caribbean and Asian people have of being victims of racism, and their common determination to oppose racism.
>
> Other groups who, together with the black communities, are usually referred to as 'ethnic minorities' also suffer varying degrees of prejudice and discrimination. These include Chinese, Greek Cypriots, Turkish Cypriots, Turks, Vietnamese, Moroccans. In a similar way, though not always to the same extent, some white ethnic groups, such as the Irish and the Jews, experience prejudice and discrimination. In using the term 'black' in this paper, it is not the Authority's intention to exclude any minority group.[10]

This kind of crude definition has two serious defects. First, it is extremely dubious sociologically in that it seeks to deny many real differences which many of those involved would like to maintain. Second, it has the effect, and in Professor Mullard's case the clearly stated intention, of ruling out, *a priori*, any explanation based on such differences.

Neglect of empirical evidence

Answers to the question as to whether racism—in the sense of discrimination solely on racial grounds—exists in this or that situation need to be empirical. Even more important is the need in these empirical assessments to distinguish and to discuss the many other factors involved. For example, it is not enough to show that the proportion of a racial or ethnic minority *within* a group in society—say, those earning above the national average—is lower than the proportion of that ethnic minority in society as a whole, and hence to infer that this is solely due to racism in employment practices.

Some of the many factors, in addition to racial discrimination, which have been found to be relevant to such questions in the USA[11] and which may also need to be considered in this country include (data refer to USA):

(1) Differences in family income for different ethnic groups—ranging from 60 per cent to 170 per cent of the national average with black West Indians at 94 per cent and indigeneous Blacks at 62 per cent;
(2) Differences in median age—ranging from 18 to 46—and age distribution for different ethnic groups;
(3) Differences in the geographic location of ethnic groups;
(4) Differences in fertility rates—from 2.2 to 4.4 children per woman aged 35–44—with West Indians at 2.5 and Blacks at 3.7;
(5) Differences in the time of immigration of different ethnic minorities—with immigration peaks for the Irish in the 1840s, for Germans in the 1860s and for Italians and Russians in the early decades of this century;
(6) Differences between the different generations within ethnic minority groups, for example in experience, language competence and education;
(7) Differences *between* and *within* ethnic groups which for some purposes may be classified together—for example, between immigrants from different European countries and differences between Chinese immigrants from different parts of China;
(8) Differences in the proportions of individuals from different ethnic groups in *any* small group due to random statistical fluctuations.

These factors are, in many cases, interrelated. This further complicates the inherent problem of disentangling correlation from cause.

Also the list given is not meant, in any sense, to be complete. It merely indicates the multiplicity of factors involved and the kinds of distinction which have to be made in any serious analysis.

Yet the 'anti-racists' do not consider these kinds of social factors and the arguments which are put forward by writers like Thomas Sowell.[11]

'Institutionalised racism'

One result of the neglect of the many factors in addition to obvious ethnic and cultural differences which may be influential in determining the economic, political and social prospects of individuals and groups is that it enables the 'anti-racists' to ascribe all problems experienced by ethnic minorities monocausally to 'institutionalised racism' in British society. This tendency is particularly apparent in Professor Mullard's writings and in policy statements by Berkshire, ILEA and Brent.[12]

Yet it is only when such a serious analysis of these many factors has been attempted—and substantial evidence presented that social institutions are discriminating against individuals or groups on *specifically* racial grounds—that it makes sense to talk of institutional or institutionalised racism and to seek to modify specific institutions or the social and political structures that established those institutions.

Such serious analysis is eschewed by the 'anti-racists'.[13] Instead they launch a generalised attack, based on a generalised charge of institutionalised racism, on any British institution or practice the actual effects of which are that the racial distribution is different from that in the population as a whole.[14] This means that, sooner or later, any institution—school, small firm or multinational, any profession or occupation, local councils, the Civil Service, Parliament—lacking the requisite proportions of ethnic minorities may be subjected to attack and condemnation.

The potential in these attacks for the endless generation of disaffection, confrontation and social conflict is obvious, as is the eventual consequence—the destruction and revolutionary transformation of all the institutions of our democratic society.

Denigration of British culture

This attack on contemporary British society is broadened in many publications of the 'anti-racists' into a generalised attack on British culture, traditions and institutions, buttressed by an extremely selective view of the contemporary and historical evidence.[15]

For example, consider Professor Mullard's paper *Racism in Society and Schools: History, Policy and Practice*[16] which is based on a lecture given to 750 trainee teachers on a Postgraduate Certificate of Education course at the London University Institute of Education. In its account of the 'racism' which has 'been an integral part of the British experience for more than four centuries', this paper makes no mention whatever of the legal prohibition of the slave trade by Wilberforce and many others in the early years of the nineteenth century or the harsh deterrent sentences passed on white youths after their conviction for racial violence in London in 1958. Professor Mullard's discussion of 'racism' in society[17] also includes an extremely crude neo-Marxist characterisation of 'the relationship between racism and capitalism' in Britain and other liberal democratic societies in what is grandiosely claimed to be '... a set of universal truths about the nature of social reality in capitalist societies ...'.

Similarly biased accounts of British history, published by the Marxist-dominated Institute of Race Relations, have been welcomed by sections of the British 'para-educational establishment'.[18]

For the 'anti-racists' any positive appreciation of British society must be eliminated. Instead they seek the complete recasting of the school curriculum so as to remove what they claim to be ethnocentric or Eurocentric bias.

Revolution not Education

The 'anti-racist' position is an intellectual morass, and it is clear that 'anti-racists' have no serious commitment to the consideration of all the available relevant evidence. Instead their writings provide fertile ground for the kinds of emotive sloganising, strident character-assassination and political agitation which has characterised recent 'anti-racist' campaigns.[19]

Yet the intellectual incoherence of 'anti-racism' is not random. A great deal of careful thought has clearly gone into its construction. The terms it uses have been defined and the facts it presents chosen so as to lead inexorably in one specific direction and to forego any

Anti-Racism—Revolution not Education

conclusion not desired by 'anti-racists' themselves.[20] That direction is towards an increase in conflict in British society with the aim of generating, sooner or later, insurrectionary confrontations.[21]

It is no accident but a natural consequence of their revolutionary Marxist beliefs and affiliations[22] that the 'anti-racists' are also prominent in recent campaigns to undermine the police.[23] This has been a constant Marxist–Leninist tactic in pre-revolutionary situations. Also, as we have seen, the 'anti-racists' do not shrink from that other settled feature of Marxist–Leninist theory and practice, the rewriting of history.

It is vital for all those concerned with education to understand the motives, the strategy and the tactics of the 'anti-racists'. Their aims and methods must be well understood by all sections of society—and all ethnic groups—if education is to be rescued from their incessant politicisation.

It is for this reason that this chapter has been written. It ends with this clear and unambiguous 'anti-racist' statement by Professor Mullard:

> Already we have started to rebel, to kick out against our jailers. Already many black immigrants, once meek, now incensed, are following their children's initiative. As more Black Britons leave school disgruntled, as more black immigrants discard their yoke of humility, the ultimate confrontation will become clearer.
>
> The battle will be a bloody one. Black and white will have no choice. The liberals . . . will be caught in the middle. In the end they too will have no choice—they will have to side with either black or white . . .
>
> Blacks will fight with pressure, leaflets, campaigns, demonstrations, fists and a scorching resentment which, when peaceful means fail, will explode into street fighting, urban guerilla warfare, looting, burning and rioting . . .
>
> Critics will argue smugly that this cannot possibly happen here. Most of them will be white, blind to what is already happening, wrapped in cocoons of isolation and utopian dreams of multi-racialism, confident that white is might. To these I say 'Watch out, Whitey, nigger goin' to get you!' Because niggers, American, British or African, will go on fighting until racism is obliterated. Others will argue academically that the analysis is wrong, ink-spotted with emotion and bitterness. So it is. For emotion and hatred become the subject; no longer is it possible to apply logic and reason to a disease which has infected the whole of white society. How can you argue with racists? Black American and African campaigns have

shown that the only argument which white society understands is force, violence and power. It is this distorted though effective logic which black Britons are using today—and will go on using.[24]

Notes

1. Thomas Sowell, *The Economics and Politics of Race* (William Morrow, New York, 1983), p.18.
2. Thomas Sowell, *Civil Rights: Rhetoric or Reality?* (William Morrow, New York, 1984), p.34.
3. Chris Mullard, *Black Britain* (Allen and Unwin, London, 1973), Preface.
4. Professor Mullard is also involved with an SSRC-funded research project on *The Social Management of Racial Policy and Practice* and with *Towards a Non-Racist Curriculum*, a collaborative research project between the Institute of Education, the ILEA and the DES.
5. For many years, sociologists—and sociologists of education, in particular—have been urging us to read between the lines of formal curricula and policies and to seek out the hidden curricula and agenda which lie behind them. Is it not therefore reasonable to ask searching questions about the hidden agenda of those advocating policies which are, as Sowell emphasises, so irreversibly divisive?
6. For further discussion see Antony Flew, *Education, Race and Revolution* (Centre for Policy Studies, London, 1984); Dennis O'Keeffe, *Racism: Neither a Sin Apart nor an Excuse for Hysteria* in Digby Anderson (ed.), *The Kindness That Kills* (Social Affairs Unit/SPCK, 1984); John Marks, *Investigating a Local Authority* in Dennis O'Keeffe (ed.), *The Wayward Curriculum* (Social Affairs Unit, 1986).
7. See reference 1, pp.143–4.
8. See *Race, Sex and Class: 2. Multi-Ethnic Education in Schools* (ILEA, 1983) and *Education for Equality* (Berkshire Education Committee, 1983). This definition has some similarity with that given in 1974 by the *Programme to Combat Racism Commission* of the World Council of Churches: 'In modern Western-dominated society racism is a special phenomenon whereby one race or group of people in power justify and perpetuate their position by making claims of biological and cultural superiority, expanding their own identity by diminishing that of their fellows and consolidating their power in structures of economic and political oppression.'
9. See p.7 of Chris Mullard, 'The Educational Management and

Demanagement of Racism,' in *Education Policy Bulletin*, University of Lancaster Institute for Post-Compulsory Education, Vol.10, No.1, pp.21–40 (1982).
10. *Race, Sex and Class: 2. Multi-Ethnic Education in Schools* (ILEA, 1983), p.19.
11. See references 1 and 2 together with Thomas Sowell, *Markets and Minorities* (Basil Blackwell, Oxford, 1981); Thomas Sowell, *Ethnic America* (Basic Books, New York, 1981); Walter Williams, *The State Against Blacks* (McGraw-Hill, New York, 1982); Charles Murray, *Losing Ground* (Basic Books, New York, 1984).
12. See, for example, the documents cited in reference 8 above.
13. A clear example of this is the furore from the 'anti-racists' which caused the Swann Committee to cancel a research project which it had already commissioned just because it attempted to investigate some of the many factors which affect the education of ethnic minorities.
14. This conclusion is explicitly stated in the Berkshire document (reference 8) and is implicit in many other reports and writings.
15. See the chapters in this volume by Tom Hastie and Caroline Cox (chapters 4 and 5).
16. Chris Mullard, *Racism in Society and Schools: History, Policy and Practice* (University of London Institute of Education, 1980).
17. See reference 16 and Chris Mullard, 'The Social Context and Meaning of Multicultural Education,' in *Educational Analysis*, Vol.3, No.1, pp.117–40 (1981).
18. *Roots of Racism* and *Patterns of Racism* (Institute of Race Relations, 1982) have been praised by some teachers' organisations and by reviewers in *New Society* and the *Times Educational Supplement*. Their sequel, *How Racism Came to Britain* (Institute of Race Relations, 1985) (see chapters in this volume by Tom Hastie, Caroline Cox and David Dale) is even more blatantly biased and inflammatory. Yet Peter Newsam, Chairman of the Commission for Racial Equality, refused to condemn it (*Sunday Telegraph*, 13 October 1985).
19. Examples include the campaign against Ray Honeyford and the anti-police propaganda produced by the GLC Police Committee Support Unit.
20. For further discussion see Roger Scruton, Angela Ellis-Jones and Dennis O'Keeffe, *Education and Indoctrination* (Education Research Centre, 1985).
21. Recent examples include the riots in Birmingham and London in the autumn of 1985.
22. See John Marks, *London's Schools: When even the Communist Party gives up!* (Aims of Industry, 1985), for some discussion of the influence

of revolutionary Marxist groups in the National Union of Teachers.
23. See the chapter by Caroline Cox in this volume.
24. See reference 3, pp.176–7. Similarly phrased sentiments expressed by almost any white teacher or educationist would, rightly, have been enough to end their careers in education.

3
Anti-Racist Rhetoric

Ray Honeyford

Language is rarely neutral, though we in the liberal West often behave as though it were. Sally Shreir[1] has recently and effectively reminded us that this is a grave error in the realm of politics; an error which can pave the way to tyranny, as the ruling classes of many dictatorships have repeatedly demonstrated. Words, and the grammar which encapsulates and controls them, not only condition our perceptions; they enable us both to describe the world and to transact our relationships with it, through the expression of cognitions, reflections and feelings. Our very concepts and categories of thought are largely a function of the words which, from infancy, we have inherited from the culture. The Soviet tyranny has survived and flourished largely because its rulers have grasped the necessity not only of using words to demonstrate, and compel support for, prevailing hegemonies by rewriting history, but also because they have created a lexis in which the tools to protest have effectively disappeared. If the state controls language, it controls the citizen. When humane dissent is used as evidence of insanity and psychiatric prisons flourish, then we may rest assured that the vocabulary of liberty has disappeared. As Milovan Djilas has reminded us, 'Tyranny over the mind is the most complete and most brutal type of tyranny: every other tyranny begins and ends with it'.[2]

Thanks to the sorts of warning signals provided by people like Shreir and Djilas we are prepared to challenge the way despots pervert language to sustain their ideology. But in our complacency—the besetting sin of those raised in freedom—we tend, I suspect, to assume that these matters do not directly concern us. They are, of course, deeply serious, but not issues about which we need to lose sleep. It could not, as they say, happen here. At the level of national politics, this may be true. There is *perhaps* a sufficient commitment to free expression to guard against the machinations of any government intent upon hijacking language to compel compliance.

However, language serves not only national intentions and overtly political purposes; it also subserves the aims of those interest groups which can flourish in our democracy precisely because the principle of free speech is the norm. And I want to suggest that language as a means of constructing the way men perceive and react to changes *within* society deserves attention. We need to look with care not only at the way those with an axe to grind push their cause, but the way they use words to convey a distinctive view of 'society'. In listening to what, on the surface, may appear a righteous cause we may well unwittingly be persuaded to adopt a highly distorted view of the world we live in.

I believe this danger is particularly evident in the single most powerful vested interest group we now have—the race relations lobby. The powers of this lobby are all the more persuasive since it is publicly funded at both national and local government level; and its voice is heard—sometimes deafeningly—in all our institutions—the law courts, trade unions, select committees of the House of Commons, education, housing, policy, child care, the National Health Service and the media. It enjoys the services of a government quango, which spends £9 million annually and employs 200 civil servants. Its doctrines are relayed, at ratepayers' expense, by an increasing number of community relations councils. And a growing number of local authorities not only espouse race relations doctrines; they make acceptance of those doctrines a condition of employment and professional advancement. In short, the powers and influence of this particular vested interest are pervasive and growing. It is time its credentials were examined. A useful way of doing that is to consider its basic vocabulary. Three key words will suffice.

Access

The underlying image is of a door, open for some, closed for others. The committed anti-racist maintains that, whilst the door to educational and vocational opportunity is always open for whites, it is closed, or, at best, only partly open for 'blacks'. The evidence for this proposition rests on the differential outcomes by the different ethnic groups in schools and the job market. If there are proportionately more whites than blacks in the professional classes, for instance, this 'proves' there has been discrimination against blacks. Now this is about as convincing as saying that, since the price of bananas and shoes has risen sharply in recent years, the one is the cause of the other—an explanation which conveniently omits the fact that an intervening variable called inflation accounts for both phenomena. It is the doctrine of the excluded middle: the error committed by the beginning, and often gullible student of sociology, who believes—often, alas, for a lifetime—that the statistical notion of correlation provides substantive explanations about cause and effect. It assumes that inequality of outcome proves inequality of opportunity, and that, thereby, egalitarian notions of 'social justice' are violated. It would be difficult to believe anyone could use the word in this mindless way were it not for the fact that the literature of race relations constantly insists that this definition is not only legitimate but self-evident.

Now the word 'access' has been of particular interest in education. The black intelligentsia—Coard, Mullard, Klein, Prophet, Woodruff, Lashley—have all, in their different ways, insisted that because West Indian children achieve less in school than English pupils, then this proves such children have been denied 'access' to educational opportunity. And the excluding mechanisms are racist teachers and an alien curriculum. The answer is to subject all teachers to compulsory 'racism-awareness' training and effect a revolution in the school curriculum through something called 'multi-cultural education'. The Swann Committee[3] endorsed this.

Now even assuming a problem exists, and that these approaches might solve it, there are objections to raise. The first of these is anecdotal, the second empirical. I have, myself, been denied the pleasure of attending a 'racism-awareness' course, but I have talked to many people who have participated. Without exception they have been upset and offended by the experience. The aim of making white people feel guilty, a central purpose of such courses, far from creating greater tolerance and enlightenment, has created feelings of anger and hostility—even in the most liberal of participants. Whether 'multi-cultural education' improves black pupil performance can be ascertained from observation. The West Indian sociologist, Maureen Stone, sat in on lessons in four comprehensive schools committed to this approach. She concluded that there had been no significant shift in black pupils' self-esteem, and no change in academic performance. What she did find was confusion and professional self-interest:

> And yet no one really has any clear ideal of what multi-racial education is or what function it could usefully serve, although it can be regarded as a part of the development of professionalism and specialisation within the teaching profession. The setting up of research and development for multi-racial education in London and Birmingham confirms this view of a professional expansion concerned as much with career advancement as with extending curricula.[4]

The fact, of course, is that achievement in school is an enormously complex question. In order to discover the mechanisms involved a whole set of variables has to be considered. Age, sex, measured intelligence, time in school, family background, social class, motivation, teacher attitude, school ethos—all these have been shown to be associated with progress in school; and some are interrelated, which compounds the problem of distinguishing causes from simple correlations.

However, there are further difficulties for those who espouse the 'access' theory. If black, i.e. West Indian, children do less well than English children because of teacher 'racism', how does this proposition relate to the dramatically better performance of Asian children? Intuitively one would predict that Asian pupils would do less well than others who suffer the alleged disadvantage of minority skin colour. After all, they come from a culture which, in an English context, is spectacularly foreign. Unlike West Indian children, whose mother-tongue is English, and whose history and culture have been radically affected by Western influences, Asian children really do have to live in profoundly different and, in many ways, conflicting cultural universes in moving between school and home. Moreover, if teachers are colour-prejudiced they are more likely, one suspects, to direct their animosity more towards Asians since, on the whole, Asian citizens in Britain have had some economic success. The progress of East African Asians has been quite spectacular. After all, if you regard non-whites as inferior, then comparative West Indian failure simply confirms your belief, whilst Asian economic success, which is likely to inspire envy, confounds it—a cognitive dissonance likely to increase rather than diminish prejudice.

Anti-Racist Rhetoric

Indeed, it is even questionable that differential outcomes actually do indicate that black pupils are underachieving. If there is a sufficiently rigorous attempt to control the relevant variables, including IQ, there is little evidence that West Indian children are doing less well than their overt ability would predict. After looking carefully at both affective and cognitive factors in a large number of pupils from ten Manchester comprehensive schools, Murray[5] concluded that black pupils showed little difference from Asian and English children: 'The result is most encouraging and suggests a rough comparability in attainment between ethnic groups when allowance is made for factors known to be related to them.' Dr Murray also produced the following observation:

> The general lesson to be learned from the research is that we must adopt a sceptical stance to some of the assumptions underlying the debate on 'multi-cultural education'. In particular the results offer little support for suppositions made about racism in schools, negative teacher attitudes, inappropriate curriculum or low expectations of career teachers/officers as these relate to ethnic minority group pupils' attitudes and attainments. If the development of attitudes is a central concern of multi-cultural education then the research suggests the focus of this concern should shift to the indigenous, white groups of pupils in inner city comprehensive schools.

This lends support to Professor Rutter,[6] who showed that where West Indian children had keen and interested parents, who allowed them to stay on after the statutory leaving age, then such children did comparatively well.

However, these sorts of complexities have little appeal for the anti-racists. No attempt to suggest that simple-minded sloganising is an insufficient response to what are extremely complex questions has any appeal for them. Consider the fate of Dr Mortimer's research. Mortimer, a leading educational researcher and statistician, was commissioned by the Swann Committee to pursue research into the fortunes of successful black pupils. However, when Mortimer produced his research proposals they included an attempt to evaluate the influence of family values and backgrounds. This caused uproar amongst West Indian organisations—whose views had a decisive influence on Swann. As a result, the research was suppressed, and the principle of disinterested search for truth dealt a serious blow.

How serious may be judged from the response of one of the instigators of the Swann enquiry, Professor Alan Little:[8] 'If, however, the study is prevented by threat of veto, then this can only undermine the credibility of the whole Swann Report, which could well be rejected out of hand by the Government and professional groups it hopes to influence on the grounds that it was loaded.' Of course, the objections were logical. If Mortimer had established links between school and home, and discovered that the structure and dynamics of West Indian family life were positively associated with poor average performance in school, then the incantation of the word 'access' to explain the issue would have been exposed as unconvincing.

In employment the access theory is even less persuasive. In the absence of direction of labour, quota systems and punitive employment legislation, then variations in ethnic representation in various jobs are to be expected in societies which are both free and multicultural. The profound differences in history and culture between the various ethnic groups are bound to influence the labour market. This question has been illuminated by the work of the black American economist and historian, Thomas Sowell.[9] He has shown not only that differential job outcomes are inevitable but, even where there is direct and official racial discrimination, this is no necessary bar to progress—as witness the socio-economic and educational success of the Chinese in South Asia, where, for centuries, they have endured appalling harassment. Dr Sowell encapsulates his arguments against the access theory by raising a series of questions. In the USA only 3 per cent of the population are Jews, yet they have won 27 per cent of that nation's Nobel Prizes. Is that evidence of a conspiracy against Gentiles? Although women account for half of the population, they commit only one quarter of the crime. Does that indicate a need for increased criminality amongst females in the name of equality? If one quarter of all American hockey players come from one state (Minnesota) is it surprising that the other fifty states do not each contribute 2 per cent of the hockey players? In Britain there is a 'disproportionate' number of Pakistani and Indian doctors in the National Health Service. Is this discrimination against English doctors? There are more black players in English league football than would be predicted from statistical probability. Does this demonstrate that managers are prejudiced against white players?

The fact, of course, is that in a free and open society disparities rather than regularities of outcome are the norm. That there is discrimination against minorities in every society is beyond dispute. But to insist that, in Britain, this amounts to systematic denial of 'access' to education and jobs is to misuse words.

Black

In the speech or writing of the reasonable person this word indicates a colour—a blindingly obvious, but, in the wake of its perpetual misuse by the devotees of the race lobby, necessary observation. One might, for instance, reasonably describe people of Afro-Caribbean origin as 'black', since the vast majority have black skins. However, in the strange, obscurantist world of race relations the word has been re-defined, so as to prosecute the cause and persuade the gullible. Leading black activists, such as Professor Mullard,[10] at some points in its rhetoric the Commission for Racial Equality, and an increasing number of local authorities all now use the word 'black' so as to describe all non-whites.

The objections to this are so obvious that the growing acceptance of this misuse of the word can only be explained by the power of the race relations lobby to shape people's understanding and perceptions. For instance, to describe someone from Pakistan or Vietnam as 'black' is to pervert perception; it also risks giving offence. My lengthy contacts with the Asian community indicates that both parents and children would reject such an epithet out of hand. They would perceive this misapplication of the word as a threat to an important aspect of their identity, and resent the crude attempt to merge their culture with those cultures which are vastly different from it. Indeed, it is scarcely appropriate to describe people of West Indian origin as simply 'black', since this conceals those traditional and deeply felt variations in West Indian culture designated by the term, 'the island question'. Moreover, it is doubtful if Africans would be happy to be confused with West Indians.

Why, then, this systematic misuse of the term? I believe there are three reasons. First, using the word this way means differences between and within ethnic groups, in terms of socio-economic and educational performance, can be obscured. Thus, the significantly better progress of Asians than West Indians—particularly by the second generation—can be masked by producing aggregate rather than specific statistics about education, jobs, home ownership and economic status. Average figures are thereby depressed. Second, an undifferentiated general term can help promote the false notion that all minority groups are equally worse off. This generates a politically very useful sense of 'black' solidarity, in opposition to the white majority. Third, since this usage abolishes the enormous variations between ethnic groups, the race relations propagandist can promote the myth that the world is divided into two groups of people—racists and anti-racists. The liberal conscience is thereby pricked and liberal support gained. If there is a simple choice, who wants to be a racist?

This misuse of the word is an important pointer to the mentality which lies beneath so much race relations rhetoric. It is a mentality which, quite literally, sees the world in black and white—the consequences of which can be seen in the attempts to create separate 'black' sections in the Labour Party and the promotion of separate 'black' state schools by a member of the Swann Committee. Those infinite, rich variations within groups, that cherished uniqueness of each individual which enrich life for all of us, these things count for little in the two-dimensional world of race relations man. This total, collectivist mentality denies the possibility of partial agreement, of the informed, complex response to complex social phenomena, of the considered view. For instance, one might legitimately applaud the marvellous way the Chinese have richly transformed that important English institution, the fish and chip shop. Also one might, equally, admire the business enterprise displayed by those victims of black African oppression who came to Britain from Uganda; as well as the willingness of Pakistani shopkeepers to work much longer hours than their English counterparts to serve the community better. And what decent man could fail to rejoice in that splendid Evangelical religious tradition brought here by West Indian Christians? But why should that positive response prevent one from expressing certain concerns about the transformation of some British cities into multi-ethnic societies? Why should fear of being branded a 'white racist' prevent a reasonable anxiety about the 'Pakistani Connection' in the alarming growth of heroin-addiction amongst young people here? How should the civilised man respond to the reported habit of Moslem women living here of seeking abortions, when they learn that their expected child will be a girl? Or to the news that in the schools of Birmingham, West Indian pupils are four times more likely to behave badly as other children?

Such a varied and honest reflection on what, after all, has been a significant transformation in the nature of British identity and urban life is not possible when the world is reduced to two groups of people, between which a grotesque linguistic sleight of hand posits inevitable conflict. It is, indeed, difficult to resist the belief that the way 'black' is now so systematically misused is to do, not with reconciliation and racial harmony, but political objectives. 'Black' is the contemporary equivalent of *sansculotte*, or 'Bolshevik'. It is an icon word whose emblematic simplicity serves as a rallying-cry to all those disaffected elements in society with a grudge against the established order— those political extremists, guilt-ridden liberals and professional opportunists who make up so much of the race relations lobby. In this sense the word is not only a testimony to dishonest thinking, it is a highly irresponsible usage in some of our highly charged inner-city areas. Of course, to many of its purveyors this consideration is irrelevant. Or, rather, it is highly relevant if your object is, indeed, to make mischief.

Racism

A 'racist' is to the race relations lobby what 'Protestant' was to the inquisitors of the Counter-Reformation, or 'witches' was to the seventeenth-century burghers of Salem. It is the totem of the new doctrine of anti-racism. Its definition varies according to the purpose it is meant to achieve. It is a gift to the zealot, since he can apply it to anyone who disagrees with him—and he often ejaculates the word as though it were a synonym for 'rapist' or 'facist'. It takes its force not from its power to describe but from its power to coerce and intimidate. It is attached to anyone who challenges the arguments or rhetoric of the race relations lobby. It is more a weapon than a word. Its misuse arises not from a desire to engage in civilised discourse about matters of gravity but from that restricted mentality which underlies all fanaticism—a mentality which insists the world is divided into those who are for or against the cause. Its proper use as a means of describing the odious doctrines of racial superiority and the master-race has long since been buried beneath the dead weight of campaign rhetoric and the strident sloganising of street-politics. In its perverted sense it is a threat to good race relations, since it serves to alienate people of goodwill who simply wish to gain access to a language which questions the soundness of the new race relations orthodoxies. Its pretensions need urgently to be examined.

If we could persuade those who use the word to stick to its proper meaning then no harm would result. If a man actually believes that one race is genetically superior to another, then he can properly be designated a 'racist'—whether he belongs to the National Front or a 'black power' movement. In this sense the word has integrity, since it corresponds to a known and verifiable phenomenon. Word and concept are one, as it were. But its current misuse involves such a degree of conceptual woolliness as to make it worthless as a tool of genuine discourse.

For instance, the separate notions of prejudice and discrimination are conflated, and an important conceptual distinction is lost. Clearly, to call someone prejudiced ought not to imply he is a neo-Nazi, or that he necessarily discriminates against other races. Indeed to be prejudiced is, simply, to be human. All men and women, whatever their origin, creed or colour, are prejudiced. We all have a tendency to prejudge, either out of social conditioning or previous experience. Sometimes our judgements are irrational and sometimes sound. This tendency is a function not of skin colour but, more likely, the result of our perceptual mechanisms, which, through a system of filtering, prevent us from being overwhelmed by undifferentiated sensory input.

Discrimination is a different matter. Whereas prejudice, in social terms, may mean no more than a preference for one's own kind—again, a universal tendency—discrimination is an attempt to implement a preference for as an hostility against. It is to penalise someone for not being in one's own group. Now a person may, of course, be both prejudiced and discriminatory. But, and this is the central point, he need not be. And a word which implies that the one necessarily implies the other muddies the water of clear thinking. My hunch, after working for several years in multi-racial areas, is that most people in Britain, whatever their skin colour, are prejudiced non-discriminators. More than that, I am convinced that initial prejudice in the majority dissipates with experience of interacting with minority groups. But the rate at which this harmonising occurs varies with the willingness of newcomers to respect and adapt to those existing values and customs of the country of which they are now citizens.

The current misuse of 'racism' also overlooks the fact that discrimination may take two forms. The American philosopher, Robert Nesbit,[11] has postulated the existence of both malign and benign racism. Malign racism is the product of that fragmentation of man which came with the Reformation. The ancient world knew little of discrimination according to skin colour. The Greeks and Romans designated men 'barbarians' not according to colour but with reference to capture in battle and the degree of acceptance of the language, culture and mores of the imperial state. Saint Augustine insisted on the essential unity of mankind. But the followers of Zwingli, Luther and Calvin, in matching the enemies of God's chosen people with strange and distant people, spelled the end not only of Christian unity but of the notion of monogenesis. The enlightenment supplied that scientific basis for the doctrine of evolution and unequal development, which ultimately issued in the institution and rationalisation of slavery, the politics of racial separation in the southern states before Martin Luther King and the appalling pass laws of apartheid South Africa. That was malign racism. And all civilised men are united in condemning it.

But the attempt, particularly in the USA, to institutionalise racial equality—to compel by law the essentially Utopian ideal of social equality—has, in reality, replaced tyranny with confusion, resentment and officially created racial hostility. This doctrine of benign racism has compelled schools, colleges, professions and business firms to recruit not according to individual merit but quota systems— a device from which the able black, who needs no props or patronage, emerges as the most embittered product, saddled for life with the false accusation that his success is a function of privileged treatment. As Professor Nesbit says, 'A plantation mentality is not made the better for being benign in intent. Malign or benign, such a mentality is opposed to everything that is essential to liberty and to the realisation of individual opportunity.' I suspect that our failure to challenge the race relations lobby's mindless, but instrumental, use of the word 'racism' may yet cause Britain to make the sort of mistakes thoughtful Americans are now regretting.

Not only does 'racism', as currently employed, fail to make

necessary conceptual distinctions, it compounds error by delimiting its target. Only white people, it seems, can be 'racists'. This allegation rests on a verbal sleight of hand—the sort which happily transforms one-party tyranny into 'democracy', or incarceration of dissidents into 'treatment'. By re-defining the term to mean 'prejudice plus power', i.e. inventing a new meaning for an established word, the protagonist successfully conveys the notion that, since most of the power happens to be in the hands of people who are white—a not surprising phenomenon in a nation which, until very recently, was almost entirely Anglo-Saxon or Celtic in origin—then only white people can be 'racists'. Thus, the uncomfortable truth that some of the worst examples of racial prejudice occur within the ethnic minority communities can be conveniently circumvented. Black racism is abolished by re-defining the word which properly describes it. This, of course, is using words not to enlighten and communicate but to manipulate, to prejudge and to bestow a guilt which cannot be purged since the language to facilitate such a process no longer exists.

In pondering the success of the race relations lobby in destroying that civilised consensus which can only survive when men accept the need for their transactions to be articulated against a background of shared, consistent meanings, I was reminded of an observation by the great Trinidadian writer, V. S. Naipaul. In *Middle Passage* Naipaul tells of hearing a Jamaican, who has lived in Britain, informing a group of West Indian emigrants about to set out to a life here that if they could not get what they wanted from the English, all they needed to do was to accuse them of racial prejudice. This never failed to evoke the desired response. This ability to exploit liberal guilt has been systematically deployed by those who run our race industry.

Just how successful this technique can be was vividly illustrated in a recent letter to *The Times Educational Supplement*. The writer, a teacher, and committed supporter of the new race relations orthodoxies, says this: '... However well meaning an anti-racist I am, I am still racist because I am white. However much I try to rid myself of the strait jacket of monoculture, some of it will surely remain tied to me.'[12] A leading article in the same issue describes this as 'chilling'. It is also, of course, irrational. If being 'racist' is inevitable in white people, what is the point of that growing, publicly funded 'consciousness-raising' movement designated as 'anti-racism'? If all white people, by their very nature, suffer from the same incurable disease, why should the state invest tax and ratepayers' money in providing a treatment doomed to failure?

Is it not time to challenge the supposed necessity for men of liberal sympathies to feel guilt-ridden about our imperial past? When such an attitude provides the soil in which such systematic untruths as I have outlined can flourish, should not sensible, civilised people adopt a better-informed, a more sceptical view of the disabling tradition that we ought, as a nation, and forever, feel remorse for what our forebears did in the name of Empire? And should we not protest at the attempt by the race lobby to so misrepresent our multi-racial character? By misapplying, re-defining and generally undermining the integrity of words, a vested interest group whose *raison d'être* is the exploitation of racial differences is distorting social and political realities. We are not a mirror-image of apartheid South Africa. We are a free and open society. Access to the franchise, the welfare state, the education system, the press and the courts is available to all. We do not seek to regulate ethnicity through the ballot box. Nor do we traditionally deny help to persecuted foreigners—the very opposite is true.

I believe the race relations lobby's view of contemporary Britain is akin to the Marxist view of history, i.e. that social appearances are determined by forces and laws, the nature and significance of which are concealed from those subject to them. The idea that only those who subscribed to the doctrines of the race relations lobby *really* understand multi-racial Britain has been assiduously cultivated by those race relations officials, who are the fountain-head of that mysterious body of knowledge and insights forming the new orthodoxies. Access to those mysteries is available only to those who employ the approved argot dispensed by our race relations priesthood. Thomas Sowell[13] has dubbed such people 'The anointed ones'. It is they who have created the language in which we are all supposed to think and express ourselves on multi-racial matters. It is a language we need urgently to call to account.

Notes

1. Sally Shreir, 'The Politics of Language', *The Salisbury Review*, No.4, Summer, 1983.
2. Milovan Djilas. *The New Class* (Harvard University Press, 1982).

3. *Education for All*, Report of Committee of Inquiry into the Education of Children from Ethnic Minority Groups, Cmmd. 9453 (HMSO, 1985).
4. Maureen Stone, *The Education of the Black Child in Britain* (Fontana, London, 1981).
5. Chris Murray and Ann Dawson, *Five Thousand Adolescents* (University of Manchester, 1983).
6. Michael Rutter, 'Staying on Helps Blacks to Exam Success', Report by Diane Spencer in *The Times Educational Supplement*, 8 October 1982.
7. Peter Mortimer, 'Study on Exams finds Asians most Positive', Report by Diane Spencer in *The Times Educational Supplement*, 13 April 1984.
8. Alan Little, *The Times Educational Supplement*, 25 July 1982.
9. Thomas Sowell, *The Economics and Politics of Race* (William Morrow, New York, 1983).
10. Chris Mullard, *The Educational Management and Demanagement of Racism* (University of Lancaster, 1982).
11. Robert Nisbet, 'Racism', in *Prejudices: A Philosophical Dictionary* (Harvard University Press, 1982).
12. Alyson Redgrave, 'Reaction to Racism', *The Times Educational Supplement*, 3 May 1985.
13. Thomas Sowell, *Pink and Brown People, and other Controversial Essays* (Hoover Institution Press, Stanford, Ca, 1981).

SECTION 2

The Materials of Propaganda

4

History, Race and Propaganda

Tom Hastie

The overwhelming majority of people in Britain today would regard as highly desirable and laudable any attempts to foster racial harmony and mutual respect for the various cultures to be found here. These worthy ends, however, are only too often being pursued by clumsy, counterproductive means which merely bring discredit to a noble cause and which call into question the credibility of the race industry, whose *raison d'être* is alleged to be the attainment of social justice for the ethnic minorities in our communities. By 'race industry' I mean community relations personnel, multi-ethnic education inspectors and advisers, vote-hungry local politicians, members of local government committees and agencies set up, for example, to monitor police attitudes to blacks, ambitious leaders of immigrant pressure groups and the like. In other words, those with a vested interest in putting race into the forefront of people's minds. The result has been a social phenomenon best described by Newsam's Law, which runs, 'The incidence of alleged racism in a given society will vary in a direct proportion to the number of people handsomely paid to find it'. Or, as the old saying more bluntly puts it, 'Never ask the barber if you need a haircut'.

My disquiet at the divisive and, indeed, disruptive consequences of the race industry's policies is experienced on three levels: as a history teacher (even if now retired), as a citizen and as a lifelong Socialist. It is on the first of these levels that I shall be putting most of my emphasis in this brief chapter.

During the past fifteen to twenty years there has been a quiet revolution in the teaching of history in British classrooms, whereby pupils have been encouraged to think and to work at their own level in much the same way as do professional historians. No longer have pupils been expected to sit like passive receptacles into which history teachers poured metaphorical jugfuls of facts, dates and statistics. Pupils were, and are, encouraged to ask, '*How* do we know all these things about the past? How *accurate* is the information from the past?' Pupils have been led to see that what we call history is merely those accounts of the past or those concrete bits of evidence such as artifacts and documents, which have survived from the past. The evidence is incomplete, of course, like a jigsaw puzzle with pieces missing, but it is all we have to work with to try to build up pictures of the past. We have, therefore, to check these bits of evidence carefully against other existing bits of evidence and then draw conclusions from the refined evidence we are left with, while being prepared to amend or abandon these same conclusions when other evidence appears to refute them. In other words, pupils are being taught to think, are being introduced to the basic principles of logic and are being shown how essential it is to check the validity of the evidence upon which we base our judgements not only in historical matters but in daily life, too.

As it happens, however, the skills of the historian are being flagrantly disregarded by the race industry, skills such as the examination of evidence to ascertain (1) its authenticity and (2) its truthfulness. An historical account may in fact be a genuine eye-witness version of some past event but yet it may be so partial or partisan that it presents a false picture of what actually did happen on that occasion. Indeed, bias is one of the historian's biggest bugbears in trying to find out what really happened in the past, and in E. H. Carr's little classic, *What Is History?* he points out, 'By and large, the historian will get the kind of facts he wants'. He claims, too, that the historian, like the rest of us, has the odd bee in his bonnet and advises us, 'When you read a work of history, always listen out for the buzzing. If you can detect none, either you are tone-deaf or your historian is a very dull dog'. The detection of bias is, therefore, of crucial importance to the student of the past—*and* the present—and E. H. Dance's *History the Betrayer: a study in bias* (Hutchinson, 1967) is essential reading for any thinking person, be he a historian or not.

Bias consists of two types, the intentional and the involuntary. The former is the tool of the propagandist and the latter is one we *all* have to guard against. Intentional bias is quite easy to reveal to pupils and it is done very effectively in the teaching kit *Thinking Through History* (a two-fold appropriate title) by Duncan MacIntyre and produced in the mid-1970s. *Inter alia*, the kit looks at two instances of propaganda in the past; Tudor propaganda vilifying Richard III to justify the Tudor military *coup d'état* and Nazi propaganda to rally support for Hitler. MacIntyre lists the six basic techniques of the recruiting propagandist and then provides a variety of fictitious examples (some based upon commercial advertisements) which pupils have to analyse and classify under their six headings. The Schools Council Project *History 13–16* makes pupils study several given case histories and then interpret the evidence, deciding which conclusions derived from the given evidence may be regarded as certainties, which may be regarded as possibilities and which may be rejected as untenable. It seems that such techniques used in the teaching of history are highly desirable in any democracy and I am all the more angry how so much of the race industry's published material for the classroom and the general public runs counter to the excellent work being done by so many of the nation's history teachers, including black colleagues I have had the pleasure of working with.

One of the latest deplorable productions of the race industry is *How Racism Came to Britain, Book three* (*HRCB* in future) written and published by the Institute of Race Relations (IRR). The format is that of cartoons with captions and frequently with 'balloons' containing what is being said by the depicted characters. Speaking as someone who was one of the midwives of the *Beano* comic in 1938 I have no objection to the cartoon format for the purposes of innocent entertainment, but I do have reservations about its use in the field of education, where its limitations can inhibit the inclusion of alternative or opposing points of view. On the other hand, a textbook can easily set out, for example, the cases of the British and of the American colonists when the American War of Independence is being studied. If the cartoon format *can* do anything similar, then the significantly anonymous writers of this publication made no attempt to do so. The result is an extremely simplistic caricature of the past which is a travesty of the truth. Any history teacher looking for examples of bias, the use of selected evidence and other logically inadmissible practices would be well advised to consult this publication and use extracts from it as examples of unsupported propaganda. Such a teacher must, of course, be prepared to be subjected to the kind of harassment and threats of sacking which have been endured by Ray Honeyford, the Bradford headmaster who dared to express opinions which were considered racist by the local race industry. He at least had the courage and integrity to sign his allegedly offensive articles, so unlike the anonymous authors of *HRCB*.

As a lifelong Socialist who has taught Commonwealth history at 'A' level, I am no stranger to the evils of imperialism, but I am also aware that those evils were made possible by men who were imperialists rather than by those who just happened to be white. Accidents of history (such as concentrations of capital, the convenient juxtaposition of coal and iron deposits, technological expertise, astronomical knowledge and consequent navigational innovations, etc.) favoured Western European societies and gave them considerable advantages over those societies lacking such a combination of fortuitous social and economic factors. Colour or race was quite incidental in the development of capitalism and its ultimate form, imperialism. Is the Institute of Race Relations prepared to insist that had black societies enjoyed these same historical advantages of Western Europe then they would *not* have exploited them *and* their fellow human beings in a capitalist and imperialist manner? To claim that they would not have done so seems to attribute to blacks the qualities of a moral *Herrenvolk*, a possibility I reject out of hand on the grounds that such a claim would be (1) the product of racial arrogance and (2) contrary to the lessons of history.

One of the main activities of the race industry is to protest, quite rightly, against the use of stereotypes in human relations, yet the race industry itself is one of the greatest offenders in this respect. Any pupil, whatever his colour, reading *HRCB* could be excused for assuming that every single white person today is (1) a frustrated imperialist and (2) absolutely riddled with racial prejudice and notions of white superiority. There is no mention whatsoever of the long-established anti-imperialist stance of the British labour movement in this country. Lancashire cotton workers suffered great hardship during the American Civil War and yet were prepared to put their livelihoods at risk when they opposed the British government that seemed on the point of supporting the Confederacy and thereby condoning the enslavement of black fellow-workers. There was also a strong voice against imperialism in the Movement for Colonial

Freedom, an organisation consisting almost entirely of white men and women. It would be tedious to provide further instances to show that the British people certainly did not think or act in a uniform, stereotyped fashion in their attitudes towards other races, but the IRR will have none of that. The white man *per se* is the villain of history and there are no exceptions. Can one imagine anything more crass? I find it astonishing that the IRR, which claims to be so left-wing, so fiercely anti-capitalist, should be so ignorant of the class struggle in human society and should advocate a simplistic view of history which can only be described as racist.

The implicit statement that the white man is the villain of history is made possibly by the use of selected evidence, by presenting whites solely in anti-social roles and blacks as being always innocent victims. For example, no mention whatsoever is made of the fact that slavery was an ancient institution in Africa and in Asia. We are led to believe that idyllic societies were the order of the day in these places till the wicked white man arrived, a view certainly not shared by anyone knowing anything about African or Asian history. We are told on page 6 that ships went from Britain to Africa 'where textiles and tools were exchanged for people caught and bought as slaves by the white traders'. Note how cleverly we are not told *who* caught these unfortunate people and sold them into slavery. White traders were hardly likely to pay for people they had already captured. Perhaps they caught some and bought others? To suggest that the crews of individual ships could land in Africa and seize whomsoever they wished strikes me as an insult to the peoples of Africa and an underestimation of their capabilities to resist. The truth is obvious. The Atlantic slave trade and the East African slave markets run by Arabs were made possible only because of the active co-operation and participation of the African ruling class and African businessmen, such as King Losoko of Lagos to name but one—and one still operating until the 1850s. By insisting that Africans were as deeply involved in the slave trade as were the white traders I am in no way suggesting that two wrongs make a right. What I *am* saying is that our pupils, whatever their colour, should be told that there were *two* wrongs. Also, I find it ironic that the race industry which keeps protesting about Eurocentricism should always be Eurocentric in its presentation of the slave trade.

It is typical of the propaganda of the publications of bodies like

IRR that no mention is ever made that whites, too, suffered the misery and degradation of slavery throughout the ages. Indeed, writing in the *Times Educational Supplement* (24 May 1985) Professor Parekh demands, 'Why were only blacks treated as human chattels?' I find it odd that a professor of Political Philosophy at Hull University should be unaware that the word 'slave' is derived from 'Slav', a people not particularly noted for their dark pigmentation; that he should be unaware of the European slaves in classical Greece and Rome; that he has never heard of Gregory's famous comment on seeing some blonde children in the Roman slave market, 'Non Angli, sed angeli'; that he is unaware that St Patrick was seized by raiders and enslaved in Ireland; that in 1212 when thousands of white children in the Children's Crusade reached the shores of the Mediterranean they were offered free passage to the Holy Land by white merchants who promptly took them across to North Africa and sold the lot; that after the 1745 Rebellion a thousand of my fellow-countrymen, survivors of Culloden, were sold to the American plantations; that serfdom in Scottish coalmines was not made illegal till 1799; that serfs in Russia were not emancipated till 1861; that for hundreds of years the Muslims of North Africa constantly raided the shores of Spain, France, Italy and Greece in search of slaves, frequently landing and looting and destroying towns and villages as well as seizing victims for the slave markets; that these raiders frequently operated in the English Channel, and that in one famous instance, an Englishman, William Okeley, was captured off the Isle of Wight in 1639; that St Vincent de Paul (1576–1660) was captured by Tunisians while making a short voyage along the southern coast of France; that various European powers—and the newly established United States of America—were constantly forced to take naval and military action to compel North African rulers to leave white ships and citizens alone. Slavery is no respecter of races, in spite of Professor Parekh.

Not only are whites deemed solely responsible for the Atlantic slave trade; they must not be given any credit for abolishing it. We are told (page 11) that it was the resistance of the slaves and their constant destruction of West Indian plantation crops by arson which made the British decide to end slavery. That is certainly news to me. I had always understood that it was the enormous competition from the vast, slave-worked plantations in Brazil that made West Indian sugar no longer profitable. Napoleon's encouragement of the growth of sugar beet in France to combat the British blockade was another factor as the growth of beet steadily spread across Europe. I agree that reduced profits were a factor in assuring the ruling class's consent to the ending of slavery in the British Empire in 1833 but the bulk of the activities of the anti-slavery movement in Britain were carried out by disinterested people like Granville Sharp, battling against powerful economic interests. To present the Christian movement's opposition to slavery as being really motivated by the prospect of better investment elsewhere (page 11) merely shows the depths to which the anonymous authors of this booklet are prepared to sink in order to 'bash the Brits' and to deny them any capacity for human compassion. Are we to understand that the desire to help the peoples of the Third World suddenly burgeoned for the first time in European hearts during today's generation of trendies?

To deny that there has ever been any racial prejudice in Britain would be absurd. Every human society is contaminated by it to varying degrees, but it has never been as universal and long-established in this country as the race industry claims. One of Francis Drake's lieutenants and companions was Diego, a black man, while Dr Johnson's black servant, Francis Barber, was a familiar figure to London's literati and was left a legacy in Johnson's will. Eighteenth-century European intellectuals enthused about the virtues of 'the noble savage' and London Society lionised black visitors like Job ben Solomon, Equiano and Omai from Tahiti, who became the darling of literary London. These may be dismissed as isolated instances, of course (although there are many, many more) yet the race industry itself excels in the technique of presenting the isolated particular as the general rule. On page 18 we read 'It is predicted that some day the menial work of the universe [sic] will all be done by Chinamen and negroes whilst the white race is to fill the high places of the earth, squeezing other races out of existence'. And what is the source of this nugget of allegedly typical white man's thinking? None other than the *Queensland Figaro*, 6 October 1883! If the *Muck Spreaders' and Rhubarb Thrashers' Gazette* printed a letter from a correspondent claiming to prove that the earth is flat, would the Director of the IRR claim this as indisputable proof that the British are totally ignorant of twentieth-century science? There are crazy people in every community, whatever its colour, and to quote them as authoritative voices merely damages the IRR's case.

As it happens, pre-war Britain was singularly free of racial prejudice as a general rule. In 1913 John Archer, a borough councillor for twenty years in Battersea, where I live, became Britain's first black mayor and in 1922 the people of Battersea sent Shapurji Saklatvala, an Indian Communist, to Westminster as their MP. I myself as a boy was in a cinema in Dundee during the Depression of the 1930s (when Dundee was officially designated as a Distressed Area) and heard working-class men and women clap and cheer when a newsreel showed Alexander Bustamente, a black militant trade unionist known as 'the Lion' and a future Prime Minister of Jamaica. These Scottish unemployed workers saw Bustamente's struggle as being linked to their own against exploitation and neglect. Again on the personal level, during the summer of 1943 a fellow-sergeant and I were stopped in a Tunis street by three black GIs. They said they had just arrived after being stationed for three months in England and asked us to be the first to drink from the bottle of brandy they had just bought because they wanted, through us, to thank the British people who had been so good to them. 'They treated us real nice, just like we was their own folks,' said their spokesman. This culture shock experienced by black GIs coming to wartime Britain from the USA is confirmed in the US Army film made for white GIs in Britain, in which the actor Burgess Meredith tells them that the British see things differently about race. White GIs were warned to avoid offending their British allies—and ruining the image of the USA as a democracy—by showing racial prejudice against their black fellow-countrymen in public. As one who spent quite a bit of time with the American 5th Army in Italy I frequently saw occasions when British troops intervened because white Americans were abusing black GIs. The USA may have a long tradition of race hatred but *we* have not.

One of the aims of education is to widen one's horizons, to open one's mind to influences other than local and traditional ones, to introduce one to the best products of the human mind and hand, wherever they come from, to train one's mind to develop as wide a perspective as possible. In spite of the race industry's allegations to the contrary, most of our schools did try to achieve that aim. At my primary school in the 1920s we read the story of Marco Polo, and it was impressed upon us how the Chinese had been ahead of the West in most things for hundreds of years. From reading *The Arabian Nights* we were introduced to the glories of Islamic architecture and to an awareness of Muslim seamanship—even our word 'admiral' came from Arabic!—while stories of the Crusades fostered in us a healthy respect for Muslim military prowess. At secondary school we learned that much of our maths and science came from the Arabs, although I for one thought that algebra was something we might well have been spared by our academic benefactors.

My history lessons certainly did not belittle other nations and peoples as is so often alleged. One of the most popular history textbooks in pre-war Britain was Marten & Carter, and if I turn to Book One, page 112, I find a very sympathetic account of Mahomet and the religion he founded, an account which says that the *Koran* is the most widely read book in the world. Tribute is paid to Arab learning, and we are reminded (page 120) that 'for some 500 years the centres of art and learning were to be found, not in Christian countries, but in cities under Mohammedan rule such as Bagdad and Cordova, Damascus and Cairo'. Another popular textbook was F. C. Happold's *Adventure of Man* (my copy, dated 1944, is the 15th impression) which (page 95) praised Muslim universities and told how Christian scholars sometimes attended them to acquire knowledge they could not find in Europe. *A Junior Outline of History*, by I. O. Evans (1932), also praises Muslim learning, and claims that the Arabs brought learning to Europe. How does the IRR reconcile these typical quotations with its own assertion that we kept emphasising how inferior other people were supposed to be?

My teachers encouraged me to have a universal outlook, but the race industry prefers to look at human affairs like sufferers of tunnel-vision, seeing only what it wants to see and yet claiming that its restricted vision presents the full and true picture. On page 11 of *HRCB* we are told, quite correctly, that British capitalists destroyed the Indian cottage industry in the interests of British factory-made cotton, with the result that Indian hand-spinners and weavers 'were driven out from any livelihood altogether'. No mention is made of the fact that because of the new factory system a similar fate was suffered by the British woollen-workers whose cottage industry over the centuries had built up the wealth of many families of the British ruling class. British rural workers were also robbed of their access to the lands held in common for centuries as Enclosure Acts poured through Parliament at the turn of the eighteenth and nineteenth centuries. The race industry's propaganda, however, suggests that only blacks have suffered under capitalism, whereas the truth is that the only social group throughout history to have a monopoly of hardship and exploitation is the *poor*—whatever their colour.

I would question the allegation (page 11) that the British not only burned Indian handlooms but actually broke workers' hands to prevent them from spinning and weaving. British capitalists were more subtle than that, and merely put a crippling tax on spinning-wheels which achieved the desired effect without a lot of messy publicity. The suggestion that the British stayed in India by force is ludicrous. At no time were there ever more than 130,000 British, including soldiers, in India, and it would have been utterly impossible for such a tiny number to hold down a population of some 300 million people. As in the case of the African slave trade, the active co-operation of the indigenous ruling class was an indispensable factor in British control of India. Also, the British presence was not as unpopular as some people claim, for it was seen by many Indians as the lesser of two evils. While the Moghul emperors were able, vigorous men, they imposed law and order on the major part of India, even if it was done mainly for fiscal purposes. When the quality of these foreign rulers declined, rebellions broke out everywhere and petty kings and princes plundered one another's territories at will. The Marathas (the origin of our word 'marauder'?) were muggers on horseback, and their armies roamed far and wide, striking terror into the population wherever they went. They even raided Delhi at one point, and exacted tribute from the Moghul emperor himself. The average Indian man and woman prayed for deliverance and did not care where it came from. Indeed, as early as the twelfth century, Kalhana, the Kashmiri historian, argued that benevolent despotism was preferable to feudal rivalries. Many Indians were, therefore, psychologically ready to accept British rule if it would only put an end to the constant killings, plunderings, extortion, enslavement and degradation. The British imperialists, aware that profitable trade was impossible in such uncertain conditions, were only too happy to oblige. Indian workers and peasants certainly preferred the British raj to *banya ki raj*, rule by the moneylenders!

Those sceptical of that last remark should consult Professor D. N. Majumdar's *Caste and Communication in an Indian Village* (Asia Publishing House, Bombay, 1962). He reports (page 299) how research students of Lucknow University studying peasants' attitudes towards Indian independence discovered that 'Comparing the present government with the British rule, some villagers say that under the British regime they lived peacefully and the government did not interfere in their affairs unnecessarily. Further, at the time of British rule, they say, justice was meted out with fairness and the wrong-doer was punished, but now, often the wrong-doer escapes and the innocent is punished, for there is much corruption and bribery among those in power'.

It has also escaped the notice of the anonymous writers of *HRCB* that the British ruling class in India despised its own soldiers in the ranks, who were almost permanently confined to barracks until needed for military purposes. Lady Curzon, wife of the controversial Viceroy, once commented that the ugliest things she had seen in India were the water buffalo and the British soldier. During the war I myself frequently seethed with impotent rage when I saw the best restaurants, cafés, bars, dance halls, etc., conspicuously labelled 'Officers only. Out of bounds to other ranks'. Once again, as in the slave trade, we are in the realm of class transcending race.

We must also bear in mind that the British in their colonies had a psychological advantage: all technically undeveloped communities tend to stand in awe of those who produce and control machines and gadgets which appear to be of magical origin. The North American Indians, for example, attributed magical properties to 'The Singing Wires' (which is how they perceived the telegraph wires that spanned the West). This effect wears off, of course, after a couple of generations or so when familiarity with the 'magical' devices reveals their mundane nature, but it is significantly potent while it lasts.

I find it rather odd that a book which is allegedly anti-capitalist should have nothing to say about exploitation by Indian capitalists—such as the Tata family, who, in 1907, founded Jamshedpur, which rapidly grew into one of the major steel-producing complexes in the world. It is also significant that the resources list at the end of the book does not include Mulk Raj Anand's *Coolie* (first published in 'racist' Britain, by the way) nor even *Reason Wounded*, by Primila Lewis, an Indian woman married to a Briton. In her book she tells of being flung into jail, on the personal orders of the late Mrs Gandhi, after trying to help Indian peasants form an agricultural workers' union to resist the appalling exploitation by some of Mrs Gandhi's friends and colleagues in government. Nor does the list include films like *Arohan*, made in 1982 by the West Bengal Marxist government to expose the continuing exploitation of the peasant share-croppers by landlords using legal trickery and even crippling attacks by hired thugs. To include works of that nature would, of course, have revealed that exploitation is a matter of class and not of race. I suggest that the IRR is not so much concerned with justice for blacks or with historical truth but more with some imagined revenge on whites—a racist policy, in fact.

My impression that *HRCB* is a work unleavened by thought is confirmed on page 17, where British education and Christianity are derided in a puerile, ignorant fashion. Christian missionaries were not sent abroad 'to impose their views on others', but to invite others to become Christians, too. Their most important work, however, lay in the setting up of hospitals and schools, not with government money but with donations from ordinary Britons who wanted to do something to help their less fortunate fellow humans. Do the writers of this book really think that Christians should have *refrained* from opening hospitals where none had existed before? And where, may I ask, did the political leaders of the new African states get *their* education? I find it very revealing that, as far as the writers of this book are concerned, the notion of altruism as a factor in human affairs is unthinkable! I also find it hilarious that in the mockery of a church meeting (page 17) there is a reference to 'Celestials and Barbarians', because it so happens that the Chinese regarded themselves as citizens of the Celestial Kingdom, i.e. China, and regarded all other people as mere barbarians. Notions of superiority and inferiority are certainly not limited to whites.

I also find it ironic that on page 22 is a cartoon of two rifles being fired into a large crowd of oddly garbed Indians to illustrate India's struggle for independence. It so happens that in one year (1947) Indians killed over a million of their fellow-Indians many times more than the British ever killed in 300 years. Anyone wishing to get some insight into the horrors of that year should read *Azadi* (Freedom), by Chaman Nahal, based on his own family's experience of atrocities committed by both sides when the family had to flee from the new Pakistan to the new Indian frontier a mere fifty miles away.

As for the British reluctantly granting independence to the colonies, that may have been true of Churchill and his cronies but it certainly was not true of the average Briton—including many of those serving in India. Throughout the twentieth century a policy of

Indianisation of the government of India was steadily accelerated with a view to handing over to the Indians completely. World War II strengthened the feeling in Britain that the colonies ought to be freed, because we ourselves had fought a long and bitter war to ensure our own freedom from Nazi domination. We felt that freedom is indivisible and the Labour landslide in 1945 was partly due to its declared policy on restoring independence to the colonies. Many Indians and Britons like myself are convinced that India's freedom could have been won at least ten years earlier had it not been for Gandhi's urging of non-co-operation with the British (which kept many able Indians out of office where they could have hastened the process of the transfer of power) and had it not been for his autocratic insistence that he alone spoke for all India. In February 1947 the British government, frustrated by the incessant rioting and wrangling among Indians over the form that India's freedom would take, announced that it would relinquish power not later than June 1948. The communal riots and the political fencing went on unabated till the British, convinced that their presence was unable to bring about agreement among the Indian factions, brought forward the date of the transfer of power to 14 August 1947. Far from being reluctant to go, we actually went earlier than we had originally promised!

On page 22 there is a drawing of a black man who has just lowered a Union Jack to the ground and is saying, 'Independence! What it means for us is: a people without land, a land without food, a work force without the capital to activate it'. I find this rather puzzling. Did the departing British take the land away with them? Or did the local black capitalists grab it? Without the evils of forced cash crops (as described on page 12) why were the liberated colonial peoples unable to grow food for themselves? Could it possibly be that the black ruling classes preferred more lucrative investment in urban industries rather than in agriculture? The notion of the lack of capital is rather hard to accept when one regards the enormous contrasts in the former colonies between the affluent black ruling classes and the poverty-stricken workers. Not for nothing is the East African black ruling class sarcastically described by their poorer fellow-countrymen as the Mbenzi tribe because of their passion for Mercedes-Benz cars. It seems, however, that black men cannot be blamed for the failures of independence and the sufferings of the black poor. It is all the fault of the wicked whites. *That* is the obvious message of this scurrilous book and many other publications of the race industry, a message which, inevitably and understandably, generates in spirited black adolescents paranoia and a hatred of whites, and anger and resentment in their spirited white (and innocent) peers. We hear a great deal about the socio-economic causes of the riots in Brixton, Bristol, Toxteth and Handsworth, but how great a factor in such riotings is the inflammatory propaganda of the race industry itself? Included in the resources listed at the end of *HRCB* is the film *Blacks Britannica* (a film the *Guardian's* television reviewer described as lacking in balance) in the course of which a black youth in Brixton says, 'We are at war with white society'. This inflammatory, one-sided film is available on hire from a commerical film library and therefore can be used in schools, youth clubs, etc. Comment is superfluous.

Thomas Aquinas said, 'Justice without mercy is brutality', and went on to say, 'Mercy without justice is the mother of dissolution'. In other words, to try to be fair to blacks by being unfair to whites is *not* a recipe for racial concord and social harmony. As a citizen, I consider it my duty to express my concern at attempts by bodies like the IRR to destabilise the community my family and I live in. These bodies constantly make sweeping statements attacking whites without providing a scrap of evidence to substantiate them. For example, on page 6 again, the emphasis is on the buying of slaves by white men, with no reference whatsoever to the selling of slaves by black men. A valid point is made, however, when ironic reference is made to the white traders' claim to be Christians as well as slave-traders. It is then asserted, however, that such Christians believed that blacks would not get to Heaven, that Heaven would be for whites only. *Some* Christians may have held such a view at that time, and the Dutch Reformed Church in South Africa even today regards blacks not as God's children like themselves but as His step-children. By far the majority of Christians at that time, however, would certainly have rejected out of hand any claim that Heaven would be for whites only, because, as they claimed, Christ died for *all* men and women, whatever their race. For that very reason it was committed Christians who were most active in the abolition movement. The unsubstantiated accusation has served the IRR's purposes, however, by stirring up the quite understandable resentment of black readers. Dr Goebbels would be proud of his new disciples in the race industry if he could see them from wherever *he* has gone.

Also, any history teacher knows that to tell only some of the truth is often equivalent to telling a thumping lie. In the section on the British treatment of immigrants we are told (page 28) 'the only schooling they could get was in run-down, overcrowded schools'. This statement implies that immigrant children were put into completely separate schools; but as we all know, that is simply not true. No mention is made of the fact that white, working-class children were attending those same run-down and overcrowded schools. Once again, needless resentment is stirred up in the minds of black readers.

As a Socialist I am constantly being astonished how the race industry, which likes to project a 'Red' image, follows a policy of blaming whites *per se* for the problems of our society and makes no reference to the real culprit, the capitalist class, which includes blacks as well as whites. Yesterday's imperialists and today's white entrepreneurs are blamed for the poverty in the ex-colonies, thereby exonerating from blame the local capitalists, who are plundering their fellow-countrymen more savagely than ever the British dared to do. To exonerate capitalists from blame seems to me a funny way of being a Socialist. I also find it worrying how the last people to make race a key social and political issue were the Nazis, for they used it as a smokescreen and a diverting tactic to distract the attention of the German people away from the systematic destruction of their liberty. As a political animal I am worried lest the race industry should serve the same purpose in diverting *our* attention from the steady destruction of our standard of living and, possibly at no distant date, of our liberty. Is the race industry to be the Trojan Horse of British democracy from which will spring the totalitarians who will tyrannise over us all, black and white alike?

I am well aware that a number of my fellow contributors to this book do not share my political views and loyalties; but I also know that in spite of these differences we share a coincidence of views on matters of intellectual honesty, on the importance of a sound and balanced education for *all* our children, both black and white, and on grounds of concern for the civic health of our communities. If Mrs Thatcher were to say that she is strongly opposed to the battering of babies to death, I am confident that even her most outspoken critics would agree with her wholeheartedly on that issue. There are some things which cut across party political boundaries. As far as I am concerned, opposition to the callous provocation of racial strife is one of them.

5

From 'Auschwitz—Yesterday's Racism' to GCHQ

Caroline Cox

Auschwitz . . . the word strikes chill into the heart of anyone who knows it to be a byword for mass extermination, horrendous torture, obscene medical experiments on living human beings and uncounted acts of dehumanising brutality. That the horror of Auschwitz occurred in the lifetime of everyone over the age of 40 is a salutary reminder of modern man's propensity to evil on a huge scale. That our young generation now in school and college were born after Auschwitz became history is good reason for teaching them about it as a major example of man's inhumanity to man.

Therefore, when the Learning Resources Branch of the Inner London Education Authority (ILEA) advertised a teaching pack on *Auschwitz* there seemed no immediate cause for concern. Preliminary inspection revealed an imaginative and well-produced pack introducing the concept of the 'Holocaust', its historical development, many facets of the experiences of those who suffered, resisted, died—and of some of the few who survived. Pertinent questions are posed which challenge pupils and students to think about the dilemmas faced by people living in a society where this phenomenon grew in their midst—with pressures to collaborate, connive or condone.

All this is acceptable—indeed, I would agree with the Introductory Notes that this is a subject which not only can but must be taught. And the notes rightly emphasise that great care must be taken because of real dangers if the subject is taught in 'the wrong way'.

'Racism' is a major theme—appropriately, given the anti-Semitism which legitimised the policy of genocide and the attempts at total extermination of Jewish people.

From 'Auschwitz—Yesterday's Racism' to GCHQ 75

However, my endorsement suddenly turned to anger, because it soon became apparent that the teaching of these most sensitive and disturbing subjects was to be used for political purposes, which could trivialise the meaning of the Holocaust and the suffering of those who experienced it. It was also manifestly designed to carry with it a political message which turns some of the material from education into crude indoctrination.

Education or Indoctrination?

One of the criteria for distinguishing education from indoctrination is the use of foregone conclusions.[1] These can be identified by the following characteristics (*inter alia*):

(1) Presentation of conclusions in such a way as to pre-empt serious consideration of alternative points of view.
(2) The use of loaded references and loaded questions.
(3) The association of ideas so that one complex issue is mentioned in the context of other issues to make it appear as if all come into the same category and can be subject to the same criticisms.
(4) The omission of relevant evidence which is needed to present a balanced, rounded appreciation of complex issues.

Before turning to criticism, it must be emphasised that much of the *Auschwitz* material is well presented and some of the contributions are appropriately challenging and disturbing. But, tragically, there are parts which are sullied by degeneration into indoctrination and cheap politicisation. These faults would be educationally unacceptable anywhere, but in a course on a subject of such profound human concern they are outrageous and offensive.

The Use of Politically Loaded Foregone Conclusions

Every now and then, among the very moving and disturbing accounts of the horrors of Auschwitz and the issues which they raise, one finds inserted some intellectually cheap and politically loaded comment. For example, in a discussion on neo-Nazis in the modern world a hotch-potch of complex issues is slipped in—with clear implications that the British action in the Falklands War is to be condemned as unequivocally as National Socialist (Nazi) activities or Amin's atrocities in Uganda:

> What is of course obvious is that whatever one particular Israeli government does in the Middle East, not all Jews and not even all Israelis are responsible—any more than all blacks are responsible for the excesses of Idi Amin, or all Arabs for the excesses of the Syrian government or the PLO, or all Irish for the actions of the IRA, or even all British for the Falklands War (15.3).

What are schoolchildren whose fathers fought, or even died, in the Falklands War to feel when parallels are drawn implicitly with Auschwitz or explicitly with Amin's barbarities? Is it altogether surprising that, if a major LEA puts out material making these insidious connections, some teachers will behave in the way of one of their profession in the West Country who told a girl whose father had fought in the Falklands that he was a 'murderer'?

The Use of Loaded Questions and References

The Teacher's Guide is entitled simply *Auschwitz*. It has a grey and white cover showing a photograph of snow-covered railway lines leading into the camp. In this Guide, teachers are encouraged to make 'Links with Today'. Here, pupils and students are to consider parallels between the horrors of the Nazi regime and:

(1) 'Questionable police behaviour (consider, for example, the circumstances of such cases as Stephen Waldorf, Blair Peach, Colin Roach, Michael Fereira, Jimmy Kelly, the Newham 8, the Deptford Fire, the Bradford 12, Mr and Mrs White ...)'.
(2) The 'denial of human rights in ... recent anti-trade union legislation'.
(3) 'Political censorship? (look at the Prevention of Terrorism Act again and the Official Secrets Act)'.

The list of topics for consideration in the context of 'Links with Today' (still, remember, in the pages of a booklet with the one word 'Auschwitz' on the cover) runs on, to include:

(1) The GCHQ trade union membership issue.
(2) Nationally co-ordinated police actions for curtailing secondary picketing.
(3) The increasing number of occasions when police are issued with weapons.

The parallels are so far-fetched as to be grotesque, and their use is inexcusable—educationally and in human terms. The use of this tactic of making grossly simplistic connections is the antithesis of careful, thorough consideration of relevant arguments and evidence. To compare the physical and psychological horrors of Auschwitz in particular and of the Nazi regime in general with 'recent trade union legislation' is an obscene trivialisation of the sufferings of those who were persecuted by the Nazis.

Omission of Relevant Evidence

Two of the canons of scholarship—surely what education is primarily about—are an accurate presentation of facts and the inclusion of available relevant evidence in any discussion of complex and/or controversial issues. The material on *Auschwitz* fails on both counts, and in a politically partisan way, reflecting the left-wing complexion of the ILEA.

Two examples suffice. First, there is a statement that the Holocaust is 'an historical event, unique in both scale and savagery: six million men, women and children were put to death in a carefully planned extermination programme, simply because they were born as Jews'. In one respect, this is accurate, but in another it is only a partial truth. It ignores completely the massive extermination programmes in the USSR, in which many more millions were liquidated—estimates ranging upwards to around 60 million or more. Granted that Soviet-style liquidation on that scale was not confined to Jews, but the scale is such as tragically to exceed the Nazi extermination programme by an order of magnitude of about 10—with no less savagery. And even when analysis is limited to extermination on racial grounds, the Soviet record is in the order of millions. As one distinguished Zionist wrote in 1946:

> Since they came into being, the Soviet camps have swallowed more people, have exacted more victims, than all other camps—Hitler's and

others—together, and this lethal machine continues to operate full-blast ... An entire generation of Zionists had died in Soviet prisons, camps, and exile.²

Surely, an honest concern with human history's record of large-scale savagery and racist genocide would require some mention of these other vast crimes against humanity, perpetrated over the same time-scale as the Holocaust—and still continuing in the barbaric labour camps of the Gulag Archipelago? Such omissions must raise some questions as to the political bias of the material.

Similarly, there is no account of a major historical fact—the Nazi–Soviet Pact. A genuine concern with historical accuracy requires recognition of the USSR's role in the development of National Socialist Germany and in the early years of World War II. But this is conveniently omitted by those who also omit serious discussion of the treatment of Jews and other ethnic minorities in the contemporary Soviet Union—treatment far harsher and with infinitely greater discrimination and deprivation of liberty than that which even the most trenchant critics could lay at the door of Britain.³ And surely it is only in totalitarian states like National Socialist Germany and the Soviet Union, with their almost complete lack of liberal checks and balances, that institutionalised mass murder—genocidal or otherwise—can occur. Once again discussion of this topic is excluded by the very way in which the Auschwitz material is presented.

Effects of Propagandist Elements in *Auschwitz*

One of the effects of propaganda is to close minds. This is the antithesis of education as traditionally understood in our society, which endeavours to encourage rational, critical thought and which enshrines the freedom to make up one's own mind on controversial issues in the light of all available relevant evidence.

Analysis of the *Auschwitz* teaching pack in this context suggests that pupils and students are being denied some important information needed to assess historical and contemporary issues of racism. For example, if they are not informed about one of the other major examples of genocide in the modern world, then it is much easier to draw direct parallels between National Socialist Germany and

From 'Auschwitz—Yesterday's Racism' to GCHQ 79

Britain. This in turn make it easier to present our society as a version of neo-Nazi oppression and as a major source of evil and of racism in the modern world.

This theme is reflected in other publications which are discussed in this book.[4] Perhaps the grossest example is the Institute of Race Relations' glossy booklet *How Racism Came to Britain*. Here there is a strikingly biased account of Britain's record of colonialism where all is evil, cruel and avaricious. There is no mention whatever of some of the advantages associated with British involvement abroad, in health care, education, law and order, administration or economic advancement. Even more politically insidious is the presentation of modern Britain as unequivocally racist, with brutally racist police, biased judges, unjust laws and unfair education.

The tone of the *How Racism Came to Britain* perhaps denotes its intent: the stirring up of racial tension, hatred and conflict. This tone is set on the front page: on one side there is a picture of a bamboo jungle and on the other are two bamboo poles held by black hands with a banner across the top proclaiming

'Here to stay
Here to fight'

What kind of 'race relations' is the Institute of Race Relations promoting? Are we really intending to fund from public money organisations producing books for children (this cartoon book is written for 10-year-olds upwards) to stir them to racial conflict?

Conclusion: 'Where there is Hatred ...'

Two themes emerge clearly from both *Auschwitz* and *How Racism Came to Britain*. They can also be found in many other teaching materials—textbooks, videos, resource packs in areas ranging from current versions of traditional subjects like History and Geography to newcomers like 'World Studies', 'Peace Studies' or 'Anti-Racist Maths', as well as in material on subjects like the police.

First, there is the degeneration from 'education' to 'indoctrination'. Some of the ways in which this occurs have been illustrated in this chapter. The effect is to bring about a preconceived 'mental set' in the form of attitudes, perceptions and emotions.

Second, there is a consistent political purpose: to create and foster disaffection, social tension and inter-group conflict. The intention is entirely compatible with Marxist-Leninist tactics of exacerbating the 'crisis' of capitalism and promoting 'class conflict'. The precise nature of the 'classes' in conflict will vary according to opportunity and circumstance. Traditionally, Marxism has focused on social classes themselves—but as the divisions have become blurred and the revolution has not been achieved on the basis of this division, other 'oppressed classes' are called into play: ethnic minority groups and women are now prime targets for mobilisation into conflict. Hence the significance of ILEA's emphasis on 'Race, Sex and Class' and its determination to change the entire school curriculum to accommodate its conflict-oriented position on these issues.

Analysis of teaching material on these topics shows a disturbing commitment to stirring up hatred and conflict. This comment does not mean that there is no place for critical analysis of our society or for consideration of appropriate reforms. But teaching material like that discussed in this chapter is characterised by its violation of basic principles of academic integrity and political balance. To this extent it is anti-educational and to the extent that it promotes, by intention or by default, hatred and conflict, it is deplorable.

Excuses have sometimes been offered. They are as yet totally unconvincing. For example, ILEA have claimed that the Auschwitz teaching pack had been approved by the Jewish Board of Deputies. However, this claim has since been challenged by the vice-president of the Board as 'misleading and inaccurate'.[5] And in commenting on *How Racism Came to Britain*, Peter Newsam (formerly Education Officer of ILEA and now Chairman of the Commission for Racial Equality) argued that it was only likely to be used by teachers who would present a balanced view. This ignores the fact that the book was on sale in shops such as W.H. Smith, where anyone could buy it and read it without the safeguard of having a teacher who would put the 'other' view. It also presumes that teachers will always undertake to present a balanced account—a supposition not always borne out by the facts.

The conclusion is thus 'naught for our comfort'. It appears that there are those in the educational field who are committed to preparing and promulgating material for educational purposes which is thinly disguised propaganda. This propaganda appears designed to undermine our society by dishonest intellectual tactics and to promote disaffection and conflict.

Whatever the faults and problems of a nation such as Britain, there is much which is good and worthy of appreciation. The alternatives which those who provide this propaganda would foist upon us are likely to prove much worse—which is presumably why a veil is almost always drawn across the realities of Socialism. It has been well said that the price of freedom is eternal vigilance. May all who are concerned about maintaining the future of freedom in Britain—including the freedom of all racial groups—maintain this vigilance and challenge those who would destroy it before it is too late.

Notes

1. Roger Scruton, Angela Ellis-Jones and Dennis O'Keeffe, *Education and Indoctrination—An Attempt at Definition and a Review of Social and Political Implications* (Education Research Centre, 1985).
2. Nikolai Tolstoy, *Stalin's Secret War* (Jonathan Cape, 1981), p.104; see also Robert Conquest, *The Nation Killers—The Soviet Deportation of Nationalities* (Macmillan, 1970) and *The Great Terror* (Penguin, 1971).
3. In this context see also Karl Marx, *On the Jewish Question*, 1844 (Collected Works, Vol.3, pp.169-74), and Leslie Page, *The Marxian Legacy—Race, Nationalities, Colonialism and War* (The Freedom Association, 1983).
4. See Tom Hastie, 'History, Race and Propaganda', Chapter 4, this volume.
5. *Jewish Chronicle*, February 1986.

6

Racial Mischief: The Case of Dr Sivanandan

David Dale

A public genuflection before the modern idol of multi-culturalism is increasingly the first test of racial righteousness. In those schools where the poor academic performance of West Indian children is brandished as self-evident proof of 'institutionalised racism' it is a foolhardy man who would suggest that such performance might be connected, however remotely, with Caribbean or, perhaps more accurately, Jamaican culture. Worse still, as the Honeyford case revealed, is the crime of judgementalism. Whilst a disparaging contempt for the history and institutions of the indigenous culture is an outward sign of inward racial grace, membership of the anti-racist elect requires that the cultures of others be treated with a benign agnosticism. Honeyford's sin was not that his judgements were flawed—indeed, they have barely been contested—but that he had the temerity to judge at all.

Given, then, that any opposition to multi-culturalism is taken as a sure sign of closet racism it may appear paradoxical, perverse even, that the organisation whose commitment to anti-racism outstrips all others in fundamentalist fervour should treat the concept with undisguised scorn. That organisation is the misleadingly named Institute of Race Relations (IRR), and it will be the purpose of this essay to examine the writings of its Director, Ambalvaner Sivanandan, a man whose suspicion of the society he has chosen to live in appears to be absolute. Opening a speech to a reverential audience of GLC anti-racists, Sivanandan usefully summarised his thoughts on both multi-culturalism and British society in the following way: 'I come as a [multi-cultural] heretic, as a disbeliever in the efficacy of ethnic policies to alter, by one iota, the monumental and endemic racism of this society.'¹

Before asking of the reasons for Sivanandan's heresy it is appropriate to give some explanation as to why space should be provided for an examination of his work in the first place. After all, it may be said, who is this Sivanandan? The question may be legitimately asked, for it is true that the man is almost entirely unknown outside of the anti-racist network. But Sivanandan's lack of public recognition is deceiving; as Professor Stuart Hall has pointed out in an admiring introduction to Sivanandan's work, 'it is worth saying that he is one of the handful of key black intellectuals who has actively sustained the black struggle in Britain over more than two decades: partly in his writing and educational work: partly—and less visibly—in political interventions of a strategic kind; partly by his defence of the Institute [of Race Relations] as a base for active political work; and partly by his own considerable personal gifts and qualities.'² Whatever the truth of Sivanandan's 'personal gifts' might be, Hall is entirely correct in pointing out the influence of his work. Despite his theoretical disagreements with them, Sivanandan's writing is a central reference point for anti-racists. That influence extends beyond the fractious factions of the lumpen left and touches the erstwhile respectable institutions of society. The Inner London Education Authority (ILEA), a body which at least purports to be concerned with the educational health of the young, has referred approvingly to his words, and his pamphlet *Race, Class and the State*, the contents of which became the left's 'adopted wisdom overnight' (Hall), is considered to be essential reading on a number of polytechnic and university degree courses. One publisher (Pluto Press, admittedly) has provided the accolade of a volume of his collected articles entitled, characteristically, *A Different Hunger: Writings on Black Resistance*,³ and as co-editor of the journal *Race and Class* Sivanandan has provided for himself a regular outlet for the dissemination of his views. Now, under the auspices of the IRR—an organisation which he has systematically purged of its once noted impartiality—three pamphlets on racism have been issued specifically for use in schools; their declared purpose is to 'question the basic assumptions and values' of British society and their content is, as Sivanandan puts it, 'unique'.⁴

Sivanandan, then, cannot be ignored; his work demands critical scrutiny for, given the political persistence of the anti-racists, it is likely otherwise to become the 'adopted wisdom' in those schools in which education is increasingly indistinguishable from indoctrination.

Let us begin the scrutiny by distinguishing between the anti-racism of Sivanandan and that of the multi-culturalists. Like Sivanandan, the latter subscribe to the notion of an 'endemic racism' within British society, but more often than not this is portrayed as an unconscious racism, a way of understanding and responding to black people which has been prejudiced and stained by the original sin of Britain's colonial past. As the ILEA condescendingly describes it: 'We live and work in a society where racist practices and attitudes permeate the whole system... Even those of us who have made every effort to rid ourselves of racism may fail to see how deep seated racist attitudes which have been prevalent in our society for so long affect our treatment of ethnic minorities.'[5] This variation on the false-consciousness theme is then magnified into the notion of 'institutionalised racism'; the absence of black people from 'positions of power and influence' becomes evidence that discriminatory attitudes, 'based on the assumption that black people are inferior to white people, [are] embedded deeply in the procedures and practices of our institutions...'.[6] The false logic underlying this unexpected support for proportional representation (which, if extended to the voting system, would consign the ILEA anti-racists to the political wastelands) is then inverted to form the movement's political demands. These amount to, on the one hand, an ostentatious display of cultural and personal self-abasement in the guise of cultural relativism and 'race-awareness training' and, on the other, the reverse racism of 'positive discrimination'.

Sivanandan will have none of this guilt-ridden liberalism. Racism, he argues, is not some cultural offshoot of history, still less is it the ingrained but largely unconscious prejudice so beloved of the ILEA. Racism is neither historical nor unconscious; rather, it is calculated, tactical and totally deliberate. Racism is the cold-blooded and systematic strategy of the white ruling class, fashioned and employed for the sole purpose of economic exploitation: '... Capital requires racism not for racism's sake but for the sake of capital.'[7] Thus 'racism is not its own justification. It is necessary only for the purpose of exploitation: you discriminate in order to exploit or, which is the same thing, you exploit by discriminating'.[8]

This is a Marxism vulgar even by the standards of vulgar Marxism. Simplistic, devoid of any subtlety or sentiment, it reduces reality to a stark struggle between the forces of exploitation and revolution. It is a fantasy in which black people, that is, real living individuals, only become recognisable if they can be made to fit the roles of prophet or class-traitor. Sivanandan's heroes are superbeings, men who, like him, have perceived the 'awful' truth of the world, his villains those who would conceal that truth by collaborating with its oppressors.

Like all Marxists, Sivanandan holds 'class-traitors' in scant regard. Time and again he uses the vocabulary of 'treachery' and 'collaboration' to denigrate any black individual who preaches the heresy of integration and racial harmony, for by doing so they have 'degraded the struggle to overthrow the system to be well off within it'.[9] For Sivanandan, 'the struggle to be well off within the system' is the ultimate crime, and those who subscribe to it he condemns to membership of a 'class of coloured collaborators who would in time justify the ways of the state to the blacks'.[10] The use of the word 'coloured' seems to be used as an insult in Sivanandan's rich vocabulary of such language, referring, as it does, not to skin colour but to a class of political lepers. 'Blackness' is no longer an accident of birth but a political medal to be earned through service to the revolutionary cause. The terms coloured or 'black' (when he uses the inverted commas) seem to be employed in a pejorative sense against individuals who achieve social or economic success. Mr. Trevor McDonald, Lord Pitt, Mr Yunus Chowdry, the first black man to be elected to a trade union national executive, all these are members of the 'class of coloured collaborators'. Even those anti-racists whose militancy within the Labour Party and the trade union movement threatens to provoke a British variant of apartheid have their racial identity summarily stripped from them. Not, of course, because their demands for separate representation and positive discrimination are fundamentally racist but because they have chosen to channel their misguided activism into the traditional, and hence racist, organisations of British society. Into this 'nascent "black" petit-bourgeoisie' are consigned the multi-culturalists ('ethnics turned "black" '), black trade union activists ('none of these gives a fart for ordinary black people, but uses them and their struggle as cynically as any other bourgeois class') and black-section advocates in the Labour Party ('no more representative of black working people than the Labour Party is of white').[11] All cases, surely, of the pot calling the kettle 'black'.

But while Sivanandan vilifies those who have 'diverted revolutionary aspiration into national achievement',[12] he bows before those he sees as the true voice of black aspirations. His language in praise of this, for the most part, motley collection of rogues, jailbirds and temporarily fashionable figures on the political margins is grotesque in its obsequious sentimentality. Consider his eulogy to Angela Davis, for example: '[One has] only to look at Angela herself to see how in gathering and focusing in her own person the varied liberation movements of our time—as woman, as black, as *intellectual engagé*, as communist—she alone could have aroused the people of the world and her jurors to justice. She alone could have shown, with the abounding love of the true revolutionary, that power belongs to the people, that justice resides in their vigilance, that if they came for her in the morning . . .'.[13] Or to Huey Newton and Bobby Seale: '[They] were leaders only in that it was they who practised most assiduously what they preached, they who took on themselves the brunt of oppression, they who went into prison and exile and they who died in the cause of the people. By precept and example, self-discipline and sacrifice of life, by their good in the community, they educated and politicised their people. And that is revolution.'[14]

Elsewhere one comes across Frantz Fanon and Julius Nyere, the murderer Michael X, even Muhammed Ali. In Sivanandan's grim fantasy these individuals become the apostles of their race, superbeings entrusted with the collective truth which only revolution can realise. But because it is a fantasy formed in resistance to reality, so the more unsavoury truths of reality have to be ignored. One can scour Sivanandan's writings in vain for any reference to Nyere's thousands of political prisoners or to his butchering of the Tanzanian economy; nor is there the barest hint of the records for criminal violence of his Black Panther heroes (Huey Newton did not 'go' to prison, he was sent). Even the fame of Muhammed Ali is misrepresented in the interests of revolutionary untruth. Far from Ali's achievements being an irritant to white society it is white society that has lauded Ali for years. Is there a white-hosted television chat-show in the world that Ali has not appeared on and delighted white audiences? One notes, too, a certain difficulty Sivanandan has in reconciling some of his heroes with their less than savoury political habits. Jomo Kenyatta's expulsion of Kenyan Asians in 1967, for example, may be explained away as 'the policy of Africanisation' but as a piece of thorough-going racism it is hard to beat. Where it has been beaten, by Amin in Uganda, even Sivanandan is unable to dredge up a sterilising euphemism.

These, then, are the heroes and villains of Sivanandan's Marxist plot. What, we are entitled to ask, of the bit-players, of those who are neither particularly 'well off within the system' nor 'struggling to overthrow it'? Those, that is, who fall somewhere between the extremes of Lord Pitt and Michael X? In short, what can Sivanandan tell us about ordinary black people? Here the reader will encounter a deafening silence; individuals, that is, real people living real lives, are largely unrecognised. The omission is, of course, not accidental; indeed it is required by Sivanandan's brand of Marxism. For if Sivanandan were to permit anyone recognisably human onto his stage then the whole shoddy structure would be seen for the fraud that it is. It would reveal that the vast majority of Asians, Africans and West Indians living in Britain are busily engaged not in 'the struggle to overthrow the system' but in the very struggle that Sivanandan condemns—'the struggle to be well off within it'. Little wonder that he must remain silent. And yet it is a silence which hides the scorn Sivanandan feels for ordinary people, a scorn which occasionally breaks through to the surface. Witness the contemptuous sting in the tail as he dismisses those Asians whose lives are informed by the best characteristics of Asian culture: '[These are] a people who are industrious and responsible, anxious to educate themselves, prepared to work hard and move up the social and economic ladder, honest, diligent, politic, cautious and meticulous—all virtues which shored up bourgeois society.'[15]

Here, however, Sivanandan encounters a perennial Marxist problem, and one which has taxed many brains more astute than his. The 'revolutionary black under-class' may, on closer examination, turn out to be both less revolutionary and more 'coloured' than his theory had allowed for; yet he is unable to simply dismiss the individuals who comprise it, for within the Marxist legend it is only when the class 'in itself' becomes the class 'for itself' that revolution becomes possible. Sivanandan may despise the values of honesty, diligence and responsibility but he needs the people who espouse them. His solution takes two traditional forms: the first is the putting to use of a grotesque anthropomorphism, the second a Leninist substitution of organisations for people.

For Sivanandan, exploitation is the plot of history, but it is a plot with its own momentum. It exists irrespective of the intentions of the actors who perform it and regardless of their awareness of its existence. And because it operates principally through the 'means and relations of production', rather than through human beings, so Sivanandan feels entitled to divest individuals of their humanity and to transfer those human qualities to abstractions. Thus it is not capitalists who exploit black people but 'capital'. It is 'colonialism' which 'perverts the economy of the colonies to its own ends'.[16] It is 'capital' which, 'having deprived the indigenous section of the working-class', now fires its weapon of racism 'in order to exploit the black section even more'.[17] It is 'racialism' which 'adjusts itself to the ordinary laws of supply and demand'.[18] And when 'racialism's self-adjustment is faulty it is 'the state' which steps in to make 'racism respectable and clinical by institutionalising it'.[19] And as for black people, they are reduced to the abstractions of 'an under-class' or 'a reserve army of labour waiting in readiness to serve the need of the metropolitan economy'.[20] And when 'the structural needs of late capitalism'[21] required more workers to exploit it was 'migrant labour' that was forced to respond.

Entirely lacking in this chronicle is any acknowledgement of individual autonomy. The process of the world follows an inevitable pattern, known in its entirety to Sivanandan, in which all subjectivity is false. Black people may think they have emigrated in order to find a better way of life, but they are wrong. Their decisions have been made for them by a monster called 'the free market economy'; they may believe that they seek out work to suit their aspirations and abilities but they are wrong again. It is another monstrous abstraction, this time the 'colonial legacy', which 'determines the nature of the work they are put to'.[22] And if, finally, the immigrant should be convinced that his migration has proved worthwhile there is the prophet Sivanandan waiting to tell him otherwise: '[The immigrant worker] had been ... reared and raised, as capitalist under-development had willed it, for the labour markets of Europe ...

[Now] everyone made money on [him] from the big-time capitalist to the slum landlord, from rejecting his labour, his colour, his customs, his culture.'[23]

But if individuals are incapable of grasping the objective truth of their own condition, political organisations (or at least those of whom Sivanandan approves) are blessed with the insights born of 'praxis'. In an extraordinary article bearing the title 'From Resistance to Rebellion'[24] Sivanandan charts the history of immigration to Britain in terms of 'the black struggles ... woven on the pattern set on the loom of British racism'.[25] As an historical account the article is a sham, a piece of revolutionary wishful thinking which, intended for other dreamers, is relieved of any need to temper fantasy with truth. As an insight into Sivanandan's fundamental contempt for people, however, it is starkly revealing.

The article itself is concerned, as is much of Sivanandan's work, with immigration laws. For Sivanandan, immigration restrictions are, by definition, racist, and he uses up a great deal of space in saying so. In reality, of course, the principle of selective immigration restrictions, in the words of the black economist Thomas Sowell, 'requires only recognition of the historical fact that some groups have indeed adapted more readily than others to the existing population, culture and institutions'. As it is only Marxists who refuse to recognise this rather obvious truth there is little need to address Sivanandan's case. Nor is it my intention to scrutinise the mendacities contained in the article, which include the glossing over of 'political' criminality (as he puts it with a wink): 'The line between politics and crime is, after all, a thin one—in a capitalist society.'[26] Rather, it is simply to note how, in true Leninist tradition, political organisations are made the repositories of truth. In 'From Resistance to Rebellion' these squib-like bodies constantly and from every direction flare into brief and flamboyant life only to peter out into oblivion. Sivanandan knows them all: The Committee of African Organisations, The Standing Conference of West Indian Organisations, The Co-ordinating Committee Against Racial Discrimination, The Racial Action Adjustment Society, The Black People's Freedom Movement, Hackney Black People's Defence Organisation, Bradford's United Black Youth League and dozens more. These bellicose and schismatic *groupuscules*, usually with a life-span of months and a membership which only sometimes reaches double figures, are given the status and authority usually reserved, by liberal opinion at least, for the United Nations. And always, waiting in the wings, there is Sivanandan, pointing out their tactical errors, chastising those who are diverted into the road of reformism and urging on the activists. These virulent bodies are, for him, the true voice of the class and therefore the people: 'Whatever the specifics of resistance in the respective communities and however different the strategies and lines of struggle, the experience of a common racism and a common fight against the state united them at the barricades. The mosaic of unities ... resolved itself, before the onslaught of the state, into a black unity and a black struggle.'[27] This is, of course, fantasy on a monumental scale. These puny organisations which fizz into brief existence are not only totally unrepresentative or ordinary black people (indeed Sivanandan, in an uncharacteristic moment of honesty, confesses that 'members of one organisation were often members of another'), but, more crucially, the notion of 'black unity in struggle' is an entirely bogus one.

The foregoing has provided a flavour of the ideology of Ambalvaner Sivanandan. It is a world only recognisable to the Marxist left and one which is easily condemned by black and white alike. Nevertheless, it is a dangerous world, not least because it has now made its appearance in the guise of textbooks for schoolchildren. My own experience as a social worker in Brixton has shown how easily 'racism' can become the Pavlovian response of young people when confronted with the possibility or actuality of failure. It would be fatuous to deny the existence of a degree of racial prejudice in British society but it is doubly facile to elevate this into 'institutionalised racism'. Prejudice can only be overcome by achievement, and any ideology which undermines the will to achieve works against racial harmony. 'Institutionalised racism' is one such ideology for, as a social 'explanation', it removes the imperative of individual endeavour. 'The struggle to be well off within the system' is made to appear an illusion, and the individual is encouraged to bask in the shallow but destructive satisfaction of condemning the system. As an all-purpose explanation 'racism' is increasingly heard from schoolchildren, particularly from those who attend schools where 'anti-racism' is the dominant educational ideology. The material put out by the IRR is undoubtedly being used in a number of these schools, and it is therefore a matter of some urgency that its pernicious influence be halted.

Racial Mischief: The Case of Dr Sivanandan   91

The three pamphlets[28] each bear an introductory commendation from the Institute's Director, A. Sivanandan. They are intended, he tells us, to provide 'an anti-racist education', an approach which 'demands the questioning and re-examination of basic assumptions and accepted values on the part of teachers and students ... They cover, in a way that is unique in either the school curriculum or in literature for young people, the history of black–white relations from the vantage of the black experience.'[29] The sort of 'assumptions' Sivanandan has in mind for 're-examination' are made abundantly clear from page 1: 'It is the white nations which have, and appear determined to keep at any cost, wealth and therefore power, grossly out of proportion to the size of their populations, and it is the non-white nations which struggle relentlessly for justice and equality ... [Race relations are defined by] the attempt to keep a particular group of people, marked out by the colour of their skin, in the lowest section of society, to keep them poor and powerless.'[30] In these two sentences the schoolchild will encounter the basic formulae of anti-racist education: 'white race = power, exploitation and racism' and 'black race = oppression, powerlessness and the struggle for justice'. He will be expected to remember them, for they are essential to everything that follows. For those with a questioning mind, who might feel slightly uneasy about the starkness of the propositions laid before them, a squiggly map of the world showing GNP per capita is included on page 2 and there, surely, is the proof; white populations do indeed appear to be richer than black populations. For remedial-level students a cartoon is included depicting grasping white merchants slavering over the words 'Make them pay whatever you can—they have no choice'.

As the child progresses through his 're-examination of accepted values' new explanatory concepts are fed to him, printed in heavy type in case their crucial significance should be missed. 'SURPLUS PRODUCT' makes its first appearance on page 4, 'PROFIT' on page 5 and by page 9 the pupil is considered ready to get to grips with 'EXPLOITATION'. Thus, bit by selective bit, a Marxist account of history is introduced. By the time the nineteenth century has been reached the term 'CAPITALIST' begins to appear in the ominous heavy type.

With this handful of categories the true meaning of history is spelt out to the pamphlet's young readers. Culture, religion, even simple human curiosity are cast aside before the imperatives of white greed and the urge to exploit. And when, on occasion, the pamphlets slip into the realms of half-truth they do so with tendentious selectivity. Slavery, for example, was an appalling human practice, but an adequate account of it must contain at least two facts which are entirely absent from their pages. The first is that black Africans participated in the practice with economic relish throughout the seventeenth and eighteenth centuries and were bitterly discontented when the slave trade was ended in the nineteenth. The second is that the notion that slavery was morally wrong was one of many Western ideas imported into the Third World. For centuries the institution of slavery aroused little moral concern anywhere in the world, and it was only at the insistence of a group of Englishmen that the trade was abolished. Anti-racist education, it appears, does not consider that the child should be burdened with such irrelevant and no doubt racist ideas.

By the third pamphlet even the heavy type has been abandoned as overly subtle. *How Racism Came to Britain* is entirely in cartoon format and, were its contents not so blatantly racist, it could more appropriately be classified as a comic. In every area of British social life white people are subjected to a racial character-assassination which is unsurpassed in anti-racist 'literature'. Whether it be housing, employment, law and order or education, the belligerent message is the same: white = power, exploitation and racism, black = oppression, powerlessness and the struggle for justice. Grinning white policemen are depicted brandishing truncheons at bewildered black youths; Hitlerian educationalists consign black children to schools for the educationally sub-normal, racist employers grind down black workers, and the media produce an endless outpouring of lies about mugging. No child, including the educationally sub-normal, could miss the message, but it is spelt out anyway on page 24. Next to a scrawled drawing of a leering white capitalist a caption reads 'From 1950 black people to be used as pawns in a new game devised by the British ... It was called "YOU CAN'T WIN".'

Stripped of its intellectual pretensions and Marxist verbiage 'You Can't Win' captures the core of the Sivanandan lie. 'The struggle to be well off within the system' is an illusion, an impossible dream manufactured and sustained by a white ruling class for its own selfish ends. There is only one path available to black people and that is to throw off the illusory individual struggle and to join the alternative, collective 'struggle to overthrow the system'.

For some young people the Sivanandan view may hold an easy escape from the difficult problems which face cultural minorities. And yet the truth of immigration to Britain is that black people, as individuals rather than as an amorphous 'class', can and often do 'win'. This evidence and the evidence of the history of immigration across the world is all but ignored by the race relations industry. One lesson to be learnt is that political organisation on ethnic grounds tends to prevent rather than enhance the social and economic advancement of ethnic minorities. Another is that the demands for 'quota systems' and 'positive discrimination' do not improve the lot of those for whom they are intended. A third is that disparities in economic outcomes are more adequately, if more mundanely explained by disparities in human abilities (what economists call 'human capital') rather than 'institutionalised racism'.

All immigrant minorities face the challenge of acceptance by the indigenous cultural majority and it is a challenge made easier for the rest each time an individual achieves success. One successful black businessman is worth a host of self-appointed 'community leaders' parroting the vocabulary of 'anti-racism', while one statement from a Bernie Grant wipes out the gains achieved by a score of successful businessmen. Ambalvaner Sivanandan insists 'you can't win', and the views he promulgates may tend to reduce the chances of the black people.

Notes

1. A. Sivanandan, 'Challenging Racism: Strategies for the '80s', in *Race & Class*, Vol.XXV, 2, p.1, 1983.
2. Stuart Hall, 'Introduction' to *A Different Hunger*, by A. Sivanandan (Pluto Press, 1982) p.ix.
3. A. Sivanandan, *A Different Hunger: Writings on Black Resistance* (Pluto Press, 1982).
4. *Roots of Racism*, *Patterns of Racism* (Institute of Race Relations, 1982) and *How Racism Came to Britain* (Institute of Race Relations, 1985).
5. 'Race, Sex and Class' No.2 *Multi-ethnic Education in Schools* (Inner London Education Authority, 1983) p.23.
6. *Ibid.*, p.23.
7. A. Sivanandan, 'Race, Class and the State' in *A Different Hunger*, p.124.

8. *Ibid.*, p.113.
9. *Ibid.*, p.113.
10. *Ibid.*, p.118.
11. A. Sivanandan, 'In the Castle of their Skin', in *New Statesman*, 7 June 1985.
12. 'Race, Class and the State', *op. cit.*, p.101.
13. *A Different Hunger*, *op. cit.*, p.72.
14. *Ibid.*, p.68.
15. *Ibid.*, p.115.
16. *Ibid.*, p.102.
17. *Ibid.*, p.108.
18. A. Sivanandan, 'From Resistance to Rebellion', in *A Different Hunger, p.3.*
19. 'Race, Class and the State', *op. cit.*, p.109.
20. *Ibid.*, p.102.
21. *Ibid.*, p.104.
22. *Ibid.*, p.102.
23. *Ibid.*, p.103.
24. A. Sivanandan, 'From Resistance to Rebellion', *op. cit.*
25. *Ibid.*, p.3.
26. *Ibid.*, p.16.
27. *Ibid.*, p.23.
28. See note 4.
29. A. Sivanandan, 'Introduction' to *Roots of Racism, op. cit.*
30. *Roots of Racism, op. cit.*, p.1.

SECTION 3

Freedom, Language and Censorship

7
Language, Race and Colour

Linda Hall

A few years ago the Inner London Education Authority (ILEA) issued a document called *Practical Guidelines to Assessing Children's Books for a Multi-ethnic Society*. This publication emanated from the Centre for Urban Education Studies (CUES), one of the many agencies for multi-ethnic education in London, and it included some dubious assertions. One such, which was later dropped after protests, was the suggestion that the English language, by using words like 'blackleg' and 'blackmail', is indelibly racist.

This accusation appeared again in print in a strident article in *Dragon's Teeth*, a magazine devoted to multi-ethnic educational matters. More disturbingly, it was repeated on BBC television in a multi-ethnic education slot intended for schools and colleges. In that programme teachers were encouraged to make a list of words and phrases involving the word 'black', and were then asked to notice how these were negative rather than positive.

Such an exercise seemed designed to prove that all English-speaking white people are inescapably guilty of racism. It implied that racism is imbibed *unconsciously* because, naturally, the language is learnt at an early and impressionable age. In a classic 'Catch 22' situation, white people cannot avoid racism even if they would like to, as they speak a language tainted at source and, therefore, insult all black people every time they use innocuous meteorological expressions like 'black ice' and horticultural ones like 'black spot'. This is determinism with a vengeance.

The largely unfavourable connotations of 'black' in the English language (and it is not alone in European languages in this) are always castigated as the inevitable product of a colonial and imperial past. It is often implied, if not openly asserted, that words like 'blackmail', 'blackleg' and 'blackguard', phrases like 'in someone's black books' arose as a result of the habits of contempt for all tanned skins that having an Empire had supposedly generated in the British people.

It is always instructive to examine the etymology of some of the words and phrases often held up as most disparaging, since examination reveals that they have nothing to do with black *people*. In fact, most of the phrases involving the word 'black', like the neutral job-description 'blacksmith', were with us long before the Empire took shape and even before the Atlantic slave trade began. 'Blackmail', for instance, is first recorded as early as 1552, which suggests that it was already a long and well-established practice. Not only was the term in use before English seamen were involved in the Atlantic slave trade, the practice it describes took place in a part of Britain well away from access to strangers, even European ones. I refer to the Highland Line and the Border counties of England and Scotland. 'Mail' had long been a name for rent or tribute. 'Blackmail' was, in essence, 'unofficial' tribute exacted by freebooting chiefs from small farmers for 'protection' from plunder. The 'black' part of the word might imply that this tribute was paid in coin and was, therefore, shining and white since, strange as it may seem, this is an early meaning of the word 'black'.

Actually, modern English 'black' derives from a confusion of two Anglo-Saxon words of similar appearance but opposite meaning—'blaec' and 'blác'. Here the length of the vowel is crucial, as the long-vowel 'blaec' meant dark whereas the short-vowel 'blác' meant shining, white. It is from the second of those two that our modern words 'bleak' and 'bleach' are derived.

In fact, it is difficult to tell in Middle English whether 'blac', 'blak' and 'blake' mean 'dark' or 'pale, colourless, wan'. We have to rely on the context in which the word appears and sometimes even that fails to make it clear. As far as the modern surnames Black and Blake are concerned, it is impossible to determine if they mean black or white!

'Blacken', as in to blacken someone's character, has nothing to do with linguistic racism either, as is often asserted. It derives from the Anglo-Saxon verb 'blâekan', which meant 'to scorch or burn'. This is how the Black Isle, that spur of very green land in northern Scotland, got its name. It was burnt by fire-raising Vikings and, of course, charred timber and crops are black in colour. Such associations may have helped to oust 'swart', the original Anglo-Saxon word for black, which is preserved in modern English only in 'swarthy'. It has, however, been retained in other Teutonic languages to this day, as in the German 'schwarz'. Possibly the Germans did not suffer so much from Viking raids.

In this connection with fire it is not beyond the bounds of possibility, and indeed is highly likely, that 'blackmail' originally meant tribute for protection against having one's home and crops *burnt*. After all, Anglo-Saxon forms and usages have survived longer in Scotland than in England, thanks to linguistic isolation.

'Blackguard' appears, according to the *Oxford English Dictionary*, in the later Middle Ages as an ironic term for the scullery lads who looked after the pots and pans in royal and noble kitchens. The lowly *social* connections of this neutral job description became associated later with *moral* inferiority, possibly because it would be a perfect term of abuse for one member of the gentry to fling at another. Indeed, by 1683 the term was being applied to bands of criminal youths in the larger towns.

'Blackleg', first recorded in 1722, was originally a disease of sheep and cattle, which caused the legs of the animals to turn black. As it was an infectious disease, affected animals were naturally kept isolated. First-generation industrial workers would have had little trouble recalling their agricultural origins. Folk-memory has kept the term with us to this day.

As for the sense of disgrace associated with being in someone's 'black books', it is Roman Catholics who have cause to complain, not people of African descent. Though the term started out quite simply as an official book bound in black and is found as early as the reign of Edward III (1327–77), it took on its metaphorical sense of being in disfavour only after Henry VIII's commissioners, like all officials before them, used black books in which to record the abuses they uncovered in some monasteries. As we all know, trouble, in the form of the Dissolution, followed as a direct result.

Moreover, the fact that most of the extremely nasty things that could happen to people in medieval Europe were black in colour no doubt helped to fix in the general mind the unfavourable associations of the colour. Fire was one of the commonest hazards of life until the eighteenth century because houses were mainly built of timber and roofs were thatched. The fire that raged in London in 1666 is called the *Great* Fire for this very reason—the largest and most destructive of many. The aftermath of such fires would be scenes of black desolation.

More common and hazardous even than fire was disease. The worst of the many awful killing diseases to which medieval and Renaissance man was liable was the plague. Not for nothing was bubonic plague called the *Black* Death. Black spots would appear first on the bodies of its victims, spreading into black patches that would eventually cover the whole body. The tongue, too, turned black. Most people died within three days of the first appearance of a black spot. The population of England was slashed by between a third and a half within a year. Black Death indeed!

One of the expressions that especially agitates the searchers after racism in the English language is 'black magic'. The term was coined in the Middle Ages long before the European voyages of exploration to Africa and certainly before the days of colonial exploitation. To study its etymology provides a revealing insight into the role often played by accident or by random factors in the process of semantic change. The original Greek *necromanteia* referred to divination by summoning the spirits of the dead from the Underworld. At some stage or other monastic translators carelessly wrote this in Latin as *nigromantia*, which was regarded as being derived from the Latin *niger* (black). In view of the Christian view of the Underworld as being the realm of the Prince of Darkness, the inadvertent switch from 'the dead' to 'black' was taken as intelligible and appropriate. The term then passed into European languages as 'black magic' with no reference to black people in mind whatsoever.

Despite the apparent attempt of the BBC's multi-ethnic education programme to prove otherwise, most of the phrases involving the word 'black' in English are not negative but are in fact neutral; that is, they are neither favourable nor unfavourable in their connotations. John Bennett[1] of St Gallen University has done a word-count of black/white collocations and finds more than twice as many neutral expressions as negative ones, 315 compared with 125. Words like 'blacksmith', 'blackthorn', 'blackberry', 'blackcurrant' and 'black king' (as in chess) do not allude to the non-white races, let alone disparage them in any way. It would take a strange mind to find offence in such innocent expressions. This is not to say, however, that demands that even neutral expressions[2] be outlawed are unheard of.

The usual complaint made by black and white detractors of the language, as reflected in the BBC television programme, is that the adjective 'black' has many negative and no positive connotations in English, unlike its opposite number 'white' which, it is claimed, has many positive and no negative connotations. A quick glance at any reasonably good dictionary reveals both these allegations to be unfounded. By my count, there are at least ten positive collocations involving 'black', three of them especially distinguished. Expressions like 'black gold' (for oil), 'to be in the black' (to be in credit at the bank), 'black diamonds' (coal), 'black velvet' (an alcoholic drink of stout and champagne), 'black belt' (the highest award in martial arts), 'black earth' (a belt of particularly fertile earth in South Russia and central India), 'black swan' (something rare and highly prized)— these are all favourable. Moreover, three expressions which might at first sight seem purely descriptive (i.e. neutral) resonate with such favourable associations that the word 'black' cannot fail to share the distinction. I have in mind the Scottish regiment justly renowned for its courage and self-sacrifice whose name, the Black Watch, seems to bring a lump to the throat of a great many Scots; the key Parliamentary official called Black Rod, without whom the annual ritual opening of Parliament cannot proceed and the figurine actually *worshipped* in many southern Italian churches as the Black Madonna. This last is unexpected, perhaps, given that Southern Italy was for many centuries subject to the ravages of (black) north African corsairs, ravages which included abducting many of its people into slavery.

There are, arguably, then at least ten positive collocations in which the word 'black' appears. This may come as a surprise, given the associations of 'black' in almost all cultures with natural phenomena that are unpleasant or downright disturbing. Ideas of evil inevitably arise from and accompany that atavistic fear of the dark and of nighttime that is universal throughout the human race. It is at night that humans without artificial light feel especially vulnerable. It is perhaps hard for adults in the well-lit twentieth century to appreciate just what fearful and disturbing things earlier minds might imagine to be lurking in the darkness. Not so long ago, until the turn of the eighteenth and nineteenth centuries even, night air was regarded as pestilential, so that all apertures were kept well and truly closed during the hours of darkness as a protection against infection.

Furthermore, the colour of decomposing organic tissue is also a slimy shade of black. It is surely not unexpected then, when we consider this example, that black should be seen to have a natural association with death and to appear therefore to be the appropriate colour of mourning. Black is also the colour of *carrion* birds such as crows, rooks and ravens, and this no doubt reinforces the association of black with death.

As I indicated earlier, it is equally untrue to claim that the word 'white' has entirely favourable connotations in English. According to John Bennett's word-count there are 31 *negative* expressions compared, surprisingly, with only 16 positive ones. If the detractors of English were right this would hardly be the case. It is startling, in fact, that a language supposedly shaped into unconscious prejudice against black-skinned races by the imperial past of its people should have only six more positive connotations to 'white' than to 'black' and also so many actual negative connotations of 'white'.

To suggest that English elevates whiteness, and by extension all white people, to a superior moral plane is quite untenable, given the cluster of words and phrases involving 'white' that actually convey notions of morally unacceptable behaviour. Many men at the Home Front or even on leave during World War I found that the 'white feather' thrust at them by belligerent females was a symbol of cowardice. To be called 'lily-livered' or 'white-livered' are also taunts of cowardliness. A person is described as 'white-lipped' or 'white-faced' with *fear*, not with racial arrogance, while to 'show the white flag' indicates an ignominious willingness to surrender. No person, white or otherwise, would care to be called a 'whited sepulchre' because it means a hypocrite, someone who professes righteousness but is inwardly wicked. Similar to this is the verb 'to whitewash', which literally means to cover a wall or ceiling with a coating of quicklime or whiting and size in order to give a clean appearance and hide blemishes. It is now used figuratively to make a person or incident appear less reprehensible than he/it actually is.

At a more materialistic level, especially where precious metals are concerned, 'white' tends to be used to convey the impression of something *inferior*. No-one would thank you for giving him 'white alloy' (a cheap imitation of silver) or 'white brass' (an inferior alloy of copper and zinc)—who would want to buy a 'white elephant', something costly but worthless?

Fifteen of the 31 unfavourable connotations of 'white' refer to diseases of people, animals and plants. For example, the 'white plague' is another name for tuberculosis; 'white leg', an illness that post-partum females can develop, while 'white rot' is a disease affecting bulbous vegetables. 'White diarrhoea' is a disease of animals and is appropriately named. There is also, of course, a large number of diseases that employ the word 'black', such as 'black spot' (a disease of roses). These, however, like the white examples, make no allusion to people but are purely descriptive of a dominant feature, sign or symptom of the ailment. Interestingly, 38 of the diseases employing the term 'black' apply to diseases of plants and animals and only four to diseases of humans.

That 'white' is symbolically equated in English with goodness, innocence and purity (cf. the lily) appears to be regarded as the ultimate racially intentioned insult. If it were true that an imperial past and a prejudice against black *people* had planted in the language the many expressions in which 'black' is used in a pejorative sense and white is used favourably, it would surely be out of the question that similarly disparaging connotations of 'black' and favourable connotations of 'white' would be found in the languages of the non-white races. This is not the case. Ancient China developed a philosophical dualism based on the interaction of two forces, *yin* and *yang*, which today's determinists could well interpret as sexist as well as racist! *Yin* represented the negative, passive, feminine features of life and the earthly principles of darkness, cold and death. It is depicted as black. *Yang* represented the positive, active, masculine features of life and the celestial principles of light, heat and life. Pictorially it is white. Are we to assume that the ancient Chinese hoped thereby to disparage the African peoples? Or was it that, as for all early peoples, the greatest contrast in life was that between day and night, i.e. light and darkness, that the one seemed good and the other bad because without light there is no life, no growth, no crops?

Even a cursory examination of the dictionaries of African languages will reveal that in these languages, too, 'black' is constantly used in a pejorative sense and 'white' favourably, not because Africans are inadvertently masochist, but because their ancient forebears were as struck as were the ancient Chinese by the contrast between the darkness of night and the clear light of dawn.

In Swahili, for example, there is a wide range of words meaning black but with a variety of usages, such as literally black in colour and metaphorically meaning dreadful, foul, dirty, malignant. A blackguard is *mkorofi*, which comes from *korofi*, one of the synonyms for black and meaning malignant. A black sheep *mbaya*, is from *baya*, also meaning black and malignant. From *tisho*, another synonym, is derived *kitisho*, something terrifying, a terror, menace, a fearful thing, an overwhelming danger. *Kisirani*, another synonym, means anything considered of ill omen or evil portent, mishap, misfortune. From *chafu* comes *chafuko*, disorder, muddle, mess, chaos, disorganisation, unsettlement, confusion, while *uchafu* means uncleanness, filthiness, dirt. By contrast, white has very few synonyms, and is expressed by *eupe* or *safi*, and from these are derived words like *kweupe*, meaning clearness, dawn, light, fine weather, and *weupe*, meaning cleanness, purity, innocence, integrity, guilelessness. Similarly, *safisha* means to make clean, correct, purify, set to right, and *usafi* stands for cleanliness, correctness, purity.

Similar correlation with black and white is to be found in Hausa, in which black is *bak'i* and white is *fari*. *Ciki* means abdomen or the inside of anything, and the phrase *farin ciki* means happiness, pleasure, gratification, while *bak'in ciki* means sadness, sorrow, displeasure, being or feeling annoyed.

We need not see in these pejorative black expressions, whether in English or African languages, any insult to black *people*—unless, that is, we are already suffering from paranoia or are creating a career for ourselves out of the perpetuation of such inaccuracies and solecisms as I have described here. This kind of simplistic and reductive approach to a complex subject like language (where recourse to a dictionary would provide rapid enlightenment) smacks of the propaganda of the demagogue. Not only is it unhelpful in promoting the cause of harmonious race relations, it is actually counterproductive. It can only serve to drive a wedge between the races, creating as it does, racist stereotypes—white people indelibly tainted by the language they speak, black people insulted racially every time a white person uses words and phrases like those examined in this chapter. This is no way to foster a genuinely harmonious multi-ethnic society.

Part of this chapter first appeared in abbreviated form in the *Times Higher Education Supplement*, 12 November 1982.

Notes

1. John Bennett, 'Some Reflections on the Terms "Black" and "White" in English Colour Collocations', in *Cahiers Ferdinand de Saussure*, No. 35 (Librairie Droz, Geneva, 1981).
2. Apparently, 'blackboard' should be purged in favour of 'chalkboard'. It is in educational circles, of course, that these demands are most insistent and most respected.

8

Reading and Discrimination: 'Anti-Racism' in English Studies

A. C. Capey

'Words', wrote Taya Zinkin in the one-time *Manchester Guardian*, 'have an unfortunate habit of imposing themselves and excluding thought.' The recently minted 'racism', however, seems not so much to have imposed itself upon a carelessly tolerant public as to have been imposed upon it; and not imposed to meet a general need for the new word, but to subserve by stealth the purposes of politically guided intruders into education. Those purposes, recognised or suspected, are not for examination here; the word itself demands immediate attention.

The objection to 'racism', as to 'sexism', 'élitism' and other modish isms, is that its application is necessarily hostile. Unlike such older isms as 'Socialism', 'feminism' and 'colonialism'—unlike even the more recent coinage of 'Thatcherism'—'racism' has no base in neutral description, but lives by the accusation it makes of an incorrect or undesirable attitude. The word is thought-refusing in both origin and intention—a slogan merely, whose employment acts as guarantee that the accuser is on the Lord's side. When, for instance, Mrs Thatcher denies that there is racism in the Conservative Party, she means to deny that candidates for membership or office may be excluded on grounds of racial origin; but the form of her denial implicitly concedes that 'racism' is a legitimately accusatory word. Or when a Bradford headmaster is required to attend a 'racism-awareness workshop' (the penalty for refusal being withdrawal of the right to appoint his own staff), he knows before he gets there the circumscribed terms of reference—knows that the key word will not itself be under scrutiny, that all the necessary assumptions will have been made by those who, 'without thinking, respond alike'.¹ Or—and here I refer to personal experience of the antagonism a dissenting voice may arouse—when the anti-racist sees that we do not choose to take the word at his own pre-emptive valuation, he beateth the air with it, chanting it as if its authority had not been questioned, or as if merely to throw down the challenge marked the challenger as a racist.

A further objection to the currency allowed the word is that the accused is ordinarily a white man. In a document addressed to the staff of an Oxfordshire teacher-training college, 'racism' is defined (in accordance with principles established in neighbouring Berkshire) as 'attitudes, procedures and social patterns whose effect . . . is to create and maintain power, influence and well-being of white people at the expense of Asian and Afro-Caribbean people'; while 'black' is described as 'a political term for a group [sic] defined by their common experience of racism'.² The white man is to be allowed no voice in the description of his attitude; the attitude is held to exist in the act of its detection, in the 'experience' not of expressing it but of being the supposed object of its presumed existence. The attitude is to be detected by the politically black man, who becomes both prosecutor and judge of the politically white man. Clearly, a teacher who had the misfortune ('disadvantage' would be the jargon-word) to be white—especially one who, through no fault of his own, happened to be white, male, Protestant and middle-class—would be well advised to undergo a course in attitude-realignment from the judge before the impending prosecution could proceed.

At one time, not a very long time ago, sixth form and college English classes would have sharpened their teeth on such absurd proclamations. Today, so vice-like is the grip of the word and the associated cult upon teachers and taught that any sort of critical examination is taboo. The fear among the intelligentsia of being branded a racist (the fear seems not to have affected the working class to the same degree) leads men to assent to propositions without even a show of the intellectual effort they would apply to a real book or a real pupil's essay. No serious challenge to the document quoted above was mounted from within the college. No serious challenge was mounted to the minutes of a meeting in a Lancashire college in 1981 which reported 'general agreement' with the masked menace of this charter for reform:

Higher Education should be concerned more with the development of skills and techniques—whether they be those of the scientist, mathematician or historian—than the acquisition of a defined body of knowledge. Multi-cultural Education can be pursued by use of an appropriate syllabus in which skills and techniques can be learned and applied.[3]

And when, a few years later in the same college, a covey of multi-cultural lecturers met to consider the decision of The Bodley Head to reissue the *Little Black Sambo* stories, no-one thought to make the point that these favourites with children were actually very good books: the meeting took for granted their exclusion from any 'appropriate syllabus', and relieved its feelings against The Bodley Head with the thought that at least the 'large-sized edition with a model that can be cut out and dressed' would prove beyond the means of most prospective purchasers.

Along with that willing suspension of intellect which constitutes anti-racist faith, even in places where one would ordinarily expect to observe the spirit and the discipline of disinterested inquiry, goes a quite shameless exhibition of ignorance. Robert Brunning, an inner London headmaster, is reported by *The Times Educational Supplement*[4] to have 'described the stories as "a cliché" for racism across the teaching profession. "It's all basically back to the jungle and dancing around the mud huts." he said. . . . "With publishing friends like this [for The Bodley Head also issues multi-cultural children's books], who needs enemies?"'[5] That the child-reader, irrespective of colour or sex, identifies himself with Sambo in his pride in smart clothes, in his lonely hour of danger and in his appetite for pancakes is simply ignored by the reported Mr Brunning, as is the self-destruction of the rival (and, arguably, imperial) tigers in their quarrel over Sambo's property. The misreading of what lies before him is not, of course, personal to Mr Brunning but characteristic of the confidence of the 'racism-aware' that, their movement being irresistibly right, the ordinary constraints of experience, logic and evidence do not apply. Here, from a group which identifies itself as the Children's Rights Workshop, is part of the introduction to *Racist and Sexist Images in Children's Books*, 'the first [in 1975] of a series of "Papers on Children's Literature" '.[6] It is a peculiarly rich example of how intellectual caution and even common sense may be brushed aside by the imperious passion of blessed assurance: 'It is the cause, it is the cause, my soul!'

> [Both Theodore Taylor's *The Cay* and William H. Armstrong's *Sounder*] have had film versions made of them ... In the face of this widespread dissemination of images about Blacks and the Black experience, we can no longer base critical assessment solely on literary merit. Content and values, explicit or implicit, deserve similar critical attention. No art, no literature can be neutral; the critical writings in this pamphlet will hopefully [*sic*] encourage the development of literary criteria that can tackle content as well as form.

Literary criticism may take various forms, as befits an activity which is neither an exact science nor the expression of the wilful individual's likes and dislikes but a place for the meeting of minds in creative quarrel—and I dare say the film of a book might qualify, by its fidelity to the text and the character of its interpretation of the given material, as a kind of creative criticism. But that is not what the Children's Rights Workshop proposes to discuss. The CRW is saying—I rub my eyes in disbelief—that when a book is made into a successful film the book 'can no longer [be assessed] solely on [its] literary merit', that such a book may no longer be discussed in its own terms. It troubles the CRW not at all that the 'widespread dissemination of images' is the work, not of the book or of its publisher's distributors, but of the film industry: indeed, so free does the Workshop suppose itself to be of the discipline of letters that it appears not to employ a single literary critical term with the honest independence of one's predilections that we expect from a responsible critic. By the 'content' of the book is meant the 'images about Blacks' in the film; the book has become, with an unintended irony, the book-of-the-film. By 'values' is meant the deducible attitude of writer or producer towards the presented 'images about Blacks'; while 'explicit' and 'implicit'—important terms in the critical examination of language—are reduced to synonyms for 'obviously or blatantly racist' and 'covertly racist', respectively. By 'critical attention' is meant the description of *The Cay*, which relates the selfless devotion of an old black man to the young white boy with whom he is marooned, as 'an adventure story for white colonialists to add to their racist mythology'; or the baleful eyes thrown in subsequent papers upon *Doctor Dolittle*,[7] *Charlie and the Chocolate Factory* and *Sounder*. By the detected lack of neutrality in art is intended the charge that art is so bismotered with unacceptable preconceptions (... watch out for 'unacceptable': it enjoys wide currency among the campaigning committed) that it must be subjected to the nit-picking procedures that have suppressed Enid Blyton's *Little Black Doll*, altered the title of *Ten Little Niggers* and presumed to tinker with *Huckleberry Finn*. There is a critical case to be made against the first book, and indeed against the second; but it is not a case that the Children's Rights Workshop, miserably bound upon its wheel of hate, could distinguish from the case for taking *Huckleberry Finn* as the author consented to leave it.

* * *

Huckleberry Finn, remarks F. R. Leavis, is 'supremely the American classic, and it is one of the great books of the world.' It is not just 'a classic for children': 'Huck himself is ... not merely the naive boyish consciousness he so successfully enacts; he is, by one of those triumphant sleights or equivocations which cannot be judiciously contrived, but are proof of inspired creative possession, the voice of deeply reflective maturity—of a life's experience brooded on by an earnest spirit and a fine intelligence.'[8] In pathetic contrast to that judgement, itself the product of a seriously applied and reflective intelligence, stands this comment on Jim by John H. Wallace, who has ventured to bowdlerise the book 'for use in the classroom': 'Jim ... is a mature, insightful older male [than Huck] seeking his freedom from the cruel and peculiar institution of slavery.'[9] Of course, if you dedicate your enterprise 'to the elimination of racism from the curriculums of schools in the United States of America and throughout the world', your invocation of the key word—which tyrannises you as much as the targets of your obsession—will inhibit you from seeing that Mark Twain has already achieved all that a respectable multi-culturalist could ask, and that by excising what for Mark Twain is the key word you contrive judiciously to destroy the 'triumphant sleight or equivocation' on which the book turns.

The key word is, of course, 'nigger', for which Mr Wallace, 'offended [as a schoolboy] by the abusive language', now chooses to substitute 'body', 'man', 'servant', 'slave' or 'devil', wherever he does not simply eliminate it. That 'nigger' is a derogatory word we are in no doubt at all, nor do we doubt that our author—equivocally identified with Huck, from whose *patois* the style of the book is created—intends us to register it derogatorily. But its every use (and it occurs quite two hundred times, we understand) is charged with an implicit criticism, if not invariably of the user (for Jim himself is free with the word: '. . . Wouldn't 'low no nigger to call me dat'), always of the use: the use of the word, without authorial comment, and indeed with an apparently genial acceptance of its currency, exposes it to the critical attention of the reader, who is effectively trained both to appreciate the subtle degrees of derogation the word must have borne before the Civil War and to recognise that Huck cannot help but use a word that is in common parlance far beyond his own illiterate circle. For between the first paragraph of Chapter xiv, when Huck approves Jim's reasons for running away:

> Well, he was right; he was most always right; he had an uncommon level head, for a nigger . . .

and the scene in Chapter xli, where 'such another clack a body never heard' from a company excited by the arranged escape of Jim from the lock-up on the farm:

> '. . . Ther's ben a *dozen* a-helpin' that nigger, 'n' I lay I'd skin every last nigger on this place, but *I'd* find out who done it, s'I . . .'

lies the problem that intermittently exercises Huck throughout, the morality of conniving at a slave's escape.

It is not a problem that may be said even to exist in *Uncle Tom's Cabin*, where good people bend the commercial rules to help Eliza elude her purchaser, and where the power of money to override the claims of kinship or affection is represented as the prime cause of individual tragedies. There are detectable connections between that tale and *Huckleberry Finn*: Miss Watson does not *want* to sell Jim, 'but she could git eight hund'd dollars for me, en it 'uz sich a big stack o'money she couldn' resis' '—and only at the end do we learn that, in her will, 'ashamed she was ever going to sell him down the river', she has granted the runaway his freedom. For Huck, however, the early realisation that he is 'to blame' for Jim's successful escape induces moral restlessness:

> It hadn't ever come home to me, before, what this thing was that I was doing. But now it did; and it stayed with me, and scorched me more and more. I tried to make out to myself that *I* warn't to blame, because *I* didn't run Jim off from his rightful owner; but ... conscience says to me, 'What had poor Miss Watson done to you, that you could see her nigger go off right under your eyes and never say one single word?'

The difference between the two books is, of course, immense. Mark Twain is no propagandist for the cause but a creative writer who apprehends that a work of art enacts its moral judgements—and enacts them the more subtly and comprehensively without the manager's explicit direction. *Huckleberry Finn* is commonly reckoned among the great comic books, and, of course, the adventures with the king and the duke and Tom's artificial orchestration of Jim's release from the lock-up are vastly entertaining. But the comic genius finds its richest expression in the presentment of Huck struggling with his conscience at the same time as Jim 'talks out loud' of his plans, in the free state ahead of him, to save up money

> ...and never spend a single cent, and when he got enough he would buy his wife, which was owned on a farm close to where Miss Watson lived; and then they would both work to buy the two children, and if their master wouldn't sell them, they'd get an Ab'litionist to go and steal them.

It is the first we have heard of a wife and children: and the shock sustained is the greater both for the expression of the information after the manner of any young man looking ahead to get ahead and for its economical incorporation in Huck's unsympathetic commentary:

> Here was this nigger which I had as good as helped to run away, coming right out flat-footed and saying he would steal his children—children that belonged to a man I didn't ever know; a man that hadn't ever done me no harm.
>
> I was sorry to hear Jim say that, it was such a lowering of him.

But, concludes Huck (temporarily, for he is mighty relieved, at the end, to know that Tom Sawyer has not *really* 'helped a body set a nigger free, with his bringing-up'),

> Then I... says to myself, hold on—s'pose you'd a done right and give Jim up; would you felt better than what you do now? No, says I, I'd feel bad—I'd feel just the same way I do now. Well, then, says I, what's the use you learning to do right, when it's troublesome to do right and ain't no trouble to do wrong, and the wages is just the same? I was stuck. I couldn't answer that. So I reckoned I wouldn't bother no more about it, but after this always do whichever come handiest at the time.

The humour is not sugar for the pill but inseparable from the seriousness of the issues raised—which are not raised as *parti-pris* statements, but freely created through 'the imaginatively recovered vitality of youth.... What the book conveys is the drama in a mind in which conscience finds that it is not single, and that the "law" doesn't speak with one voice, and that... "sympathy" itself engages a moral imperative. In fact,' Leavis concludes, '*Huckleberry Finn* has as a central theme the complexity of ethical valuation in a society with a complex tradition—a description that applies (for instance) to any "Christian" society.'

That 'nigger', in its time (which is the time of Mark Twain's boyhood, not of his 'reflective maturity'), should be seen to have imposed itself on the vernacular of the complex society represented in the book, the assumptions behind the word being altogether too strong to question, might have given the anti-racist pause before he hastened to suppress its historic and literary manifestations. In the cause of the new puritanism, however, he is moved to apply the sort of patriarchal rectitude that John Wyndham characterises in *The Chrysalids*, where a close and closed community treats any deviation, human, animal or vegetable, as a blasphemy against the true image of God. We should not suppose that the anti-racist will draw the line at altering *Huckleberry Finn*. Some juicy fruit awaits the picking of a vandal who cannot even recognise in *Uncle Tom's Cabin* a useful friend.[10] Crusoe's man Friday is an obvious target: no matter that Defoe introduces him as a fugitive from the pot boiled by his similarly coloured enemies, man Friday and pot-boilers alike are candidates for 'alternative representation' (... beware 'alternative': it no more means alternative than 'positive', another word much used in progressive circles, means positive). Conrad's deeply considered anti-colonialism is unlikely to save *Heart of Darkness* for the classroom—unless Marlow can be made to mend his language. In *The Pilgrim's Progress*, the pair of energetic scrubbers who labour in vain to 'wash the Ethiop white'[11] are sure to be put on Other Duties when John H. Wallace tracks them down. A bishop's recent detection of 'racism' in the New Testament is enough to warn us that even Shakespeare may not prove immune to the depredations of the new censor: Othello's sooty bosom is indubitably unacceptable, as is Iago's foul-souled baiting of Brabantio—

> Even now, now, very now, an old black ram
> Is tupping your white ewe.

I do not mean to put ideas into the adversary's head. The point to make is that our literature, the achievement of several centuries of creative effort, is altogether too rich and various for accommodation within the total exclusion-zone that the anti-racist would throw around the classroom, and that the pupil is entitled to access to that wealth and variety. For a literature provides 'a record of explorations in interest and feeling, of compassions, brutalities of attitude, subtleties and crudities of personal relations, varieties of humour, conceptions of holiness, of tragedy, of generosity—*possibilities of feeling inexhaustible by any one person or contemporary group*.... A literature [for no single author stands alone] does not sanction any particular outlook or scale of values; it is committed only to the belief that human experiences and our ways of evaluating them must be brought to light and looked at, probed and discussed' (D. W. Harding—my italics).[12]

But the leopard would have to change his spots to take that point.

Notes

1. F. R. Leavis's interpretation of C. P. Snow's idea of cultural assumptions: see 'Two Cultures?—The Significance of Lord Snow' in *Nor Shall My Sword* (Chatto, 1972).

2. The document, entitled 'Westminster College and Multi-cultural Education', and addressed to 'all staff' on 6 March 1984 as ideas 'we can kick around', was composed by a teacher who had been seconded to the College to help in the establishment of multi-cultural principles and practices there.
3. 'Continuing Education in a Multi-cultural Society', a series of resolutions and suggestions distributed for discussion in subject-departments in the City of Manchester College of Higher Education (November 1981).
4. 16 March 1984. News of the 'cut-out model', which seems to me an acceptable and appropriate reading-aid (and which Mr Brunning is reported to deplore), comes from this source.
5. To attack the publisher, rather than to take issue with the published article, seems to be a growing (and distinctly sinister) practice. Two recent cases: (1) SPCK came under fire for issuing *The Kindness that Kills*, edited by Digby Anderson, £3.95—a collection of essays on the Church's official attitude towards such things as race, industrial relations, spending on education and the condition of the poor. (2) When the *Universities Quarterly*, in January 1984, printed a lecture of mine entitled ' "Sex", "Race" and English Matters', it was not the editor but the publisher—Basil Blackwell—that was reviled, along with me (personally, for I received no critical reply), by the targets of my polemic.
6. The address of the Writers and Readers Co-operative (the publisher) is 14 Talacre Road, London, NW5.
7. *Doctor Dolittle* is also pricked down, and pricked out, by Gillian Klein in an article entitled 'Print and Prejudice' (*Junior Education*, October 1980). Mrs Klein shows us the illustration of Prince Bumpo 'reading fairy stories to himself', alters the caption to suit her purposes to ' "If I were only a *white* prince!" said he, with a dreamy, faraway look in his eyes', and remarks: '*The Story of Doctor Doolittle* [sic] reflects the racial attitudes of 1922, and has no place in Britain today.' 'Hard though it seems,' she advises her teacher-readers, 'you should destroy all the offending material or, better, ... return it to the publishers telling them why it is not acceptable in your school.'

I first made that descriptive-critical observation in the lecture referred to in note 5; and I bring it forward here for the further light it sheds, in conjunction with a published retort to it, on the purposes and the tactics of the professed anti-racist. It seems that, in pressing the claims of an 'inter-national, inter-actional world' and 'a multi-racial and multi-cultural Britain' free of 'preconceptions and prejudices about race, sex and class', Mrs Klein and her associates may assume a license to tamper with the truth that would be deemed unscrupulous in ordinary civilised discourse. Writing, with their mentor's approval, in the *Universities Quarterly* for Autumn 1984, Miss Ann Miller and Mr Christopher Gaine blandly ignore the matter of the altered caption and choose to interpret Mrs Klein's destructive and suppressive intentions as a 'message [*sic*] . . . that teachers should be alert to stereotypes . . . , not, as Capey seems to think, that any literary portrayal of blacks or women which does not meet with her approval should be banned, censored, burned, etc.'

8. Introduction to *Pudd'n'head Wilson* (Chatto, 1960). (I discuss *Pudd'n'head Wilson*, along with *Uncle Tom's Cabin* and *The Nigger of the 'Narcissus'*, in the printed lecture referred to in note 5.)
9. Published by John H. Wallace & Sons Company, Falls Church, Virginia; and obtainable here from Sam Lee, 3 Knowles Close, Halstead, Essex. (Among the patrons of the responsible charity, 'Roots of Culture Foundation', are Professor John Eggleston, Professor Harold Rosen and Bev Woodroffe.)
10. 'Uncle Tomism' is a common ism of abuse in the anti-racist's vocabulary.
11. The phrase in fact is Charles Wesley's, in a verse (of the cento 'O for a thousand tongues to sing . . .') expunged from the hymn-books in this century. The incident referred to constitutes a scene presented by the Shepherds of the Delectable Mountains in Part II of *The Pilgrim's Progress*.
12. See 'The Bond with the Author', in *The Use of English*, Summer 1971.

9

Here be Witches! 'Anti-Racism' and the Making of a New Inquisition

David J. Levy

In the last week of August 1985 the British Association for the Advancement of Science met in conference at Strathclyde. The reports of the conference which appeared in the educational press made it clear that, by and large, its proceedings had encompassed the usual range of addresses and debates, by turn, predictable, provocative and profound. The British Association is a prestigious body whose annual conferences provide an opportunity for representatives of the natural and the social sciences to meet, together and in separate subject-based sections, in order to discuss matters of mutual interest. In an age of increasing specialisation, when even within a single discipline communication between researchers in different areas is often all but non-existent, gatherings like the British Association conference have a particular importance. The British Association is not a forum for detailed examination of arcane research projects. It provides a platform for reporting general trends in research and introducing new developments in scientific inquiry in ways that are accessible to the reasonably educated non-specialist. Beyond this, the annual conference gives natural and social scientists a chance to voice their concerns about the present state of their disciplines; to publicise both the problems intrinsic to their fields of investigation and those, like funding, which derive from the relationship between the sciences and the society in which they are practised.

On the whole, it is the pronouncements of the natural scientists which tend to receive the greatest publicity in the press. This is not surprising. Natural science retains a considerable prestige in the eyes of the general public; and the voices of those who present themselves as its representative spokesmen are listened to even when they choose to pronounce on matters far removed from their fields of expertise. Natural scientists, particularly those who like to spend their time at non-specialist conferences, are often keen amateur philosophers and enthusiastic moralists. Such people are assured of a ready audience among a populace which, unable to penetrate the complex codes of scientific discourse, believes that those able to use them must be figures of superhuman wisdom and intelligence. It was therefore striking that in the reports of the Strathclyde conference which appeared in *The Times Educational Supplement* and *The Times Higher Education Supplement* on 30 August 1985, the lion's share of attention was devoted to the day-long meeting of the British Association's sociology section; a session given over to a critical examination of what its organisers called 'The New Right'.

Under the banner headline 'Assault on Honeyford's multi-cultural views', the *Educational Supplement's* reporter devoted half a page to an account of David Oldman's paper 'The Rise and Fall of the Concept of Educational Opportunity'. The *THES* report ranged rather wider; mentioning not only Mr Oldman's contribution but also Professor Robert Moore's paper, 'Sociology, Social Change and the Sociology of Race Relations' and Professor John Eldridge's 'British Industrial Relations in the Eighties'. The report of Moore's paper, subsequently confirmed by examination of all three papers, made it plain that he, like his Aberdeen colleague Mr Oldman, was concerned with detecting the cancer of 'racism' in the writings, not of Mr Honeyford alone, but in those of other writers who had contributed to the conservative journal *The Salisbury Review*. Moore had perused the pages of *The Salisbury Review*, as well as a couple of other essays by Roger Scruton and John Casey, in search of a justification of what he called 'old-fashioned "scientific racism" ' which he never seemed quite able to find. Oldman had examined a number of Ray Honeyford's contributions to the *Review* and supplemented his rather narrow data base with references to a few articles in *The Spectator* and to Antony Flew's book *Sociology, Equality and Education* (London, 1976). Like Moore, Oldman apparently found it rather difficult to make the charge of 'racism' stick, preferring to argue that the writings of Mr Honeyford and others are symptomatic of a trend toward 'authoritarianism' in British society in the 1980s.

No doubt such accusatory discourse has a place in debates about the direction of social and educational policy which are part of the life of a free society. Quite what it has to do with the advancement of science, or of social science for that matter, is altogether more obscure. Moreover, for there to be debate there must be debaters, and what was remarkable about the Strathclyde conclave was that in the course of the day there was no opportunity for any of the academics whose work was variously described as 'slipshod', 'inadequate' and 'without scholarly content' to answer the charges. When challenged on this Professor Moore replied, in a letter to the *Times Higher Education Supplement*, that the subject of the session had been announced well in advance, and that anyone interested in attending could have journeyed to Strathclyde to do so. While that may be true, it still seems an odd sort of academic conference at which a group of university teachers are provided with a platform for the critical appraisal of the work of colleagues, none of whom is even invited to deliver a prepared response.

Seen on its own, such a meeting may seem objectionable but unimportant. Unfortunately not only have its tendentious proceedings been given an undeserved aura of scientific respectability because they were held under the auspices of the British Association, but the gathering cannot be seen, let alone understood, in isolation from a growing number of 'anti-racist' initiatives which range in type from the hideous hounding of Mr Honeyford in Bradford to the almost comic purges of such 'racist' literature as *Hucklebury Finn* and *Tin-Tin* from the shelves of childrens' libraries in Inner London. Whatever their occasion, they are characterised by the same inquisitorial mode of procedure displayed by the sociologists at Strathclyde. Increasingly, self-styled 'anti-racists' operate according to the logic of the witch-hunter. Convinced, as their writings make plain, of the near-omnipresence of 'racism' in British culture and institutions, they see the forces of evil at work wherever anyone expresses an opinion opposed to their own or dares to suggest that their proposals and the assumptions underlying them are far-fetched or simply wrong.

The absence of one side of the argument gave the Strathclyde meeting an appearance not of a forum of debate but of a sort of showtrial at which opponents were condemned before an audience already convinced of their failings.

It is important to recognise that the initiatives proposed and instigated by 'anti-racists' go far beyond what most of us might recognise as legitimate attempts to defend our fellow citizens from abuse and discrimination on grounds of their ethnic origins; and that the results of their activities are not always confined to the relatively harmless practice of ritual condemnation. The institutionalisation of what now passes for 'anti-racism' in the policies and directives of numerous local government and educational authorities has already damaged the lives and careers of quite a number of competent and conscientious teachers and public servants.

'Anti-racism', as it is understood by academics like Professor Moore as well as by ideologues like Dr Sivanandan, director of the publicly subsidised Institute of Race Relations, implies much more than a commitment to oppose racial discrimination. The views put forward by such men reflect a particular, largely Marxist, ideological perspective on British society and its history. Their writings sometimes seem to be inspired less by concern at the problems of the ethnically diverse newcomers who have chosen to settle in Britain than by the inner requirements of a jaundiced and intentionally subversive attitude toward the country and its institutions. 'Anti-racism' increasingly provides a morally acceptable cloak for the pedalling of tendentious Marxist history and discredited political and economic nostrums.

It is essential that the character of this 'anti-racism' be understood for the ideological phenomenon it is; and that the creditable aim of promoting racial harmony should cease to be associated with a rag-bag assortment of Marxist intellectuals who regard racial tensions as a stick with which to beat our present political, social and economic system. The future of the ethnic minorities in Britain depends upon their capacity to build for themselves a secure and respected place in British society and upon the willingness of the wider population to accept their presence. Despite the best efforts of small and politically insignificant genuinely racist groups and the setbacks which occur whenever there are inner-city riots, there is every reason to suppose that the process of integration and adjustment can be successfully completed. It is, nevertheless, a difficult and sensitive process which involves the fears and feelings not only of the ethnic minorities but of the people among whom they must live.

To the extent that the Marxist version of 'anti-racism' prevails, it threatens to make the attainment of harmonious inter-communal relations more difficult, if not impossible. By encouraging resentment and suspicion in the minds both of the ethnic minorities and of the indigenous population, whose history, loyalties and traditions are held up for contempt and condemnation, the proponents of this view do a terrible disservice to the cause they claim to have at heart. The main danger in this, as I see it, is not that they will succeed in inducing the sort of social transformation they so obviously desire, but that, by associating the interest of the Afro-Carribean and, to a lesser extent, the Asian communities with their own ideological ends, they will discredit the very notion of integration with all the consequences that would entail. The activities of 'anti-racists' too often make real the very fears of cultural and social transformation which fuel suspicion of ethnic minorities in the first place. The combination of radical political rhetoric and mob-violence, which was a feature of last year's riots in Handsworth, Brixton and Tottenham, was disquieting enough. But, in the long term, it is far worse to read, in Robert Miles' and Annie Phizacklea's *White Man's Country*, for instance,[1] that riot is a legitimate form of 'resistance' to a supposedly racist state. Such writings encourage further disorder and so provoke the inevitably bitter reactions of police and populace alike. They bring the whole effort to improve inter-communal relations into disrepute by offering moral justification to forms of mass violence that already, in themselves, have the effect of confirming the suspicions of those who believe that the integration of Britain's black population is impossible. Nothing could be more calculated to make the position of Britain's ethnic minorities less secure or to hinder the attempts of the vast majority among them to succeed in the society they have chosen to make their own.

The ideology of 'anti-racism' permits of many nuances but, underlying its various expressions, is the assumption that inter-communal tensions, far from being endemic in every situation where ethnically and culturally diverse communities live alongside each other, are the product of a particular 'capitalist' form of society. In the extreme form represented by Dr Sivanandan, a propagandist whose monolithically Marxist view of the world renders him not so much against discrimination as incapable of it, 'racism' is something deliberately engineered by 'Capital' in order to divide a potentially revolutionary working class.[2] In the more sober version of the case presented by Miles and Phizacklea (*op. cit.*), racial tensions are seen as the incidental but inevitable by-product of an economic system in which labour is treated as a commodity and population-movements are encouraged for the sake of profit, only to be curtailed when no longer economically advantageous. 'Racism,' they argue, 'should be viewed more as an ideology around which class struggle occurs rather than as an ideology of the ruling class' (*ibid.*, p.160). Professor Moore himself presented an early variant of this theme in his somewhat anecdotal *Racism and Black Resistance in Britain*,[3] in which, after presenting the now-familiar case that Britain's adoption of immigration controls more or less similar to those of every other non-communist industrialised nation represented the 'institutionalisation of racism' by the state, he concluded that inter-racial tensions are 'problems rooted in the very nature of the economic system in which we live and which create the everyday problems that are familiar to ordinary people at work and in the supermarket' (*op.cit.*, p.114).

Through all these versions runs the typically Marxist assumption that the roots of every social problem are to be found in the character of the prevailing economic system. It is not surprising, then, that Moore's book, like that of Sivanandan and of Miles and Phizacklea, was published by the Pluto Press, a publishing house closely associated with the Trotskyite group once called the International Socialists and now renamed the Socialist Workers' Party. Given the ideological preferences of the press, it is no more surprising that each of these 'Plutocratic' authors reserves a particular scorn for anyone working in the race relations field who regards his role as the integration of immigrants in society rather than the attempt to undermine it. 'Integration' has indeed become something of a dirty word in 'anti-racist' literature, suggesting, as it does, that adjustments are required from the ethnic minorities as well as from the white population, and that, once these occur, race relations can be improved *within* the established social order.

Contempt for those who choose the path of conciliation rather than revolution as a solution to the problem of racial tension is most vividly expressed in the colourful rhetoric of Dr Sivanandan; for whom no prospect is more frightful than the emergence of a Black and Asian bourgeoisie in Britain. Sivanandan stands, it must be admitted, at one end of the spectrum of 'anti-racist' writers. He is an overtly revolutionary writer who makes no secret of his belief that 'racism' is merely a surface symptom of the 'underlying contradictions' of world capitalism, and that the 'anti-racist' struggle is only an episode in the battle for universal, socialist revolution. Moore, who now holds the chair of sociology at Aberdeen University, is more circumspect. In his Strathclyde paper, for instance, he goes out of his way to stress the usefulness to society of the knowledge acquired by students on his and other sociology courses.[4] On the other hand, in his writings on race and racism, he seems to endorse the view that the problems of inter-communal tension are insoluble within the established social order. Scepticism concerning the resolution of these problems, described predictably as products of 'capitalism', is matched by cynicism about the motivation of government initiatives in the area. Thus, in 1975, when *Racism and Black Resistance* was published, he dismissed the organisations established by government, the Race Relations Board and the Community Relations Commission, as bodies created, not in order to do anything about Britain's racial problems, but as cosmetic gestures designed to show that the government 'cared'. One may well share Moore's scepticism about such bodies, which he describes as living off the conflicts they were supposed to resolve, without accepting his questionable analysis of the motives behind their creation.

In *Racism and Black Resistance* Moore's distaste for officially established organisations stands in stark contrast to his undiscriminating enthusiasm for every initiative perceived as originating within the Black community itself. 'We have,' he rightly observes, 'something to learn from trying to understand the various responses of black people,' continuing, 'something to gain from supporting them and everything to lose by opposing them' (*op. cit.*, p.102). One begins to wonder who this 'we' may be when one notes that among the 'responses' picked out for special emphasis on the previous page was the Black Workers' Co-ordinating Committee and the Black Unity and Freedom Party—organisations whose aim, Moore tells us, is the development of 'the working class ideology of revolutionary and scientific socialism amongst all workers, especially Black workers'.

There is no evidence that such ultra-left groups were ever more representative of the opinions of Black workers than is the SWP of the generality of the British working class. Nevertheless, small extremist organisations, which may merely have a nuisance value in the broad perspective of national politics, can have much more pernicious effects when they enter an emotionally charged area like that of race relations. The significance of such groups must be judged in the context of the results of their activities, not only on the minority community, where they encourage dissaffection and a fruitless political activism, but on the majority of population which perceives them as more representative than in fact they are. Every time one of their members puts himself forward as a self-styled 'community leader' he damages the interests of the community for which he presumes to speak. In large part the remedy to this problem lies in the ethnic minority communities themselves; but the more politically responsible members of these communities are hardly helped by the pronouncements of 'anti-racist' academics whose analyses of the situation reflect the same Marxist assumptions that underly the ideologies of the most extreme factions.

In the eleven years that have elapsed since the publication of *Racism and Black Resistance in Britain* the centre of effort of Marxist activists has shifted from the creation of more or less ephemeral, openly revolutionary groups and parties to the mainstream of British politics. The sort of person who once found his political home in one of the schismatic factions of the Trotskyite left, now works patiently in the Labour Party's corridors of power. The well-publicised and carefully orchestrated confrontation between the present Labour leadership and the Militant Tendency at the 1985 Labour Party Conference cannot hide the fact that views scarcely distinguishable from those of Militant now inform the policies of a large number of Labour-controlled local authorities, including local education authorities. 'Anti-racism' is only one of the anodyne labels behind which such authorities seek to introduce their own ideology into the educational curriculum. The experience of racial tension and the moral opprobrium in which doctrines of racial superiority are rightly held provide the opportunity for initiatives whose fundamental purpose is not the integration of ethnic minorities in British society but the revolutionary transformation of that society in a Marxist socialist direction.

Notes

1. Pluto Press, London, 1984.
2. A. Sivanandan: *A Different Hunger: Writings on Black Resistance* (Pluto Press, London, 1982).
3. Pluto Press, London, 1975.
4. Available from The British Association for the Advancement of Science.

SECTION 4

Culture and Value

10

The Myth of Cultural Relativism

Roger Scruton

Britain contains many cultures, several of which are likely to be represented in any single classroom: so we are told by the advocates of 'multi-cultural education'. The observation is used as a ground for rejecting the 'anglocentric' curriculum of our parents. In such circumstances, it is argued, we cannot justify the adoption of a curriculum which is wedded, in both form and content, to a single culture. Our curriculum should be either 'multi-cultural' or 'culture-free', so as to offer equal advantages, and equal opportunities, to every child, whatever his social, ethnic, religious and moral background.

What do we mean by 'culture'? In educational debates, the following have all been included as part of 'culture':

(1) Language, including dialect, speech melody, and idiom.
(2) The 'deep' customs and beliefs of religion.
(3) The 'shallow' customs of social intercourse: feasts and ceremonies, manners and courtesies.
(4) Morality, and especially sexual morality.
(5) Popular entertainment, sport and leisure.
(6) 'High' culture, in which aesthetic values are paramount.
(7) 'Political' culture, including a sense of law and justice, and expectations as to the correct way to resolve conflicts.

Only some of those could conceivably be the subject of a 'choice' on the part of the person who learns them, but clearly all *are* learned, and all are of concern to a person who educates children. It cannot be said that Britain is a 'multi-cultural society' in all seven respects.

There is a common language, a dominant religion, a settled pattern of social expectations, a shared network of entertainment and sport, a common morality and a common law. Most of those whose ancestral religion is not Christianity belong to another monotheistic cult which grew from Christianity and Judaism. The Bible is a sacred text for most Britons who are believers; and even the unbelievers share, as a rule, the Judaeo-Christian values of the surrounding order. In 'high' culture there is indeed a radical divide within British society—between those who understand it and those who do not: but it is a divide that has always existed.

This is not to minimise the real difference between the child of Moslem, Urdu-speaking parents, and the child of English-speaking Christians. But there are also great similarities between these two children, who are equally different from the morality of Polynesia, the religion of the Incas or the customs of ancient Japan. To some extent the similarity between them is explained by the pressure exercised by law. Polygamy, for example, is forbidden by English law, as is *suttee*. The caste system is legally ineffective and any attempt to act upon it is tortious, if not criminal. Divorce is permitted, and is also a matter for the civil courts. There is freedom of religion, of speech, of opinion. In these and other respects our law exercises a powerful homogenising force, and in no sphere is law more effective than in the sphere of education. For the law, rightly or wrongly, compels people to send their children to school; and if parents cannot afford private schools, the children must perforce mix with those who are gathered into the same classroom as themselves.

It is partly because people overlook the power of the *political* culture of Britain that they imagine such vast differences between the various ethnic groups. If it were the case that one group lived by the caste system, practised polygamy, *suttee* and the stoning to death of adulterers, then it might seriously be suggested that there are vast cultural differences among British citizens. Perhaps a true 'multculturalist' would seek to undo the laws which prevent that way of life so that another 'valid alternative' might flourish. As things stand, however, the differences are less significant than the similarities, and the pressure to conformity is enormous. Only in certain crucial matters concerning religious observance are there grounds for thinking that teachers *must* be presented with a problem by their attempts to teach according to the 'anglocentric' curriculum.

That, however, is not the way that the matter is seen by the 'multi-culturalists'. The fact that the teacher can make do with the anglocentric curriculum does not mean that he *ought* to make do with it. For one thing, it is argued, the anglocentric curriculum discriminates against children whose mother tongue is not English. So great is the aversion to 'discrimination' that educationalists argue that children ought to be taught in their mother-tongue, *even though* the surrounding social order is impervious to its utterances. The disastrous consequences of such a policy should be obvious. Deprived of their only opportunity to learn the language of the public world which surrounds them, the children would be destined for a life of social and cultural isolation, in ghettoes, cut off from the larger world and hostile to its law and politics. Of course, there are advocates of 'multi-cultural education' who desire that result, but their disposition to use the ethnic minorities as pawns in the political game of revolution is hardly likely to be shared by the normal British teacher.

No educational process can avoid imparting some culture to those who participate in it. It is impossible to teach children without also teaching them language, good manners, polite and peaceful behaviour and the elements of morality. Without those precious attributes, children could not stay peacefully together in a classroom, nor could they listen to a teacher. It follows that every genuinely educational process must recognise certain cultural expectations as legitimate, and endeavour to support them.

Why, however, do we group together those seven types of activity under the single word 'culture'? All the activities mentioned have this in common: that they serve to bind people together in a common enterprise. To put it another way, they are ways of 'belonging' to the larger world of human society, and of affirming one's reality as a social being. Unless people acquire the habit of 'belonging' they cannot live peacefully together, nor can they be happy. Not all ways of belonging have the same structure. The rehearsal of our shared nature in ritual, ceremony and faith is more profoundly rooted than the patient resolution of conflict through law, and the educated obedience to a civil order. The bond which comes from a common religion sincerely believed, and from a solemn enactment of the identity of the tribe, is stronger, more immediate, more overwhelming than the feeling for law. Hence people often look with admiration and nostalgia upon the organic communities in which law is undeveloped, and in which ritual and ceremony carry the principal burden of social existence. Our culture is not—primarily—dependent upon the organic bonds of religion and ceremony. It tries to accommodate conflict and to forge bonds between people by means of contract, law and a shared sense of justice. Indeed, it is frequently argued that this is precisely what distinguishes the modern from the medieval state. The modern state has emerged from that 'prophetic' order, in which people are united behind a revelation of transcendent truth, embodied in ritual and ceremony, to become a 'civil society', in which various religions, various customs and various tastes may co-exist beneath a common rule of law. Many of the philosophers of the European state—Spinoza in particular—advocated just such a transition, believing that the cohesive force of religion is also a source of violent confrontation. Hence, Spinoza argued, religion must be displaced from the centre of political life, and the secular sovereign must be given (through the law) the principal power to administer justice, to uphold association and to establish a common code of conduct. Large questions of political philosophy and sociology are raised by those thoughts. But we can at least see that the *law* of England, and the parliamentary procedure through which it is developed and enacted, are as much parts of the public culture of Britain as is the Christian religion. Any attempt to impart British culture to the children (or grandchildren) of immigrants quite reasonably involves an instruction in the nature of, and the feeling for, the English law: in the *Rechtsgefühl* (the feeling for law and justice) of England, upon which the 'English peace' is ultimately founded.

'British culture' includes any activity, under our seven headings, which facilitates the participation of the individual in the peculiar social order which is Britain. It therefore involves the English language, and the literature that gives to that language its field of reference and its principal communicative power. It also involves the customs and leisure activities that are common to the British people, and—muted though they may be in their consciousness—the religion and history which have given to the law of England its particular force and application.

It is surely a prime duty of a teacher of British children to prepare them for their acceptance into this culture. This does not mean that he must induce a blind obedience to surrounding imperatives or an uncritical acceptance of the myths and dogmas whereby other people live. It means only that, in the end, he will have failed in his duty if the children within his care find that they do not, as a result of their schooling, 'belong' to the surrounding world. For to what other world can they turn for the consolations of society? If their education alienates them from the only world to which they have access, what value does it have for them, and why should we compel them to undergo it?

The answer that is often given to those questions is this: British culture is a tawdry and disheartening affair. We should prepare children to free themselves from its grip, not to feel bound by the manacles of history, not to be tied to a particular culture that has outlived its usefulness. But this gives no real argument for rejecting British culture. A child is not free from the grip of a culture simply by being *alienated* from it. On the contrary, alienation is merely a particularly painful form of attachment. Freedom from British culture can be induced only by inducing a state of culture-lessness, or by attaching the child to *another* culture, which is not that of his surrounding world. Neither of those are feasible projects. To void a child's mind of culture is to leave him isolated from fellowship, without the possibility of social fulfilment. If that is what education is supposed to do, then we should all fight to the death against education. To attach a child to another culture, on the other hand, supposes that the teacher himself possesses that culture, and also that he is able to provide the environment that will enable it to thrive. Neither assumption is reasonable, and both lead one to ask why a teacher should really bother with this exercise. Our ancestors did their best to teach their pupils about other cultures: about the culture of Greece and Rome, and that of early Palestine. But they did this in full consciousness that these cultures were extinguished. Hence their teachings were not, in any real sense, a method for presenting children with an existential choice. To attempt to present a genuine *choice* between cultures, to say to the child, this is *one* way of living, this *another*, and now you choose, to do this would require skills, understanding and moral courage beyond the normal or desirable level to which our teachers can aspire.

To transmit the *particular* culture of Britain to the children of Britain is not simply to indoctrinate them in beliefs and values which they are not to question. Almost all cultures contain a principle of internal criticism. It is permissible to question beliefs, even to question values, provided this activity of questioning is contained within the recognised limits of cultural stability. This is particularly true of those cultures—the European—which are founded upon *Rechtsgefühl* as their dominant social perception. The child brought up in the British way of doing things is encouraged to question and to criticise, to seek fair play and impartial judgement, and to receive as doctrine only that which he has independent reason to believe to be true. A child brought up in such a culture does not *need* that presentation of 'alternatives' which so many educationists wish to foist on him. Nor is this openness to question and to other experiences a feature only of our modern culture. Any reader of Shakespeare will recognise the ease with which the poet enters into situations and cultures which are totally outside the ordinary experience of contemporary Englishmen. (Consider Othello, Shylock's daughter, Hamlet, Caliban, Brutus, Cleopatra, Troilus—and a hundred more.)

Advocates of the thesis of cultural relativism often argue as though no culture can really be criticised except from a point of view internal to itself, so that anybody who attempts to judge another culture—a culture with which he does not identify—would be engaged in argument that is without foundation. This thesis, if true, would make the whole idea of a 'choice' of cultures absurd: since each culture is insulated from external criticism, there could not conceivably be any reason for choosing between them. However, this kind of relativism is unacceptable. A culture is a pattern of social unity, and can be judged as such; it can be praised or condemned on account of the society that it engenders, and the actual unity which it founds. A culture which holds people together in a state of fear, or which brutally extirpates the natural inclinations of those who share in it, is surely inferior to one that permits peaceful and open dialogue. Nobody would argue that Nazi culture, for example, or Communist culture, are really unjudgeable from any point of view except the one that they themselves define.

This is not to say that there is some *particular* culture that is superior to all others, or that we could establish any canon for evaluating the cultures of other peoples. It is only to say that the very enterprise of social existence is answerable to absolutes of right and wrong. The moral law is universally valid and universally binding: anybody who fails to receive it as such is without morality. A culture that forbids or distorts the truths of morality is objectively undesirable. Of course, it is a difficult philosophical question how we might *justify* the laws of morality. But *what* they are, and *that* they are—these are given to us unquestionably. One of the most important functions of a culture is to rehearse and to support the dictates of morality—to embody them in laws, legends, ceremonies and manners, and so to make them inviolable. Morality therefore provides us with the Archimedean point from which cultures may be weighed, and unless morality too is 'relative'—a view which no-one really believes in his actual dealings with his fellows—cultural relativism is false.

That said, we have not yet justified the teaching of *British* culture: all we have done is to propose a test which all cultures must meet if we are to regard them favourably—a test which is met, by and large, by the major cultures of Christendom, Judaism and Islam. Nevertheless, there is already contained in what I have said an intrinsic justification of the British curriculum—and this on two counts:

(1) Children have a prior interest in acquiring the prevailing culture of their surroundings. If they do not acquire it, then their strangeness becomes apparent, and they themselves become victims of discrimination, unable to secure the full advantages of social existence. Hence British children have a prior interest in acquiring British culture.
(2) British culture is a prime example of secular culture, sustained, it is true, by the religious traditions and institutions of Christianity, but based more in open communication and the feeling for law than in any slavish adherence to custom. As an 'open' culture it is manifestly permeable to outside influence, and therefore able to adjust itself to the demands of other customs. (Consider the rapidity with which British language, cooking and costume were penetrated by the language, cooking and costume of India.) Such a culture prepares children for the mobile, mixed society to which they are destined far more effectively than does, for example, the culture of modern Pakistan.

As I have already indicated, this openness of British culture is a long-established feature. One of the reasons for teaching the *high* culture of any society is that it shows this openness at its most developed. A high culture is a sphere of maximum influence, of maximum exposure to what is strange and interesting, of maximum alertness to the human in all its forms: it is the ultimate expression of man's sympathy for his kind. To understand the high culture of Britain is to understand its links with the high cultures of France, Holland, Germany and Spain; with the dead cultures of Greece, Rome and Egypt; with the cultures of Arabia and Persia, and even with those of China and Japan. It is no accident that our culture has reached out to so many others, or provided those cultures with new forms and styles. (To take a few random examples: consider the mutual influence of English and Arabian culture, through such adventurous personalities as Sir Richard Burton; of English and Indian culture through Rudyard Kipling; of English and Balinese music through Benjamin Britten.) This, indeed, is one of the major justifications that could be offered for what has been called a 'liberal' education, but which might just as well be called an education in the high culture of our civilisation.

In the light of those considerations, it seems to me that there can be no real argument for a 'multi-cultural' curriculum. To adopt such a curriculum is to fail to transmit either the common culture of Britain or the high culture that has grown from it. And no other culture is put in the place of those: the result is nothing more than a void, existing in the child's consciousness at precisely the place where certainty, immediacy and competence is needed if he is to engage spontaneously and peacefully within his surrounding world. Teachers have a duty to place their pupils within the broad context of British culture, and, where possible, to foster the development of those wider and more enquiring sympathies that are the substance of a liberal education.

What does this mean in practice? It seems that teaching in our schools ought always to be in English, even if children are encouraged to retain and to develop the mother-tongue which informs their first experience of the world. And the first concern of the history teacher must be to teach the history of Britain, so that a child may understand the past in terms of its present and observable residue. To teach the history of distant and unknown places is, of course, a splendid educational exercise—and one which has always been conducted, under the guise of 'ancient history'. But it cannot substitute for that informed awareness of history as a living process, a form of communication with the past and the future, which stems from an awareness of the 'pastness' of everything one touches, and of the evolving nature of existing social and political arrangements.

Those are only two suggestions, but they point the way to many more. Once the myth of cultural relativism is rejected, we can surely see the way to an improved curriculum, which will be both British in its cultural background and also open to the world, permeable to experience and sympathetic to languages, customs and religions which are not those of modern England.

11

Swann and the Spirit of the Age

Simon Pearce

The memorably bland title of the Swann Report, *Education for All*, gives no clue as to the scope of its ambitions. Nor did the inadequate media coverage which greeted its publication in March 1985. Such lack of daylight, however, has served its purpose. The Report has grown out of a philosophy of manipulation inimical to free debate for which its premises are ill designed.

Swann (properly, the Report of the Committee of Inquiry into the Education of Children from Ethnic Minority Groups, chaired by Lord Swann) is a profoundly dangerous document aiming at the reshaping of British society in conformity with an outlook which would be rejected if its intent was understood. It argues for a fundamental change in a national culture regardless of national opinion. It is to be implemented by the subordination of education to political ends regardless of the educational consequences.

There is no plot, of course: the committee was simply in thrall to one of the powerful spirits of this present age, that faith in the mutability of society by political action which is best described as 'progressive' (though the connection between it and the forward movement of humanity is largely incidental). It possesses a secular version of religious zeal, the end of which is to purge Western civilisation of evils which are seen as ingrained or 'structural'. It is born of both liberal and Marxist thinking and older, less rational, urges. A desire to free the oppressed is a powerful motive but not its only one—there is also hatred for the 'system'. The progressive temperament rejects the past and is thus enabled to accumulate the grudge-holders and those whose satisfaction it is to be against. It is egalitarian, of course, Utopian certainly, relativist at bottom and incipiently totalitarian.

Education, the shaping of a new generation still unsullied, is central to its philosophy, but not as a means of seeking and transmitting truth; rather as an engine of social change.

The Guilt of the British

The Committee of Inquiry was established in 1979 in response to concern over the generally low level of West Indian attainment in our schools. Swann claims that this phenomenon cannot be detached from what it sees as an 'underlying climate of racism'. It uses hard words about the white population. It 'resents moves by ethnic minority groups to advance beyond their "prescribed place" in society' (page 19). The public peace is threatened since 'having rejected' the minorities 'they are now in turn choosing to reject' (pages 6–7). Swann drips with a sense of the culpability of the native British population. There is a current demand for the creation of an offence of 'group libel' to allow action over racial slurs. The chances of convicting the Committee of Inquiry under such an offence must be high.

In addition to this it must be remembered that Britain's institutions and customs 'ignore, or even actively work against the interests of ethnic minority communities' (page 28). Swann attributes this to inertia rather than intent. 'Institutional racism', we are told, springs from the unsuitability of many of our institutions to a multi-racial society.

Education is tainted by its social context. Swann is careful not to point the finger of overt racism at the teaching profession, whose resentment would not assist the implementation of its plans. But British teaching is 'ethnocentric', based implicitly on a sense of superiority and riddled with unconscious racism.

Swann reflects the anti-racist doctrine that disparate levels of achievement between ethnic groups are proof-positive of discrimination on the part of the majority and/or dominant group. Yet 'what stubborn things are facts'. One single but massive fact undermines the anti-racist view of the extent and influence of racism in Britain. Racism, it has been loudly claimed, is the primary cause of West Indian underachievement. However, Swann's findings show that Asians (hardly less likely candidates for discrimination) perform considerably better than blacks and about as well as whites. Swann is obliged to conclude that 'the reasons for the very different school performances of Asians and West Indians seem likely to lie deep within their respective cultures' (page 87).

Swann failed to examine the causes of underachievement (pages 79–80). It failed to examine the internal problems of the black community, such as the high level of fatherless households and the aggressive behaviour of sections of black youth reported by many teachers (page 76). Yet such studies could only profit black people.

White prejudice and ignorance of minority life-styles are *a* factor in underachievement and other ethnic minority problems. The progressives have helped to open eyes to the problem of prejudice and insensitivity. But that is a very different proposition from one that sees Britain as soaked in racism. Is this the nation that has constantly rejected racialist parties? Which has accepted an unwanted and, in modern times, unprecedented migration with remarkable passivity? Judged by absolute standards the white English working class (the main object of anti-racist scorn) is easy to reproach. But by the test of history, of international comparison and the standards that frail creatures have the right to expect of each other, it has on the whole shown up well. Hatred and violence there has been but they cannot be laid at the door of a whole people. Might it not be more profitable to point to the growing multitude of inter-racial friendships, of co-operation and a host of little yet significant kindnesses? They too should be taken in evidence. But, of course, Swann's opinions were not to be shaken by facts. Its plea for social upheaval required a striking moral justification, and what more so than the plea that the British were a pretty rotten lot? A belief in widespread white racism is an essential prop for Swann's policy.

Reshaping the Nation

The spirit of our age is one that itches to start the world over again, to clear away the past which stands as a reproach to its vision of perfection. The growth of state power and an apparently unshakeable faith in its efficacy provides it with the opening it requires; education is one of its chosen instruments.

The mixture of customs, attitudes and institutions that we call British culture has always disappointed such thinkers. Although some of their ideas have been gratefully taken aboard our nation has maintained an obstinate continuity. The arrival of large number of settlers from the New Commonwealth and their multiplication has provided an opportunity to demand radical changes. This is to be done, in part, by 'fostering' via the state education system the 'linguistic, religious and cultural identities of ethnic minority communities' (page 771).

The committee makes it clear that is far more than the promotion of tolerance or even the use of foreign cultures in the curriculum:

> We are perhaps looking for the assimilation of *all* groups within a redefined concept of what it means to live in Britain today (page 8).

This remarkable statement is fleshed out by specific proposals for 'changing the attitudes of coming generations of the white majority culture' (Lord Swann—*A Brief Guide* to the Report). There should be a fundamental change in the education of *all* children in *all* parts of the kingdom whether or not they are likely to have contact with ethnic minority children (page 315). Their parents' cultures would play a major role in all parts of the curriculum—'this is not just a separate topic that can be tacked on to the existing curriculum; it must permeate every aspect of the school's work' (Lord Swann). British history, political institutions, religion, all must be subject to major reappraisal.

There is no doubt that Swann is proposing a dramatic break in the continuity of our national life. The burden of change will fall on the indigenous population, few demands being made on the ethnic minorities. It is, after all, the way of life of the former that stands in the path of what Swann calls a 'pluralist' society. This, while possessing a 'framework of commonly accepted values, practices and procedures' (page 5) (though, as we shall see, these may not be our currently accepted ones) will mean an acceptance of Britain as an archipelago of ethnic cultures maintained by a policy of state. Traditional native values will no longer be the norm to which minority cultures relate; British culture will simply be the largest amongst many and the only one not positively promoted by public education.

British schools have, according to Swann, no special obligation to ensure the transmission of our attitudes, faith or heritage: 'we do not see schools as having a responsibility for cultural preservation' (page

322). One LEA is quoted with approval when it proclaims that 'education is not concerned with teaching children their culture. This is too presumptuous a role for education to attempt to undertake' (page 322).

Swann has no special affection for the ethnic minority cultures. One of its motives for maintaining them is that they will be the building-blocks of a new national identity (page 322). This must involve a loss of identity for the native British since the transmutation of their culture is the essential element in the creation of a pluralist society. The *status quo* which consists of the predominance of British ways is the obstacle to multi-culturalism—it cannot, on Swann's terms, escape from radical change.

Specious consolation is offered. Apparently we are already a multi-cultural society—when culturally distinct ethnic groups constitute much less than one-twentieth of the people (page 7). To seek to 'preserve' a culture is, apparently, 'self-defeating' since it will always be 'changed and being changed' (page 323). This, when people after people, African, European and Asian can in their languages, literature and customs point not only to change but deep continuity. Our regional and class differences, the presence of ethnic minorities and the heterogenous origins of the English nation do not add up to our already being a multi-cultural society. Such facts, when viewed in isolation, ignore common ties of language, religion, geography and all the unity that has evolved out of common government, common foes and common economic interests. No sophistry can hide the injustice that Swann seems to do the British.

There is no grass-roots demand for full-blooded multiculturalism from the ethnic minorities (page 238). They ask for equality of opportunity and are naturally concerned about religion and better English teaching. Many, however, accept that their British citizenship involves some adaptation (though not conformity) with British ways, which is the historic and successful pattern of most migrations to this country.

The crucial question is whether indigenous British culture will maintain its predominance (though never a tyranny) in our schools and national life. There can be no doubts about the full equality under the law of ethnic-minority citizens and their right to equality of respect. Their communities also have a right to seek to preserve their own heritages by voluntary action. But all this is a world apart from the notion that the state should foster foreign cultures and place them on an equal footing in public policy with that of the nation. Britain's culture is open to the modifications that arise naturally from the ebb and flow of social life, and the ethnic minorities are already playing their part in this. But they have to come to share in a long-established way of life, not to found a new society. The native British have a right to preserve their way of life and this must mean that it is their culture which predominates in our schools. The ethnic minorities' right to cultural preservation is already guaranteed. Any attempt by the state to promote it in education will, however, entail a downgrading of the rights of the indigenous population, since their heritage must move over to allow room for multi-culturalism. They are to be treated as a people whose interests are entirely secondary.

Swann and the multi-culturalist lobby seem to have learned little from the long, bloody history of racial and cultural strife. They say that minority cultures must not be suppressed—but they tilt at windmills: no respectable or influential group advocates that they should be. But the majority's culture is to be remoulded and its rights outraged. The ethnic minorities will be encouraged to assert their separateness. The slow process of integration, whereby race becomes a less important factor in our society, will be disrupted. Both white blacklash and black and brown intransigence will be encouraged, and no amount of emphasis on tolerance in our classrooms will bridge the growing gap.

Swann talks of encouraging diversity. That diversity already exists and will never disappear. Racial and cultural difference, however, can be fostered and aggravated. The Utopian frame of mind of the Report is nowhere so evident as at this point. History's lessons are ignored. Human nature cannot be so easily dismissed.

The Curriculum: Closed Minds and Empty Souls

If a multi-cultural education means a drawing on the insights and achievements of the world outside the West, inculcating not only tolerance but respect, then it is a sound concept. Jeffcoate has in this context quoted Matthew Arnold's view that the good education should embrace 'the best that has been thought and known in the world'.[1]

It would be a grotesque nationalist parody of education to insist on a curriculum that drew a line at the water's edge, which deified Britain and her culture. If a backlash against pluralism led to such a state it would be one of anti-racism's most bitter fruits.

Swann's version of multi-culturalism is about social engineering rather than education. It is a method of implementing items long on the progressive agenda. The radical character of these changes may be seen in the curricular reforms of two authorities that Swann singles out for praise (pages 320 and 353); the notorious Inner London Education Authority (ILEA) and the less well known Royal County of Berkshire (respectively under Labour and Conservative control; multi-culturalism is a bipartisan form of madness).

Swann says that no LEA has fully adopted the principles of *Education for All* but ILEA is in the van of progress. It has had particular impact in history teaching. Its guidance for its staff in such papers as *Race, Sex and Class* (1983) and *Marches* (a handbook for teachers, 1981) emphasise that coloured immigration is a consequence of Empire, not of political ineptitude in the 1950s and 1960s. This ties in with an emphasis on British guilt. Accounts of the slave trade rightly blame English attitudes and policy but ignore both the black and Arab contribution to it and the successful agitation against the trade in Britain. Plenty of space is given to colonial iniquity, again not unfairly, but there is no balanced discussion of colonial achievements. History is brought up to recent times, and account of post-war immigration (which Swann regards as very important, page 330) are laced with anti-white prejudice.

Swann wishes to ensure that pupils' horizons 'are not limited by an exclusively Anglo- or Euro-centric view'. Quite so, but it must be remembered that an emphasis on the overwhelming importance of British and European history is not a chauvinistic luxury. It is a matter of *relevance*, essential for both coloured and white Britons to understand their nation's contemporary context. The story of migration to Britain and of the non-Western world should not be ignored, but it needs to be kept in proportion. Swann's attitude gives one little confidence that it will be: 'we believe,' says Swann 'that all areas of the curriculum can contribute towards the development of an education which is more appropriate to the contemporary world'. In science and geography, for instance, one LEA states that 'the issues of regional or group differences need to be worked out and developed in the context of interdependence and unequal resources'. This is suspiciously like the 'Brandt-speak' of the Third World lobby, a progressive sect which holds that the West causes poverty in the underdeveloped nations. (Little attention is directed to the cultures and institutions of the countries concerned.)

Whatever might be the educational justification of a reform of the curriculum the attitude of both Swann and the LEAs that excite its admiration provides great cause for concern. Leaving to one side the indoctrinatory aspects of their policies there is a danger that the curriculum will be distorted by the introduction of materials that may be inherently worthy but which are irrelevant in the context of a British education. It is difficult to avoid the feeling that Swann is intent on inserting multi-culturalism whatever its effect on the quality of instruction.

Religious education requires some separate considerations. Swann does not side with those who would remove it from the curriculum but favours what it calls an 'undogmatic approach' (how good progressives are at appropriating useful terms). This is 'the only response which accords with... the ideal of cultural pluralism' (page 475). It would involve teaching about all faiths without reference to their respective merits. Swann feels that 'all the religious communities in this country had the right to expect the education system to respect and to reflect their faiths, not by comparing them negatively with Christianity, but as valid belief systems in their own right' (page 473).

Swann reflects the view of a wide religious and educational consensus. It is less certain that it reflects majority feeling in the country. If Britain can be said to have a religion it is a form of commitment to Christianity. An 'undogmatic', or to use plainer English, a 'multi-faith' RE must involve considerable reduction in the time devoted to that faith (it is unlikely that more time will be allocated to RE lessons. Once again a cultural change will be imposed on the majority). And not only them. Most West Indians profess the Christian faith and many are very devout. The pressure for change comes from some Asian immigrants. But again it must be repeated that they already possess the right to teach, and indeed propagate, their faiths. The 1944 Education Act explicitly grants the right of withdrawal from RE lessons and other minorities have not been afraid to exercise it. Moreover, Asian communities have a higher level of religious involvement. Their children hardly require extra teaching about their own faith at school. Yet many white and black pupils, whose parents are not churchgoers but who would wish their children to receive a grounding in Christianity, will certainly lose out on a syllabus which allows it to compete for the scanty time allocated to RE with other religions. As with so many of Swann's proposals, the benefit to the ethnic minorities is dubious and the harm to the majority evident. The white British heritage is of slight importance and the problems of the minorities exploited to further the 'cultural revolution'. Swann is a profoundly anti-democratic document, out of touch with the values of the people of Britain.

There is another, deeper, objection to the multi-faith syllabus. The essentially non-religious motivation of Swann's approach to RE and its desire to avoid pointing towards conclusions is likely to lead to an emphasis on the common ground between the faiths. This is all very well up to a point. It is worthwhile to demonstrate the universal nature of the fundamentals of social morality and to develop respect and understanding; but it can also result in a shift of emphasis away from spiritual things and towards a purely moralistic course of instruction. After all, if Christ's claims are true they stand in contradiction to the essential tenets of, for instance, Islam. An RE which is based on cultural pluralism, which demands that all faiths (*all*?) be presented as 'valid belief systems in their own right' is likely to fudge these basic questions and, by majoring on ethics, convey the impression that spiritual matters are less important. There will be an inevitable temptation to imply that, at bottom, all faiths are the same. Would that not be in the spirit of the cultural egalitarianism that Swann desires?

The drift towards syncretism implied by Swann's views on religious education brings us back to the 'Spirit of the Age' that is its source. It is good not to be 'culture-bound', to respect ways of life that are not one's own. It is another thing to flee from judgement and take refuge in moral relativism. Swann's dedication to cultural pluralism is a means of avoiding commitment, of detachment from the cultural bonds that most of us form. Swann's egalitarianism is not perhaps an indication of equal esteem but a way of not making any judgement at all.

Such relativism is a particular feature of our time, which has indeed proved to be an age of uncertainty and moral doubt. It has also seen a rise to power and influence of doctrines whose motivation is a hatred of that which is established. The two are fusing to create a creed which zealously propagates its lack of certainty by the abuse of power. Swann is one of its manifestations.

The Inconvenience of Freedom

Something may be learnt from the spirit that motivates Swann. One of its mainsprings is an outrage at inhumanity. Is our nation, our civilisation, so aware of oppression, so brim-full of compassion that it can dispense with disturbing voices? The progressive error, however, is to allow its insights to denegrate into alienation from the culture that nurtured it and to deny its freedoms to others.

Anti-racism and other progressive causes may draw upon what were originally Christian insights and certainly they have a likeness to religion in their zeal, certainty and sense of evil. But many of their adherents lack Christianity's understanding of our common imperfection. To seek perfection without the love of God can produce dreadful things.

The dream of 'eradicating' prejudice is too grand an aim for politics or education; and resentment will grow out of disappointment. When we or our children's generation fail we shall be viewed not with resignation but as transgressors of a high moral code. The anti-racist philosophy equips them for rooting out opposition from every nook and cranny of society. This stage is already commencing and people have been persecuted in Bradford, in Waltham Forest, in Bristol and in Islington. We can be sure it is only the beginning.

Swann's outlook is basically illiberal. No legitimacy is conferred on other opinions—all are products of intentional or unintentional racism and therefore invalid. Its own logic demands a narrowing-down of freedom, the closing-off of options and the restraint of expression to an approved band of views. Swann's proposals on political education and teacher training demonstrate this clearly.

The brazenness of the Report's views on political education evaded the vigilance of our media—who confined their attentions for the most part to the DES press release and Lord Swann's *Brief Guide* (which obscures much of the central thrust of the Report). Many would agree with the committee that teaching about our institutions and the range of political viewpoints in our society would be valuable. Most would also agree that great caution would be required. Swann has no such worries and makes its motivation plain. Political education

> should involve a consideration of how particular structures and procedures have evolved and their appropriateness to today's multi-racial population. Learning how some long-established practices were originally developed to cater for a relatively homogeneous population should lead youngsters by extension to consider whether such practices are still appropriate to the changed and changing nature of British society today. It should also lead them to consider whether some can now be seen to operate against certain sections of the community, especially the numerically smaller ethnic minority groups, by depriving them of equality of access... In thus learning how racism can operate youngsters... may be better able to understand and challenge its influence and to consider positive and constructive changes to reflect the values of a pluralist democracy. This process should not be seen as a threat to democratic principles... [it] should also lead youngsters to consider fundamental issues such as social justice and equality and this should in turn cause them to reflect on the origins and mechanism of racism and prejudice at an individual level (pages 335–6).

This passage is awash with loaded concepts and controversial judgements. Terms like 'social justice and equality', for instance, carry party-political connotations, and there is no general agreement as to their meaning. The notion of widespread, institutionalised racism is a disputed opinion yet it is presented as a fact. The very image of sixteen-year-olds meditating on our constitution strikes a false note. The trail of reasoning portrayed as inevitable in the passage is nothing of the sort; pupils would have to be led down it; and the tone leaves no doubt that teachers would be briefed by the syllabus to do so. One wonders exactly what the failings of our political institutions are supposed to be. Whatever they might be, Swann is obviously eager to begin the work of demolition.

'Pluralism' has become the cover under which ideas long advocated by the political left (but which would be difficult to have approved on their own merits) are advanced. The accusation of 'racism' can be used to discredit opposition, to suggest that certain ideas are unthinkable for decent people.

A foreclosing of certain political positions for an entire generation is the aim of the Report and its supporters. Children are to be predisposed to disaffection and the support of radical ideologies. What has this to do with education in a free society?

Swann takes care to strengthen its hand by presenting nothing but the unpalatable alternatives. Thus we are offered 'assimilation' with its total elimination of minority identity; 'separate development' with its South African echoes; and pluralism (pages 4–5). John Rex, one of the latter's leading exponents, has gone as far as to claim that 'to promote equality of opportunity without allowing for cultural pluralism is to move towards a policy of forced assimilation' (page 239).

There is a spirit of manipulation at the heart of Swann's philosophy. There is a blackguarding of opposition and a dangerous impatience with freedom. The unfettered expression of opinion is undoubtedly one of the 'structures' that require reform. It is an inconvenience, a barrier to the new order.

The success of pluralism in the education system requires the fullest 'permeation' of its personnel. In-service courses and, most importantly, initial training are to be soaked in 'multi-culturalism'. All student teachers must be given an 'informed awareness' which consists of a slanted history of immigration to Britain, 'the theory and practice of racism' and how it might be challenged and such like (page 560).

Swann's view that students who dislike minority pupils and who cannot be educated out of such views will make unsuitable teachers is a valid one. But Swann goes on to demonstrate that its definition of prejudice embraces not only character but political opinion: 'if a teacher has negative attitudes towards ethnic minorities *and the development of a culturally plural society* then he or she will in our view remain an inadequate teacher of *any* child in *any* school in this country' (page 568).

Disagreement with the Swann Report is to be placed on a par with crime and sexual perversion as a disqualification for teaching (indeed it would probably be considered very much worse). Dissent is to be equated with professional unworthiness.

The normal meaning of pluralism is turned on its head by Swann. Whatever it now means, it does not extend to free speech on race relations. The charitable explanation is that a majority of the committee did not understand what it was doing. But some of them did. The 'totalitarian temptation' was proffered and accepted.

Conclusions

This chapter has attempted to examine the central proposals of the Swann Report and their moral base. In some respects it is the latter which is the more disturbing. It throbs with all the ugly passions and inhumane ideals of the twentieth century.

Swann's proposals are, in themselves, contemptuous of the rights of the native inhabitants of the UK and threaten all by their promise of social disintegration. The spirit that has inspired or latched onto them, however, promises nothing but a closing of society and ever-growing opportunities for the intolerant, the arrogant and the malign.

Swann speaks for, and has encouraged, a powerful body of opinion in both politics and education. The government's criticism of some of its views has not prevented it from allowing multi-culturalism to develop. In any event, our decentralised system means that central government cannot fight the battle alone. Swann's semi-official imprint will mean that its views are given increased weight, and opposition to multi-culturalism and anti-racism, already growing difficult, will grow more hesitant. It can be emboldened if their implications and inspirations are made more widely known. At present, Swann's policies parade under the banner of justice and toleration. They must be made to march under their true colours.

Note

1. Quoted in *Ethnic Minorities and Education* (Harper and Row, London, 1984).

12

Moral Understanding and the Ethics of Indignation

Frank Palmer

Underlying the claim that education should serve the cause of 'anti-racism' is a moral injunction. If an example is needed, consider, for instance, the ethical vocabulary deployed in a recent book by Jon Nixon, entitled *A Teacher's Guide to Multicultural Education*, in which it is made clear that educationists who do not share Mr Nixon's sense of urgency for institutional reform need, according to him, to be 'shaken out of' their 'mental laziness' and their 'torpor'.[1] Mr Nixon's adversaries—rendered thus by their inactivity—are, clearly enough, not accused of being merely mistaken. He is not alone in exerting this moral pressure, nor in dismissing as 'armchair theorists'[2] those whose willingness to campaign is subordinate to their concern for conceptual clarity. In comparison with some of the more strident and even violent demands, Nixon's moral *obbligato* is relatively serene.

Clearly, then, there is a need to consider 'anti-racism' *as* a moral argument. The first obstacle that lies in our path here is a politicised conception of 'racism' which defines the sin into existence by locating it not in individual attitudes nor in the free and conscious interplay between one individual and another, but in societal 'structures' and institutional 'arrangements' of which individuals are merely products. This view of human beings as will-less, and surely therefore amoral, representations of an environment has grown to the status of a ubiquitous dogma. Frances Morrell, Leader of the Inner London Education Authority, claims that she is not concerned with 'remedying deficiencies in *children*' but, instead, with improving 'institutional arrangements'.[3] The almost unrecognisable concept of personhood implied by this view helps to weaken critical resistance to the preposterous suggestion that *all* white people and *only* white people are, and cannot *but* be, racists. The 'endemic racism' of Britain is established not by empirical observation but by a form of conceptual chicanery, which defines 'racism' in such a way that all possible counterexamples are precluded *ab initio*. The argument not only 'proves' the conclusion that all whites are racist by assuming it as a premise but also 'proves' in advance that no non-whites can ever be racist. This is in effect the form of 'argument' used by twelve signatories on behalf of the Sheffield Anti-Racist Group NATFHE in a letter to *The Times Educational Supplement* on 24 May 1985: 'The statement that "racism works both ways" and that "racism is one form of prejudice" ignores the power dynamic inherent in racism ... Black people do not have that power—they are not therefore racist.' (It is a strange sort of 'power' white people have if they *cannot help* being racists.) This simulacrum of logical reasoning is so well entrenched that it is almost without surprise that one hears the activist leader of a Labour-controlled council declaring to the cameras in the aftermath of the Tottenham riot, which took place on 6 October 1985, that no attack upon a white police officer could ever be construed as a racist attack, since 'racism' *means* white against black. Given this conception of 'racism', the moral argument is at an end: for there is no logical space for it even to begin. 'Racism' could only be an object of moral evaluation if considered as a *failing*. Since we cannot choose our parents or our place and time of birth, it is certainly not clear how we could be *blamed* for the results of such contingency. And it is not clear how educators brought up in 'white society', imprisoned in what Chris Mullard has called 'white reality', could be blamed for their reluctance to engage in campaigns for reform; for such reluctance would *ex hypothesi* result from an accident of birth.

If, on the other hand, we are not mere slaves to our social circumstances but have some part to play in the formation of our own attitudes—a position which is at least robust enough to re-admit the concept of a person—the moral claim for education to 'combat' racism would have to be transposed into a claim about the development of *individuals*, who are not therefore mere members of cultures or ethnic groups, products of institutions or indeed 'products' *tout court*. There are those who reject the views of political extremists, yet feel that education should do something about 'racism', not as a political problem but as a defect in human nature. In order to let the argument proceed on *this* basis, let us be generous enough to make out the strongest possible case for anti-racism. First, let us assume that 'racism' is now taken to denote racial prejudice, racial discrimination and racial intimidation, conceived as failings in individual people. Second, let us assume that 'racism' in this sense is even more widespread than some of us are prepared to concede. Granted that there are racists and that racists are sinners, what follows? The impulsive answer would be to draw the conclusion that we should plunge headlong into an anti-racist curriculum and that the ripples should encircle every aspect of school life (the usual metaphors are 'permeate' and 'pervade'). The haste to draw this conclusion, however, is directly related to serious misconceptions about the nature of morality, of education and of human life. My remaining task is to show how these misconceptions are related.

Anti-Racism as a Moral Position

Drained of its 'structural' predilections, the moral argument against 'racism' is no *argument* at all. Unlike fox-hunting, smoking and meat-eating, which admit of a *prima facie* defence, 'racism' (like 'murder') denotes something which is wrong by definition; the pejorative force of the word is built in. 'Bullying', cowardice', 'cheating' and 'lying' are also pejorative terms. But the difference is that these words do not prevent the possibility of moral argument, a precondition of which is that a person's intentions are a relevant consideration in determining what he can be said to have *done*. (The 'liar' who was simply mistaken and had no intention to deceive was not lying after all.) In contrast, the new orthodoxy of anti-racism does not permit moral argument. The office-worker who forgets to invite a black colleague to the office Christmas lunch[4] or the nursery assistant who sings *Ba Ba Black Sheep*[5] may no more intend disrespect to black people than the actor who recites '... the native hue of resolution is sicklied o'er with the pale cast of thought' intends to cast aspersions on white people. But this does not defeat the charge of 'racism'. Where it is not intentional, we are told, it must be unconscious or unintentional (an axiom of, sometimes compulsory, racism-awareness courses).

This is a desperate move. The more unconvincing the example, the more we are persuaded 'we know not what we do'. Now, to begin with, 'unconsciously' does not mean 'unintentionally'. I may not be conscious of changing gear whilst driving, but that does not make my operations with the gear-lever unintentional (they do not happen by accident). These operations are knowingly, though not necessarily consciously, performed.[6] It is possible to make some sense of 'unconsciously racist acts'—taken to mean 'intentionally racist acts of which we are not consciously aware'—but that does not mean the concept can be legitimately invoked to settle, or prevent, disputes about allegedly racist acts or practices. For that would be to posit 'unconscious racism' in order to preserve the concealed assumption that where racial offence is *taken*, it is necessarily rational and justified (which begs the very question at issue): it cannot be assumed *a priori* that the anti-racist is always correct in his *perception* of racism.

Recourse to '*un*intentional racism' does not settle the matter either; for it relies upon the same concealed assumption that the anti-racist accuser is to be invested with judgemental omnipotence. Apart from other difficulties with the idea of racism being 'unintentional' (would we ever speak of unintentional cowardice, unintentional generosity or unintentional murder?), whatever grounds there are for doubting that a given act or a given practice is an instance of *racism* are equally grounds for doubting the judgement that the act or practice is *unintentionally racist*. Against this, it is often argued that 'negative uses' of the word 'black' (as in 'black magic') express 'negative beliefs' about black people, irrespective of the intentions of the speakers: a view which suggests it is language which is racist (as though *language* could have beliefs and intentions). It is at least a necessary condition for the expression of belief, that such 'negative beliefs' could only be 'expressed' by people who *believe* that black people are evil, deadly, dangerous and so on. Yet the 'negative uses' are cited to prove the existence of the beliefs. The argument is circular and assumes the very thing it seeks to prove. Moreover, the presence of such beliefs would not in any case be a *sufficient* condition of the claim that 'negative uses' of 'black' express 'negative beliefs' about black people. If it is true that I hate Chinamen, it by no means follows that my scorn for cowardice, expressed in the term 'yellow-bellied', is an expression of my dislike of Chinamen. (Nor does it follow that I believe Chinamen are *cowards*). If it is to be argued that such 'negative beliefs' must be lodged in that *deus ex machina* known as '*the* unconscious' then there are two replies. First, why should it be assumed that anti-racists have privileged access to the contents of our unconscious? Second, even if they were right about that, why should it be assumed that it would be a sensible policy to bring such beliefs to consciousness? Some thoughts, beliefs and desires are best left repressed.

Used within anti-racist discourse, to prohibit in advance any attempt to question the proscription of *allegedly* racist acts or practices, the term 'racist' is little more than a boo-word—as empty of content as 'wretch' or 'infidel'. But even if it were not used as a question-stopper, the fact that it is pejorative (in the ordinary sense) raises an immediate question about the status of '*anti*-racism'—which suggests not only that there is a conceivable alternative called 'pro-racism' but that it is the only alternative. It implicitly denies there can be a distinction between anti-racism and non-racism. Either we are anti-racists or we are racists. But why? The anti-racist answer would be that it is only possible to be a non-racist if one is actively opposed to racism. But if active opposition is a criterion of moral worth, why do we not equally insist that the only way of not being a cheat is to be an anti-cheat, and that the only way of not being a liar is to be an anti-liar? Why does our moral vocabulary not insist upon 'anti-cowards', 'anti-gossipers' and 'anti-bullies'? There are two connected reasons. The first is that the world is not neatly divided into the matter of evil and the anti-matter of good. The second is that the kind of life a person leads is its own testimony to the values he holds. And it would be nothing less than dogmatism to insist that such values must be expressed negatively. Not only is it a trivial truth to say that the kind or generous person is *ipso facto* opposed to behaving otherwise, but to express it in this way may be to disfigure what is of importance and value about the way such a person lives and sees his life. It is possible to be kind without campaigning against unkindness and without the self-conscious avoidance of being *un*kind. True kindness is not laboured or derived from a formula; nor is it enkindled by sparks of contempt for an opposed attitude. Why, then, should it not be thought that the true non-racist is more profitably considered as a person for whom the racial difference between himself and another person is not of overriding importance, or for whom this issue might not even arise. When I engage in friendly conversation with my next-door neighbour, must I keep reminding myself that he is an Asian, a Jew or a Welshman? If the answer is yes, and that is precisely what the concept of race-awareness suggests, then we must conclude that anti-racism forbids natural relationships.

The upshot of this discussion is that any moral claim upon our attitudes should have to do with *non*-racism. 'We ought not to be racists' is by no means equivalent to 'we ought to be anti-racists'. In fact the latter is grotesque, for it suggests that our duty consists in making an issue of race and, still worse, an issue of the racism of others (who are not as enlightened as we). It is a prescription for obsession and fanaticism. And, with respect to the *Times Educational Supplement*, which on other occasions has taken a more sensible view, such obsession is practically advocated by a writer of the *TES* 'Comment' for 25 October 1985, which concludes: 'All teachers need to be on their guard against their automatic prejudices: *white* teachers of *black* pupils must be alert to the danger *every minute of the day*' (emphasis mine). Any teacher following this advice is committed to a view of black pupils that is so guarded it might justifiably be called 'racist'.

A second level of difficulty with anti-racism as a moral position is that the word 'racism' purports to pick out or denote a specialist brand of vice in the same way that 'gluttony', 'pride' and 'lust' are thought to pick out chart-busting sins. It has, if you like, become the eighth deadly sin (though clearly not in eighth position). This is misleading, because particular instances of (genuine) racism, whether of prejudice, persecution or intimidation, are instances of more general failings which are not themselves exclusively concerned with the matter of race: irrationality, greed, intolerance, fear, aggression, insensitivity and so on. I can find no more clarity in the idea of 'the racist mentality' than I can in the notion of 'the criminal mentality' (or, for that matter, in 'the concert-pianist mentality'). It would be no more enlightening either at the level of psychology or at the level of moral evaluation to be told that all racists have racism in common than it would to be told that all criminals have criminality in common. (Would we for one moment suppose that someone who is irrational enough to judge another person's character by the shape of his nose is displaying a form of prejudice which is *sui generis* and can be labelled as 'noseism'?) We are right to be horrified at the prospect of someone being physically assaulted or abused because of his/her colour or racial origin. But we have no right to be *less* horrified if someone is assaulted or abused because he/she is left-handed, academically minded, opera-loving, rival-football-team-supporting or of a nervous disposition. If racial victimisation is wrong, it is wrong because no-one should be victimised. If racial prejudice is irrational, it is irrational because it is *prejudice* and, as such, is neither more nor less irrational than many other forms of prejudice.

The traditional basis of moral training—often misleadingly called 'socialisation' (as though it were a *process*)—assumes a much wider network of concerns housed within the generic term 'respect for persons'. The child who ridicules the disfigured or the handicapped, the child who refuses to share, is corrected not by having his misdeeds brought under artificially narrow concepts such as 'disfigurism', 'handicapism' or 'non-sharingism', but by learning to feel shame and remorse and by having his behaviour brought under increasingly wider concepts: rudeness, selfishness, insensitivity, unfairness and so on—a family of moral concepts which give substance to the general principle of respect for others. To single out 'racism' as a sin unrelated to all others and bearing special pre-eminence narrows rather than widens the moral understanding. Bradford council's instruction[7] that all children involved in 'racist incidents' (verbal or otherwise) must be reported to the Town Hall is an example of such moral narrowness. To make a song and a dance about racial bullying and name-calling and not to lay equal stress upon other kinds of intimidation is a defect in moral integrity. It is tantamount to claiming that there is nothing wrong with intimidation *per se*.

A third level of difficulty is that anti-racism, *qua* moral position, is aggressive. As the tell-tale prefix and the inevitable cadence of 'ism' reminds us, it belongs to a growing community of other fashionable 'antisms': anti-sexism, anti-ageism, anti-classism, anti-genderism and, latterly, anti-heterosexism, anti-adultism and anti-able-bodiedism.[8] This community is one of clamour and protest against which lesser mortals are to be judged, either for committing the new sins such 'isms' define into existence or for failing to join in the war against those who commit them; as a recent GLC poster puts it: 'If you are not part of the solution, you are part of the problem.' This suggests there are such things as moral experts who have provided their own conception of virtue and vice according to which the rest of us, not merely ought to lead, but must be *compelled* to lead our lives. One might suspect here the recrudescence of the self-righteousness that fired the Puritan ethic. Certainly there is nothing new about it. And it was against this conception of moral rectitude that Bertrand Russell inveighed in his essay 'Nice People': 'Those whom the nice people condemn are fair game; at their call of "Tally Ho!" the hunt assembles and the victim is pursued.' What *is* new about it, however, is that with the assistance of radical sociology the Puritan ethic is now suffused with the ability to create new sins by means of the powerful sorcery of language and thus keep itself in business.

The really important issue lies deeper still, and has to do with the conception of 'morality' implied by this moral position. Beneath the 'antisms' lies the unexamined assumption that moral concerns are a type of crusade. Along with its sibling neologisms, anti-racism begins from a position of weakness. It posits the *summum malum* and represents 'morality' as the fight against it. Morality is reduced to a species of 'action' and the moral agent to a busy 'actor' who puts acquired policies into practice. There is no room for informed passivity or critical reflection and no room for the notion of a self, except as the noble self which opposes external evil, a self which cannot be extricated from the mass movement that carries it into battle. With the loss of the individual is a divorce between thought and action, and therefore loss of concern for truth. The ethic of indignation upstages all other values which stand in its way and, incoherently, makes truth subordinate to 'justice'. Its indifference to wider concerns turns it into a form of sentimentality which never has the world as its object.

There is a 'tradition' of moral philosophy which runs from Plato through Spinoza, Kierkegaard and Wittgenstein to Simone Weil which begins from precisely the opposite position, and one that has to do with love: love of the beauty of the world. This love has nothing to do with sentimentality; for sentimental emotions are hostile to the truth which threatens their continuance. Nor should it be confused with romantic love. Love, here, means patient attention to the truth about things, which is intimately connected with attention to beauty—not in the sense of 'prettiness' but in the sense of order. Such an attitude is an attempt to see oneself in relation to the world and feel at home in it, to see the world as an object of reverence. Recognition of oneself as a finite creature lodged between birth and death cannot be separated from recognition of a world that transcends the self in space and time. This is what I understand Wittgenstein (and Spinoza before him) to mean in saying that the good life is the world seen *sub specie aeternitatis*.

The life according to the flesh—to be contrasted with what Wittgenstein called the life of knowledge—is one which disposes us to view all things in the world as nothing more than a means to our satisfaction, or as 'amenities' (cf. 'the ordinary way of looking at things sees objects so to speak from within their midst...'[9]). Seen in this way, the world is nothing more than a vehicle to the pleasure or displeasure of the self. The man who is malicious, greedy, dishonest, power-worshipping or opportunist is one who thereby rejects any kind of acceptance of a world which might transcend his own importance or be indifferent to his whims and fancies. He is not happy with the world *whatever it might be*, but only happy with himself, hence not happy in the ethical sense. There is a connection between Wittgenstein's remarks and Plato's discussion of the impersonal part of the soul. It is from this perspective that we can renounce the self-interest that makes us see others as mere instruments to our satisfaction (the world-view of an Archelaus).

An important consequence of this argument is that although the good life is one of knowledge, it is knowledge which is non-propositional. That is, it cannot be expressed as a series of propositions to be passed on and obeyed or in a set of maxims to be followed. Early moral training is, by definition, something which is *imposed*, and without which no further moral development would be possible. But at the highest levels of moral understanding, virtue in this sense cannot be taught. It must be grasped by each man 'in the silence of the heart' (as Kierkegaard would say). Stuart Hampshire's 'to copy a right action is to act rightly' is therefore inadequate: a right action is one which has not been copied. The good life is not one in which particular virtues are merely exercised or put into practice. It is not the possession of virtues which make a man good but the part they play in his life as a whole. It might be thought, for example, that we approve of King Lear's servant, Kent, because he is sincere and loyal. But the real grounds for admiration are rooted in the way these qualities dovetail with his other qualities: his courage, his sense of justice and his capacity for caring about the man he serves, come what may. In other words, we have to consider what part sincerity and loyalty play in his *life*. It is possible to admire a man's sincerity and loyalty without admiring *him*. Had Ben Jonson given Volpone's servant, Mosca, the qualities of sincerity and loyalty he would not have thereby created a character deserving our admiration. Indeed, such qualities may have even increased his complicity in the sordid enterprise he and Volpone embark on; certainly they would not have *de*creased it. Even a Nazi could be sincere and loyal.

This view of ethics is one which draws attention to the intimate connection between a man and his acts. It can be clarified by considering a view of ethics diametrically opposed to it: utilitarianism. According to the utilitarians, 'morality' is a kind of policy or instrument and the moral agent is a centre of practical reason for whom 'morality' is a means to a further end and for whom 'altruism' stands in need of an 'external' (empirically describable) pay-off. Given this world-view, 'good' means expediency and 'harm' means frustration (and such a thought lies at the heart of the empiricist ethic of consequentialism, of which political activism—and anti-racism—is a species). Wittgenstein's remarks on ethics belong to a tradition of thought which challenges this relation between a man and his acts. Utilitarianism can never fully allow us to *belong* to what we do, and restricts the role of morality to a kind of veneer or damp-proof course. In locating goodness and badness solely in the effects or consequences of our actions it implies a severance between the doer and the deed.

When Macbeth consented to kill Duncan he thereby consented not merely to perform a deed but to become the kind of person who was prepared to do such a thing. At that moment he chose to become a butcher. And the blood that flows through the rest of the play is, in a sense, the blood of Duncan. The subsequent murders are a symbolic illustration of what he has *already* become in freely consenting to kill Duncan. A utilitarian/consequentialist reading of the play would insist that Duncan is the one who is harmed and the harm that befalls Macbeth is purely contingent (he might have got away with it). A closer identification between the doer and the deed (and surely the one portrayed by Shakespeare) would suggest that Duncan is not harmed in the sense that Macbeth is harmed:

Duncan is in his grave;
After life's fitful fever he sleeps well;

> Treason has done his worst; nor steel, nor poison,
> Malice domestic, foreign levy, nothing,
> Can touch him further.

Macbeth's harm is not contingent on how things turn out. He is not harmed 'by one of woman born'. His harm lies not in the *results* of killing Duncan, but *in* his free consent to commit the act of murder. His loss is the loss of his soul (his 'eternal jewel') which makes him unable to respond to the souls of others. The harm resides in his immersion in a perspective that *necessarily* prevents him from seeing anything that has permanent significance. This is the world not seen *sub specie aeternitatis* but seen from within the meaningless flux of physical events—

> A tale
> Told by an idiot, full of sound and fury,
> Signifying nothing.

—a world in which there is no reason why the 'firstlings' of his heart should not become the 'firstlings' of his hand.

A prerequisite for moral understanding may consist in the kind of early training that insists upon unquestioning obedience. But subsequent higher forms of moral understanding can only be intelligibly predicated of individuals who, though they share a common humanity, do not merge mindlessly with a social tide like Aldous Huxley's 'drops within the social river' but possess the 'inwardness' which we describe as the soul. The soul is not a puff of gas; neither is it a spiritual substance, as it was for Descartes. Talk about the soul is not talk about an *entity*; rather, it is an attempt to distinguish our attitude to people from our attitude to objects. Unlike objects, we are responsible for our actions. And, unlike our responses to objects, our responses to other people presuppose that they are something more than carcasses of flesh and blood or causally determined products of a social environment. We see people as free autonomous agents with intentions, beliefs, desires and feelings; and this perception is not an appendage to human existence, but is written into our very conception of human life.[10] Recognition of oneself as a finite creature lodged between birth and death enables one to consider the sense of one's life as a *whole*; and this cannot be separated from the attempt to understand the relation of a single life to the lives of others. Moral understanding does not consist in the acceptance of slogans and maxims; it aims at nothing less than an understanding of the world: a task which has no terminus and ultimately no utilitarian purpose, because it is a task of selfless attention to that which is not oneself. In short, we perceive the wrongness of 'racism' not because we have been drilled with 'anti-racism' but because we have been awakened to much larger concerns.

Anti-Racist Education

Since education is education of *persons* this needs to be reflected in the way that education is conceived: as a personal transaction, rather than a 'system' or depersonalised set of processes to produce a narrowly circumscribed set of consequences. It is better to suppose that education has no purpose than to claim that its purpose consists in, say, the training of soldiers for warfare, the replication of CND supporters, the production of disembodied 'skills', the reproduction of anti-racists or the ideological procreation of citizens who display the 'right' political beliefs and fixed repertoire of social attitudes. To suppose otherwise is to collapse the distinction between persons and 'things'. Different social customs come and go, but Kant was surely right to emphasise that respect for persons as ends in themselves is paramount and universal as a *moral* principle. It would militate against such a principle if education were not conceived as an end in itself. To regard education essentially as a *means* to the production of a certain type of society or particular kind of citizen is tantamount to regarding *people* as a means towards some further goal. The price of freedom is uncertainty; not the uncertainty of the ditherer but the absence of unreasonable certitude. There is no guarantee that the educated man will be a good man, for the simple reason that the good life is not imposed from without but created from within.

In his *Réflexions sur la question Juive*, Sartre argues that the anti-semite is not a man who holds an *opinion* about Jews (a word which implies that all judgements are of equal value) but is a consenting victim to a passion that must affect the way we are to describe his world-view and his personality as a whole. According to Sartre, the anti-semite has found premature certainty where the rational man 'seeks the truth gropingly'. Sartre is renowned for exaggerating the nature and extent of human freedom and the way that 'choice' necessarily predominates in human affairs. But, given that *caveat*, it is unreasonable not to concede that we have *some* responsibility for our attitudes. If anti-semitism is a passion freely 'chosen' it follows that it can only be freely renounced. And freely renounced by the man who learns to appreciate the beauty, wonder and mystery of a world that dwarfs his own concerns, 'thwarts his own self-love' (to misappropriate Kant) and often calls his judgements into question.

This is, in essence, the 'purpose' of a traditional academic education, which from its inception in ancient Greece was never narrowly concerned with purely local problems or the exigencies of the moment. A true academic education and an ethos of firm discipline (both now being eroded) does everything possible to foster the development of 'the person' into a decent rational being who, *ceteris paribus*, will neither be 'racist' nor hopelessly vulnerable to the other snares of moral turpitude and excesses of irrationality that await the untutored. Having spent a large proportion of my life teaching in comprehensive schools I am aware, however, that this view is not widely shared. In fact there are those who would treat it with derision. It is necessary to examine some of the assumptions that inspire disagreement with my own view.

The anti-racist thesis not only begins from the assumption that education must have an aim beyond itself ('education *for* . . .') but further assumes that it must be instrumental to the production of certain attitudes of which it approves and to the elimination of attitudes it condemns. An early article by Robert Jeffcoate (I do not say he still holds this view) claims: 'We want . . . [the pupils] . . . to have developed certain *identifiable attitudes* and *behaviours* [*sic*] by the time they leave school'[11] (emphasis mine). If we allow behaviourism its voice (a philosophy which clings to the shirt-tails of positivism and consequentialism) we will have no qualms in agreeing with Jeffcoate that 'the function of formal education is to bring about desired changes in children'.[12] We will then be brought one step nearer to the 'Community, Identity, Stability' of Aldous Huxley's *Brave New World*. Education is not the attempt to produce 'attitudes' or pieces of 'behaviour'; it is the attempt to offer to an individual that which will develop his or her individuality; a chance to develop the capacities, the knowledge, the love that raises human life above the level of mere existence; a chance to become someone who is in a better position to make his or her *own* evaluations. It is in other words (and the words are those of Michael Oakeshott) an invitation to share in a 'transaction between the generations'. If we value it highly enough we will not see it in a vacuum but will instead attribute to it the nature of a sacrament. It is the medium through which the generations of the dead can speak to the living, and through which we enact our duty to the yet unborn. If, on the other hand, we fail to value it in this spirit we will not object to its decline into a form of social engineering.

In order to 'make sure' and 'not leave to chance' that pupils emerge brandishing the 'right' beliefs and 'behaviours' (the very word denies the unity of the self which expresses itself *in* action) anti-racist attitudes are concentrated into a focal point from which the whole curriculum and all aspects of school life are to be seen. The idea of a subject or an academic discipline is first disinherited (by a form of nihilism known as 'the sociology of knowledge', which reduces knowledge to socially shared fiction) and then recruited in the service of 'the cause'. If this is not a *prima facie* case of indoctrination, and if education has the narrow purpose (both morally and intellectually) this world-view assumes, there is nothing to stop us from rivalling this demand by inventing a new 'antism'. Why not an anti-handist, anti-hairist, anti-dressist—or even an anti-wardenist—curriculum? Since it has recently been argued that education should combat the rampant 'heterosexism' of the school curriculum—because it does not actively and explicitly challenge prejudice against homosexuals—it should not surprise us if already existing courses of anti-racist mathematics are soon augmented by anti-heterosexist arithmetic.

Education, thus conceived, is not something which is *offered* but is instead a species of causality which brings about pre-specified empirical effects; it becomes a matter of *doing* things to people. It cannot abide the risk involved in the idea of people shaping their own destiny, having the ultimate freedom to reject its 'enlightenment' and eventually choosing the path of sin. Deprived of such freedom, there is equally therefore no freedom to choose the path of virtue. Even taken on its own terms, anti-racism is its own worst enemy, for it lacks a clear concept of what 'racism' is. Racial prejudice and racial victimisation involve failures in the human heart; they stem from unkindness in the human spirit. In other words, they are not reducible to the level of a simple intellectual mistake which can be corrected by constant exposure to the 'true facts about race' (whatever *they* might be); for the failures here thrive upon a willingness or a determination to disregard such 'facts'. Unlike racial *preconceptions*, racial prejudice is hostile to that which challenges it, and is hardly likely to be sustained by any form of reasoning that can be called sensitivity to evidence. This does not mean that 'racism' is simply a torrent of hostility which has *no* purchase upon an individual's capacity for reasoning or logical thought. Brentano's insights into the 'intentionality' of mental life (that our thoughts and emotions are *about* things) are enough to rob us of the illusion that attitudes and emotions are blind forces randomly erupting in a vacuum; we could make no sense of human life if that were so.

However, the anti-racists' concentration upon the cognitive elements of 'racism' is, paradoxically, one which ignores the kind of relations which do exist in the life of the mind. The idea that 'racist beliefs' can be expunged from the mind via exposure of pupils to 'the true facts' and exposure of teachers to 'racism-awareness' belongs to a view of education as a type of mental dentistry. Beliefs are not like teeth which can be extracted and the cavity filled with a new epistemic denture. In so far as 'racism is connected with our powers of cognition, it can be counterveiled at that level only by facilitating *general* powers of rationality by means of a good education that is far more committed to traditional academic values than is often now considered 'appropriate' or 'relevant'.

In so far as 'racism' is related to a deficiency in human kindness, hence a moral failing, the remaining question is: what can education do about that? I have already tried to show that it is misconceived to single out 'racism' as an ethical 'target'; so what this question now amounts to is: how, if at all, can education help to facilitate moral development? If this is taken to mean: how can education ensure moral development? the answer is that it does not and cannot 'ensure' *anything*. Provided that teachers have done everything they possibly can (and that includes being firm with disruptive pupils), the ultimate responsibility for a pupil's moral and intellectual development must lie with that individual pupil—if he or she is to be regarded as a person rather than as a product, or object of policy. If, however, the question is taken to mean: what does education have to *offer* at the level of moral development? my answer may come as a surprise to those who conceive of moral education as a form of moral instruction or social-skills module tagged onto the curriculum—or, indeed, as any kind of 'extra'.

I shall approach this answer by rejecting the assumption that traditional education has no purchase upon the development of 'the person'. That this assumption is a popular one is evidenced in recent attempts to swell the curriculum with new 'subjects' like *Life* Skills, *Life* Studies and other 'subjects' redolent with social utility: Peace Studies, World Studies and—the latest to reach me—Consumer Studies (shopping 'skills'). Even worse, it is evidenced in diabolical attempts to politicise traditional subjects, making even English 'an *essential weapon* in the *armoury* of the working-class' (emphasis mine).[13] Chris Searle's view of education—which can be sniffed through these words—would be better termed recruitment. It is no longer enough that language is the indispensible medium through which we are enabled to experience and to express understanding of the world; it is a useful addition to the accoutrements of war against the 'system'. Mr Searle's discontent does not confine itself to expression in journals advocating 'global transformation'. It is trumpeted to schoolchildren through Young World Books, sponsored by an organisation called Liberation, and is available for topping up library shelves with anti-racist fiction that reveals its dour and provocative message. In circulation from the same source is an anthology of children's verse, edited by Mr Searle, entitled *Our City* which results from a collaboration between Young World Books and teachers from no less than twenty-one London schools. Despite the presence of the occasional good poem, many are mediocre renditions of the moribund sentiments anti-racism likes to encourage, and one or two are execrable even by the standards of graffiti. Moreover, it is not without irony that the reference on the fly-leaf to 'London, 1984 (Year of Anti-Racism)' should be complemented later with, on page 77:

> The English are the First Class Race
> They lead the world in hatred.
>
> (13-year-old pupil)

Might it just be that anti-racism leads *children* into hatred?

Though it can never be its purpose (for, as Leavis said, literature can only afford sociological insight if it is studied *as* literature and not as sociology), the study of *good* literary works affords rich opportunities for understanding human life and the human condition, not least on the moral plane. Because it contains characters, a novel or a play engages our capacities for moral understanding. Literature helps, or can help, to foster the moral insights, the imagination and emotional sensitivity that enters into our understanding of other persons. Morality is not simply a 'social matter', for our engagement with others is necessarily affected by what we, as individuals, bring to such engagement. The enrichment offered by an academic education is one which, if offered and received in the right spirit, enriches our relations with others.

The voice that decries 'mere' academic values is a voice whose power to convince succeeds only at the cost of a crude reductionism that sees no more in mathematics than a mere juggling with symbols and sees no more in novels and poems than scratches on paper. It reduces the idea of study to that of an immobile figure seated at a table, staring at ciphers; and then asks of this skeleton it has created, this matchstick man, what it is doing to help the world: the world of 'social reality' in which the individual is an abstraction against the datum of the collective. If this is one's conception of study it follows that study has no value at all. And the attempt to *give* it value by making it 'relevant' is as self-defeating as trying to build a house where there is no ground to place it upon.

Traditional education is often disparagingly referred to as the mere pursuit of knowledge, as though all this means is the acquisition of facts. But the reduction of 'knowledge' to 'facts' is positively Gradgrindian. Study, conceived in the right spirit, is not just a matter of facts-gathering nor (its vulgar antithesis) skills-gathering. In all its forms, it is essentially the pursuit of truth. It calls upon a willingness to confront, and where necessary abandon, comfortable presuppositions and preconceptions and learn to love the truth, *whatever it might be* and *wherever it may lead*. This is why such love is unconditional and why it demands courage. Reality is no respecter of wishes and wants.

It would be easy to mistake these remarks about the value of study for a claim that *what* is studied has no value in itself but is merely instrumental to the progress of the soul (a progress which Simone Weil reminds us is not to be confused with measurable performance). But nothing could be further from the truth. An individual subject can never be the proper object of selfless attention or 'patient suffering' (or what Russell called 'glorious torment') unless what is focused by the mind is valued for its own sake. There is as much beauty in mathematics as there is in music or literature, though perhaps of a different kind. Nevertheless, in each case the willingness to engage is one which is written into any genuine attempt to understand the world; and that engagement has to do with love.

This is why education is a *leading out*. Far from being primarily concerned with the premature escalation of 'self-confidence' or promotion of 'positive self-images' that fashionable theorists would like to see, it urges caution, patience and striving, where there would otherwise be rush and meaningless bustle. Pupils do not enter classrooms with blank minds to be filled, but with all kinds of preconceptions: about their own wonderful ability or lack of it, about the nature of subjects they have barely begun to study and about the world in general. A significant part of education consists in challenging preconceptions and prejudices—though not always, and not necessarily, directly or head-on. We do not need a checklist of all possible preconceptions (which, in any case, would have to be infinite). Rather, education consists in offering pupils the wherewithal to challenge their *own*. This 'wherewithal' is not simply a matter of skill or *savoir-faire*; it calls upon the deepest capacities in the human character: a willingness not to seek refuge in palatable falsehoods; a willingness to admit (admit to *ourselves*) that we are sometimes mistaken.

Anti-racism seeks, we are so often told, to 'tear out racism by the roots' but has no plausible conception of what and where these 'roots' may be. Though it can never be its 'purpose', traditional academic education, if restored to a place of importance in contemporary society, would do more to challenge the real 'roots' of 'racism' than the anti-racists' myopic doxology could even begin to do. The study of history, mathematics, science, music, literature and art cannot be indifferent to a concern for truth, which may at times require moral courage. The historian, scientist, composer, dramatist, poet or art critic who lacks integrity is not only deficient as a practitioner but is deficient in his attitude to his fellow-men. For these pursuits do not exist in a vacuum; they are important elements in social life which have their roots in the traditions and cultural heritage of the past. The pursuit of truth in this sense cannot be disassociated from appreciation of beauty, and a sense of wonder. It involves reverence for past civilisations, respect for great achievements, celebration of individuals who, against all odds, created something of worth and lasting value or who, in their own person, provided a vision of the world that raises it above a pointless concourse of mere events. Such a view of human existence must affect one's very conception of human life, and therefore of moral values. The child who is brought, however minimally, to cherish the sublime achievements of the human spirit, or at least have some glimmering of what it means to see the world in this way, has far more done for his moral development than the child who is on the receiving-end of disenchanted policies that decry 'mere' academic values and become narrowly preoccupied with the latest social 'issue'. The values thus decried are ones which provide access to a much wider respect for humanity that transcends the narrow divisions of race, class or nation and the fleeting concerns of here and now.

Anti-racism accentuates these divisions and makes a meal of them. It is hostile to the spirit of true education, and, in its wish to proselytise, redefines it as 'ethnocentric', 'monocultural' and 'racist'. Inconsistent with the pluralism it advocates, it imposes its single-minded and repetitive slogans on teachers and pupils alike and denounces those who dare to question it. It *uses* subject areas to promote its message. It censures, prohibits, compels. Like any good consequentialist theory, it sanctions the doing of evil (violence, revolt, or mendacious distortions of history[14]) that good may come. What 'good'? Even in the hands of the moderate, anti-racist education is fundamentally misconceived. In the hands of the enthusiast, it shares the moral failings it professes to condemn.

I am grateful to Roger Scruton, Jessica Gwynne, Ray Honeyford and David Dale for their comments on earlier drafts of this chapter.

Notes

1. *A Teacher's Guide to Multicultural Education* (Blackwell, Oxford, 1985), p.164.
2. 'What is offered is not abstract definition for armchair theorists but a programme of action...' *ibid.*, p.1. Mr Nixon's 'programme', however, is hardly free from 'theory'; it rests upon an arcane ideology.

3. *Race, Sex and Class 1* (Inner London Education Authority, 1983), p.5.
4. It was reported in *The Times* (11th May 1985) that a woman employed in the housing department of the London Borough of Islington was found guilty of 'racial harassment' for this very 'offence'. The finding by the council carried a reprimand, and she was instructed to attend one of the council's racism-awareness courses.
5. As part of their 'racial-awareness' training programme for those who deal with the under 5s, the company *Building Blocks* has produced a worksheet entitled *Practicing [sic] Non-Racist Language*. An accompanying glossary states: 'black = gloomy, dirty, deadly, sinister, wicked' and 'white = light, clean, good, pure'. Among expressions to be proscribed are: 'black ice', 'black sheep', 'Black Widow Spider'; and 'White Paper', 'White House'.
6. On the distinction between knowledge and consciousness, see D. W. Hamlyn, 'Unconscious Intentions', *Philosophy*, Vol.46, No.175, pp.12–22 (1971).
7. LAM 6/83, *Racialist Behaviour In Schools*, Bradford Council, 17 November 1983.
8. Catherine Itzin advises parents how to 'spot' seven such 'isms' committed by schools, three of which include 'Heterosexism', 'Adultism' and 'Able-bodiedism'. *How To Choose A School* (Methuen, London, 1985).
9. Ludwig Wittgenstein, *Notebooks 1914–1916* (Blackwell, Oxford, 1961), p.83.
10. As Peter Winch puts it: 'Unlike beasts, men do not merely live but also have a conception of life. This is not something that is simply added to their life; rather, it changes the very sense which the word "life" has when applied to men. It is no longer equivalent to "animate existence".' ('Understanding a Primitive Society', in *Ethnics And Action* (Routledge and Kegan Paul, London, 1972), p. 44.)
11. 'Curriculum Planning In Multiracial Education', reprinted in *The School In The Multicultural Society*, edited by Alan James and Robert Jeffcoat (Harper & Row, London, 1981), p.8. (It is only fair to indicate that Jeffcoate has since spoken out about the arrogance of anti-racist programmes which seek to delve into the psyche of pupils.)
12. *Ibid.*, p.6.
13. From a flyer advertising *World Studies Journal*, Vol.5, No.3 (1985), in which Searle's article is featured.
14. Apart from other evidence given in this book, see Tom Hastie, 'History, Race and Propaganda', this volume, Chapter 4.

13

Pentecostalists and the 'Black Movement'

Roy Kerridge

> Satan is an evil foe,
> Caused many a man to roam . . .

So runs a song sometimes heard in any one of Britain's seven hundred or so Pentecostal churches, with West Indian ministers and congregations. However, it was not Satan who had caused the West Indians to roam to Britain but the hope of a better life and greater prospects in the Mother Country. Most Black Britons, grandchildren of the original immigrants, feel as if they have two nationalities, and go back to the Caribbean for holidays. Very many elderly West Indians, having saved during a lifetime of hard work in a cold climate, are now returning to their home-island in retirement.

British West Indians, for the most part, have *always* felt as if they had two nationalities, their home-island and Britain. In London, Manchester or Birmingham the different islanders met one another for the first time—Jamaicans, Barbadians, Trinidadians and others. The unexpected prejudice of white landlords (whether of house or pub) made them aware that in Britain West Indians were 'foreigners' and members of a different race. As early as the 1940s, however, Africans in Britain had been welcomed by one type of white person, the Communist. This coalition of negroes and the Left paved the way for the Black Power movement of the early 1970s, which attracted many unsettled young West Indian men and led eventually to the racial politics of the present day. Black-power politics is a vague, unthought-out form of Marxism, in which the black race has replaced the 'proletariat' and the white race the 'bourgeoisie', one destined to be exploited by the other until the explosive Day of Reckoning. The 'black consciousness' or 'racial-awareness' movement is hard at work, trying to bring the Day nearer by tireless progress and mischief-making in schools and social service departments.

'Racial Marxism', however, is too tortuous an idea to appeal to most West Indians. A spiritual people, British West Indians usually prefer churchgoing to politics. Few English people expected West Indians to go to church. I have been told of one old-established Pentecostal church whose English members began to leave as West Indians moved into the pews. It is now a wholly 'West Indian church'. Anglicans, Methodists, even Roman Catholics from the West Indies often felt snubbed or uncomfortable in English churches, and joined Pentecostal fellowships where everyone came from the Caribbean. In the new Pentecostal churches, the humblest factory-sweeper can be a pastor or deacon, a benevolent king or prime minister of the church rostrum on Sunday. Every church-member is expected to take over a part of the lengthy service, to sing, preach or 'testify'. The most fleeting thoughts and deepest experience is listened to with equal respect, amid many a cry of 'Preach it, Sister!' or 'Sing it, Brother!'

Church-members are addressed collectively as 'Saints' and individually as 'Br'er' or 'Sis'. Bible characters belong to the same cosy world as the congregation, and many a sermon is preached on the exploits of Brother Paul, Brother Moses or Sister Sarah. When the fashion for Black Power waned during the 1970s, as did the later fashion for Rastafarianism, such churches became very popular among younger people. Clean-cut youngsters vied with one another in forming choirs and 'gospel groups' of drummers and guitarists.

West Indian family life had been broken by the traumas of immigration, and a lost generation of youth had appeared as a result. These youngsters, many of them brought up in children's homes, looked to community workers at black youth centres for guidance. As a result of such misplaced devotion, they were used as an instant mob by the council Left in its cold civil war against the government. When this generation became adult, the supplies of youth 'on tap' for protest marches came to an end. Young people looked to their parents for guidance and the churches boomed.

It is a Pentecostal paradox that while the unfriendliness of white Christians has led many West Indians to gather in their own churches, these same West Indians seek to reach out to white people and save them from hell.

At last the racial politicians became aware of the churches, and considered how best to absorb them into the council-backed left-wing 'Black Movement'. Souls, not race, were the stuff of which Christian dreams were made. Attempts to convert Pentecostalists to race-consciousness are now being made, with varying degrees of success. In this chapter I propose first to describe a type of Pentecostal church and then to examine the ways in which it is being subverted. For although many people on the council Left are well-meaning and wish to help West Indians by giving grants to their churches, and many Pentecostalists are self-satisfied and inward-looking, the two have no common language. Councillors and politicians will do no good until they eschew jargon based on Marxism for the language of honest men. Then they will be able to explain their views to church people without throwing deacons and pastors into miserable bewilderment.

In 1985 the Thirty-second Annual National Convention of the Church of God of Prophecy took place at Brighton Conference Centre. Five thousand or so Brothers and Sisters from all over Britain, wearing suits or bright dresses with hats, sat in the tiered seats of the auditorium. An organ played a slow Jamaican version of 'He's Got the Whole World in His Hands'. The 'Prophecy' church seems to me to be the archtypical Pentecostal ministry. Church leaders are aware of the political threat to the church, which they denounce as 'nationalism' or 'causing divisions'.

'We say we are not a black church, but then the visitor looks round and sees only black people!' as Pastor Joseph Aldred remarked, in a plea for further evangelism among Indians and white people.

A popular song at the Brighton Convention went like this:

My shackles are gone!
My spirit is free!
Oh, praise the Lord,
He lifted me!

Later, I learned that this 'chorus' is also a hit among white Pentecostalists, and no-one knows who started it. After the anguish and passion of a West Indian service, the 'jolly sing-song' atmosphere of English Pentecostalists seems pale indeed. 'My shackles are gone' has an extra meaning for West Indians. Fast, repetitive choruses, mounting in excitement, are an important prelude to 'speaking in tongues', the noisy and impassioned culmination of a Pentecostal service. An English-born church-member once told me that he hated the impassioned electric atmosphere in the church, as it reminded him of 'slavery and spirituals'. He preferred 'Jesus loves me' jollity.

Meanwhile, at the Brighton Convention, a gospel group sang 'There'll Be No More Crying Over There', and a lengthy Message was preached, accompanied by waving programmes. 'I need two programmes, one to read and one to use as a fan,' a young Sister remarked.

A small choir took the stage, and the leader paid tribute to Thomas Dorsey, the 'Father of American Gospel Music'. Dorsey had begun his musical career as a blues singer named Georgia Tom, and went on to compose modern spirituals with a slow, bluesy rhythm. 'Take My Hand, Precious Lord', Dorsey's masterpiece, rang through the hall, the refrain taken up by church-members.

Later, after a pastor's warning against 'shouting, bawling and hollering' in hotel corridors at night, the Mayor of Brighton rose to speak, heralded by enthusiastic applause.

'We are always pleased when the Church of God comes to Brighton, as we always have good weather!' the Mayor said, echoing the views of most Brightonians. The West Indian visitors are supposed, by the locals, to have great spiritual powers, their prayers for sunshine always answered. If the Mayor had known that the church had prayed confusion on IRA bombers, he would have been doubly delighted.

'The Mayor is a third generation Italian, so there is hope for us all,' Pastor Aldred remarked, as His genial Worship stepped down, followed by a black-clad RC chaplain.

Spread over four days, the Convention was enlivened by girl cheerleaders with pom-poms, flag-wavers, marchers in red, white and blue uniforms and a play based on the story of Esther and Mordecai. This last had a very African atmosphere, the barbarian Babylonian King shouting 'What!' exactly like a Nigerian. In the audience, Brothers and Sisters from Cardiff waved the Welsh dragon emblem. Guitar and drums struck up a secular tune, 'The Bluetail Fly', as the National Overseer, J. C. Cagle, took the stage. A white American, Cagle told a rapturous audience: 'You are the Church in Europe! You are not Jamaicans! You are Europeans!' If he had said 'British' instead of 'European' he would probably have been chaired shoulder-high through the streets of Brighton. As it was, he and his wife were garlanded with flowers, and thousands of people queued to shake his hand. 'Don't leave your seats while I'm talking—a sign of madness!' a Birmingham pastor joked.

The American founder of the Church of God was a white man, and when he died, his church was divided between his two sons. One half became known as the Church of God of Prophecy, the other as the New Testament Church of God. In England both churches are West Indian-attended, and have an attitude of friendly rivalry towards each other. As if to be contrary, the New Testament Church of God *welcomes* the apostles of 'black consciousness' and holds seminars on black history and the like. Members dutifully attend, but continue to regard individual souls as of greater importance than race or class. It is another Pentecostal Paradox that most 'black churches' have been founded by white men.

> When I do the best I can,
> And my friends don't understand,
> Make the work that I've done
> Speak for me

a young male choir sang tragically as the Convention ended.

In general, the political attitudes of West Indian Pentecostalists seem to be as follows. Mrs Thatcher is considered to be a bogey-woman, though if the churchgoers knew her ideas they would probably agree with most of them. Almost all churchgoers pay lip-service to Labour, while voting for no-one at all. Labour is thought of vaguely as the coloured man's party, while 'Socialism' is never mentioned or discussed.

'There are no police in church!' a Church of God pastor once announced, hoping by this message to entice some visiting young men into regular attendance. 'Never in all my days as a minister have I seen the police come into a church and arrest a Brother! You are safe here.' This could be interpreted either as an anti-police message or an anti-young man one. Probably it was the latter, as the pastor's views on crime and punishment were rather drastic.

'Do you think snakepits is the answer?' he mused at a deacons' tea party. 'If you put a criminal in a pit of deadly snakes, he would no longer be a wrongdoer.'

'Cutting off fingers!' a deacon shouted, inspired. 'They do that in the Arab country dem. Imagine what it must feel like, to know that each day, one by one, your fingers are going to be cut off!'

'The only time justice is done in this country is when the police beat up someone in the cells,' a third deacon remarked, and everyone agreed.

The above attitudes on politics and opinions on justice are, generally speaking, almost exactly those of the white working class. 'Correct' left-wing opinions, those discussed in universities, polytechnics, school staffrooms and social services departments, have almost to be *forced* on West Indians and white working men and still make little headway.

Many associations of 'black', 'West Indian' or 'Afro-Caribbean' churches now exist, their literature couched in familiar, dreary left-wing jargon. My friends' conversation on 'snakepit justice' was at least expressed in vigorous English and meant something, however absurd.

Not one Pentecostalist in a hundred has heard of the 'black church associations', whose organisers create jobs and apply for grants in a council-backed world of their own. In this world, simply being black is a criterion for a grant application. Important personages in the 'black church movement' are Dr Ashton Gibson, Sybil Phoenix, MBE, and Paul Boateng—all Socialist Methodists. There is no anti-Methodist feeling among Pentecostalists, but they feel little in common with this church. Some Pentecostal pastors, however, have turned to the 'black movement' of their own accord, and others may follow. Their flocks seem to find 'black politics' tedious, and attend occasional meetings out of politeness before bursting into song, prayer or 'tongues'.

Dr Ashton Gibson is the Chairman of the Afro-West Indian Council of Churches. As such, he often speaks of the 'black church movement'. Dr Gibson is very much at home in the larger world of secular racial politics, and is known in social service quarters as a 'black spokesman for the black community'. 'Black politics' usually leads to calls for 'black separatism', and seems as undesirable a phenomenon as the 'white politics' of the National Front. West Indians who dabble in these murky waters, sometimes feeling that they are doing their best for 'their people', are often disconcerted by the eagerness with which white social workers greet each 'blacks only' or 'whites only' scheme. Apartheid appears to be used with unholy glee, as a means of excluding West Indians from English life. If I were Dr Gibson, I would proceed carefully. At the moment, among 'black politicians', white people are sometimes shut out of 'blacks only' meetings. A white visitor to a Pentecostal church full of West Indians is almost always greeted with happy surprise, welcomed by the pastor and invited to become a member of the church. Until this happy state of affairs is brought to an end by the 'black church movement', I cannot see how any Pentecostal church can be called a 'black church'.

The Afro-West Indian United Council of Churches was founded in 1977 at a meeting held in the New Testament Church of God at Willesden. This is an historic church, for it was among the first West Indian-attended Pentecostal churches to be founded in Britain. Despite a slight taint of 'black movement' that appears occasionally, the New Testament Church of God services, at Willesden and elsewhere, are unspoilt and moving. When a service at Willesden was televised, viewers throughout the country were enraptured by its fervour, poetry and passion. It was a typical Pentecostal service, with a banjo-player, a Brother testifying that prayer had cured him of cancer, a choir, praying and preaching. English viewers called for more, but many of them could have found similar churches in their own neighbourhoods.

Pastor Ira V. Brooks of Willesden has far more 'black consciousness' than the average Pentecostal minister. This may be because he is an academic man, aware of the world of ideas but not aware that so many of the ideas are rotten ones. He has written an interesting book, *Where Do We Go From Here?*, in which a slight anti-white bias is perceptible. ('You may pass verdict on me as a racist Pentecostalist,' he writes). The book makes use of jargon never heard in church, such as 'inner-city area'. It appears that the British Council of Churches has given grants to 'inner cities' through the Community Relations Unit.

Moth and rust cause decay, and so do grants, which confer a dreary collective left-wingery to all who taste of their bounty. Long may Pentecostalists and all other honest folk be spared from grants! Bank loans, on the other hand, fulfil one purpose of grants (money) without the other (left-wingery). It could almost be said that the bank loan is Nature's grant, and I advise all needy ministers who wish to remain

Christian to go to the bank. Both the World and the British Council of Churches support revolution, which is to say, civil war.

I have heard Pastor Brooks preaching, and although he begins with a sprinkling of left-wing phraseology, this falls aside as he grows ever more impassioned, showing that he is still a Pentecostalist at heart. All the same, I preferred his predecessor, Pastor Peterkin, who played the saxophone while the whole church danced.

Sometimes the Afro-West Indian United Council of Churches works in conjunction with the Community Roots Trust. Personally I never trust anything with the word 'community' in it. This Roots Trust promotes gospel concerts in aid of 'black causes'. One such concert, in which innocent gospel groups sang 'People Get Ready, There's a Train a-Coming' and similar songs to a rapt Pentecostal audience, was actually in aid of the 'Black and Ethnic Women's Forum'—whatever that is! However, the singers and their audience seize every opportunity to get together without bothering overmuch who their promoters are. Gospel music in Britain is so much the preserve of strong-minded females that 'GLC feminism' can make little impact on it.

Reverend Ira Brooks, in his book, lists the black 'leaders and heroes' whom he thinks the 'black Christian' should follow. They are Nkrumah, Kenyatta, Marcus Garvey and Martin Luther King. What is a Christian such as Martin Luther King doing in such company? If the list had been made with Christians in mind, not 'famous black people', then Martin Luther King might have found himself in better and more appropriate company. Racial thinking can lead to curious and non-Christian conclusions. Even Pastor Brooks, at times, must wonder at the company he finds himself in. At a church seminar on 'Community Service', held on 13 July 1985, he found himself playing host to Valerie Wise of the GLC Women's Committee, Brent Labour Councillor Martin Coleman and the newt-loving eccentric Ken Livingstone. It was a unique opportunity to convert them to Christianity, but nobody grasped it. Instead the bemused members of the congregation, mostly kindly Jamaican housewives in hats, listened as the Co-ordinator of the Church Community Project announced a season of 'counselling projects'.

Fortunately, such goings-on at a Pentecostal church are almost unique, and seem to have had few ill effects. The white Left are eager to preach their secular gospel to a new West Indian audience but that audience keeps half an eye on Heaven and cannot concentrate. In the war between collectivity and individuality, individuality is winning hands-down. The 'black movement' could be said to represent the frightening idea of a 'collective soul', made up of units swept on to do another's bidding. Pentecostalists, as yet, still think as individuals, and often change churches, a fact which progressive pastors should bear in mind.

Another progressive pastor, out to change Pentecostalism from within, is the formidable Esmé Beswick of Brixton's New Testament Assembly. At a Black Pastors' Conference for Racial Awareness which she organised she apparently sought to 'enhance an infrastructure of organisations conducive to the existence of black-led churches'. Her infrastructure became the Brixton Council of Churches, and, as its leader, she wrote to Mrs Thatcher in August 1985 blaming the Prime Minister for the rise in football hooliganism caused by 'alienation'. Beswick and Brooks are virtually the only jargon-speaking pastors, and most people who seek to organise 'black churches' are non-Pentecostalists working ineffectually from outside.

My young friend Erskine, a tall, cheerful and immaculately dressed youth of Barbadian extraction, left college a year ago with a string of 'A' levels to his name. After a year of applying for jobs in banks and insurance he grew desperate and began to apply for the 'black jobs' advertised at the back of West Indian newspapers. This was an unusual procedure for a keen Pentecostalist.

Erskine's applications for work coincided with the Welfare State's discovery of Caribbean Pentecostal Churches. Before long, he was enrolled at what I shall call the Brixton Black Youth in Crisis Outreach Workshop. By the time I got round to visiting him there, he had been made the Director! He and a secretary ran the large empty office between them, paid for by IIEA and the British Council of Churches. From outside, the Workshop seemed yet another Socialist haven, but inside the political posters were replaced by evangelical ones.

'I've just finished my Director's Report,' Erskine smiled. 'Hang on, I'll read it to you. I've put that more attention must be paid to monitoring school books for signs of possible racism. It's disgraceful that there should be books like *Huckleberry Finn* that enforce stereotypes of black men as slaves. There should be more black history, to teach young people to be proud of their past, the slave trade and so on.'

At church, Erskine blended with all the other young people, but in his 'black job', one based on the idea of a 'black church movement', he seemed capable of writing and speaking only in jargon. On the very first page of his Report, my eye fell on phrase after nonsensical phrase: 'participation ...', 'the community ...', 'single-parent families', 'motivation ...', 'cultural differences ...', 'the ethnic community ...', 'the racism that is inherent and ingrained within our society.'

Repeating jargon words and the ideas of the Welfare Party line has become a way of making a living, so that people do it with the mindless ease of a man whose only job is to pull a lever in a factory all day long. At night he stops pulling the lever and does whatever he likes. If a Director's Report contained an atom of sense or a crumb of Christianity, the Director would be assumed a naïve half-wit and fired. So harmful lies, in our Welfare State, seem to go on forever. 'Outreach means going out to sing and preach at schools, youth clubs, hostels, Borstals and churches,' Erskine said. 'We do classes in English, Maths, Business Studies and Law, and we have a Saturday school.'

'Why Has the Educational System Failed Black Children?' a headline on the Report caught my eye. Erskine had blossomed in the educational system, and had many happy memories of school. I would like to know Why the Educational System Leads So Many Clever West Indians into Proving that West Indians Aren't Clever? As the children *are* clever, they soon learn to use juggled or invented statistics in order to prove whatever welfare opinion is in fashion.

'More black teachers', Erskine had written, falling easily into the cast of mind that sees members of a race as 'deprived' whenever it has dealings with another race. Thus 'black children need their own black teachers', or black doctors or black social workers. No-one can help anyone of a different colour—if they try, they are (if white) guilty of 'cultural imperialism'. The sense behind this argument is that apartheid provides more jobs for black people.

An important part of anti-racist writing is the reference to Racism Overt and Covert. So often are Overt and Covert mentioned that I fancy I see them, partners in an old-established firm of solicitors, Overt and Covert, Commissioners for Oaths. With his church background, however, Erskine had written 'Overt and Convert' throughout, so there's hope for the boy yet! Putting his work away, Erskine's conversation led from the 'black church movement' to his own church in particular. 'How can we get white members?' he asked piteously.

A very different type of West Indian Pentecostalist Church is the Mount Zion Spiritual Baptist Church. Deaconesses, known as 'Mothers', wear gorgeously coloured robes and turbans. Hand-bells and holy water play a great part in church ritual, and sometimes the first serves as a chalice for the second. Holy water, sipped from a bell, is used during lengthy healing services. This church, too, was ostensibly founded by a white man, the mysterious Bishop Boltwood. The repetitive 'choruses' evidently date from slavery days, the liturgy from the Church of England and the occasional magic practices from the pagan rituals of the Yoruba tribe of Nigeria.

Yorubas, together with Ashanti from Ghana and Ibos from Biafra, were often brought to Jamaica as slaves. However, a few emigrated there as indentured labourers after Emancipation. Tribe-spotting is an interesting pastime. Celtic, Iberian and Neolithic features can be found among the Welsh. Danish characteristics can clearly be seen among Yorkshiremen in fertile regions, at the mouth of rivers such as the Tees and the Humber. In other parts of Yorkshire, such as Pickering, where the medieval painting of Hell as a dragon's mouth recalls pagan drawings of Nidhug, the World Serpent, the people are obviously Saxon. In just the same way, a knowledgeable man can make fairly accurate guesses as to the original tribes of all New World negroes. Most Jamaicans seem to be Yorubas, the Mount Zionists in particular. When Yorubas in Nigeria form 'spiritual churches', Christianity presented with local pagan forms instead of with English ones, their services almost exactly resemble those of the Mount Zionists.

Mount Zionists from Oxford, Reading, Swindon, Manchester, Birmingham and Huddersfield join their London Brothers and Sisters for conventions, in the same way as other Pentecostalists do. However, Zionist conventions are modest affairs, taking place in large churches rather than in enormous auditoriums. In July 1985 an open-air Convention was held under the concrete flyover beside Ladbroke Grove Tube Station. 'Mothers', dressed in red and gold turbans with white aprons tied over their crimson robes, scampered into the middle of the road to poke tracts through the windows of cars in heavy traffic. The surprised drivers chosen for this honour were usually white. The imposing priest, Father Noël, wore a scarlet robe and a rope tied round his neck, below his black Assyrian beard. He rang his bell vigorously and emptied holy water onto the pavement from a glass. Mother Noël, his wife, had an equally stately bearing. A table with a white cloth, flowers, bottles of healing oil and holy water, a bell, book and candle, did duty as a rostrum.

Surrounded by women in robes, less exalted Brothers and Sisters in neat Pentecostal clothes and children who played on some nearby railings, Mother Noël led the prayers. She used the Book of Common Prayer. Everyone recited the Creed, and then began to sing in most unAnglican tones

> Let us roll, let us roll the old chariot along!
> If a sinner's on the road, we shall help him in!
> If the devil's in the way, we shall roll right over him!
> We shall roll the old chariot along!

This old song was adapted by seamen, in the age of sail, for use as a sea-shanty. It did not interest the passers-by of Ladbroke Grove overmuch. Drug-derelicts who had survived the 1960s lurched by unseeingly, an insane Rasta who swore at nobody and everyone, and haggard former fashion models, once on LSD and now on heroin. A fierce, mad old lady with a beard ordered me to call a taxi and then shuffled on her way.

Strangely enough, the Mount Zionist Spiritual Baptist Church, rather than the more Westernised Pentecostal churches, was among the very first to be addressed by the Left in an attempt to recruit a 'black movement'. This may be because one Boltwood's Chapel is situated opposite a council Community Centre and so got noticed. Paul Boateng, as Vice-Moderator of the World Council of Churches' Programme to Combat Racism, first addressed them several years ago, under the auspices of the GLC. What poor Mother Noël and the others made of being called 'blacks' I cannot say, but the church appears to have received a grant at the end of their ordeal. Among other grievances, Boateng discovered that Pentecostalists were paying too much rent for the church halls they hired off Anglican vicars. This is true, but the Mount Zionist mind, dwelling on the mystical and on messages in dreams, is not attuned to the protest-mentality. Boateng's well-intentioned remarks puzzled them and may even have terrified them.

The Zionists addressed by Boateng appeared to go into a decline, the Mothers and Fathers apparently stunned and in deep depression. A notice, in scrawly writing, appeared on the Chapel door, announcing a 'Senior Citizen's Club Especially for Ethnic Minorities'. The New Testament Church of God eagerly brought such clubs into being, following a Welfare Party Line, but the Mount Zionists seemed at a loss. Far from being "old dears" to be patronised, West Indian old ladies are usually extremely vigorous, and virtually run the churches. One of the Mothers owned a shop that sold West Indian food, and 'black militant' pamphlets appeared on the counter, their contents a mystery to the church people. Officials from 'multi-racial Brent' photographed the Chapel, the pictures appearing in a library exhibition to show how multi-racial they were. Notices on feminist issues, demanding abortions and contraceptives for schoolgirls, were plastered on the shop-walls. One particularly mad one read 'Rights for Embryos are Taken Away from Women'.

Boateng, whose father comes from Ghana where similar churches thrive, did not appear concerned to understand the beliefs of the Mount Zionists. These beliefs appear to have been thought irrelevant. The ideological onslaught has been strictly one-sided. Far from becoming a self-consciously 'black church', however, the Mount Zionists have acquired a small sprinkling of white members. This has cheered everyone up, and the 'Ethnic Minority' notice has disappeared. Its successor, announcing church evening classes in various subjects, bears the explanatory footnote: 'GLC Funded.'

The third type of negro Pentecostal Church in Britain is the West African 'Spiritual Church'. Such churches deal not in spiritualism, but are more or less 'Mount Zionist' with Africans replacing West Indians. Nigerians are increasingly making their homes in Britain, sometimes by means of a short-stay visa, a change of address and a talent for success and intrigue. Not long ago, I was walking along a Liverpool street when I saw a ruined church, with most of the roof slates missing. 'Church of the Lord (Aludura)', the sign read. An African girl, noticing my curiosity, stopped and told me a little about the church, advising me to attend.

So next Sunday morning, I knocked at the door of the 'manse' that adjoined the church. A tall, formidable Yoruba man in mauve robes greeted me, at first almost speechless with surprise. Recovering himself, he welcomed me in, and I was shown into a small parlour, transformed by rows of chairs and a table-altar into a place of worship. Three candles burned brightly in a candelabrum, beside a handbell and a bottle of oil. The service had not yet begun. A Brother in a white robe was joined by three spirited young ladies, one in a Princess Anne hat. These were the minister's daughters. Two Nigerian seamen completed the congregation.

'"Aludura" means a place of prayer,' the minister explained. 'We are a full member of the World Council of Churches, and they helped us to obtain this church. At first we had white members, but they fell away. Then the children of the neighbourhood began to invade this very compound! The whole church has been vandalised, again and again. It is now too smashed to use, and we will have to build another. Sometimes we have caught the children, and they have said their parents sent them, to steal the lead. How can this be? In Africa no one would do such a thing. They would never smash a house, let alone a church. Perhaps you would like to share?'

This phrase, in white evangelical circles, means a soul-baring testimony of faith. The Aludura minister, however, only wanted an explanation of vandalism.

'Well, the council in Liverpool has been pulling down houses for so long, leaving ruins everywhere, that generations of children have grown up regarding empty buildings as places to play in,' I told him. 'They have no respect for a church because many secondary school teachers are atheists, and the boys have not been taught anything about Christianity.'

The Nigerian looked deeply shocked, and the service began. At one point he hissed angrily as someone read the wrong verse from the 'Good News Bible'. Dreams were recounted and songs sung in the Yoruba language. A goblin-like boy of six, mischievous-eyed but mute, sat or wriggled by my side. Prayers were said both for the vandalised church and for the vandals.

'We will now sing spiritual choruses', the minister announced, ringing the handbell to set up a rhythm. He held the clapper inside the bell instead of the handle. At once his daughters began brisk, pistol-shot criss-cross hand-clapping, a typical Yoruba style, and we all sang:

We are expecting Jesus!
We are expecting Jesus!

We are expecting Jesus!
We cannot tell you when.

Afterwards the minister told me of the Aludura custom of 'Tabora', thirteen days of fasting and prayer. He also showed me a rude and unhelpful letter from the British Council of Churches who refused to pay towards the church repair costs. Yorubas in Nigeria, and their descendants in the West Indies, seem of all tribes to be the most church-minded and the least politically inclined.

African spiritual churches have not yet been discovered by the apostles of the 'Black Church Movement'. Far more internationally minded than West Indians, fond of intercontinental congresses and Youth Fellowships, West Africans have managed to get their churches into the World Council as fast as sects can be invented. In Britain the World Council helps them by (as far as I can make out) providing them with redundant churches to revitalise. If the Aludura church is any guide, the Councils of Churches, World and British, begin by raising the minister's hopes to the skies and end by abandoning him. Some very odd, almost pagan, churches are now in the World Council of Churches.

Although the World and British Councils of Churches are rather fond of non-Christian guerrilla fighters and have given grants to Marxist groups and 'black activists' in Britain and elsewhere, they have not unduly disturbed the beliefs of African church members. African churches, such as Aludura, seem more aware of the Church of England than are Caribbean Pentecostalists. If they are ever politicised, it will probably be from an Anglican source. Already the Anglican Bishop of Croydon, the Right Reverend Wilfred Wood, a West Indian, has made a speech addressed to 'black pastors', urging them to 'get more involved in social action'. When 'doing good' is described as 'social action', how much good in fact can be done? Can the Church of England now be described as a tool of Satan?

The answer to the last question is almost certainly 'No', but the antics of a few city vicars sometimes makes me wonder. At a sophisticated dinner party in a Chelsea club a stout, vivacious clergyman in a black cassock gave a comic Grace, and later on lit an enormous cigar. A dessert shaped like a naked woman's torso, life-size and covered in icing, was passed around the table. Helping himself to a slice of breast, the churchman told me that he was 'high up in the

Church bureaucracy' and asked my advice on how to influence and take over the West Indian-run churches. 'Leave them alone!' I begged.

'Too late for that, old boy, the Church is deeply involved. One suggestion is that we should have black Anglican churches and white Anglican churches.'

This idea struck me as a bit too South African. It may well be that all the churches in Britain, black, white or whatever, will one day be combined as a Church of Social Action. If so, I can only remind Christians of the song sung by kindly Mother Noël and her flock in their little shop-front church, Sunday after Sunday:

> You can walk as you like, you can talk as you like,
> But you can't get to Heaven as you like.
> For the angels hold up a record
> And you can't go to Heaven as you like.

14

Preference and Prejudice: The Mythology of British Racism

Dennis J. O'Keeffe

A readiness to criticise present social arrangements is crucial to the survival of a civilised order. Indeed, such a spirit of criticism was essential to the emergence of the free society. It is no accident that the British, who produced the world's first industrial economy, had also evolved over a period of some centuries the most open-minded and intellectually free society that had ever existed. A critical and questing spirit, an outlook at once sceptical and humane, is probably a necessary condition of material progress.[1]

If one were to weigh criticism against self-satisfaction in the scales of progress one would undoubtedly prefer criticism to tip the balance. A look around the world is enough to convince one of that. Neither Marxism, nor—to take an example further from mental stasis—the trans-Atlantic version of Whiggism which prevailed in the United States until the 1950s, nor indeed any form of triumphalism, can supply a proper moral or intellectual basis for the social order. Nothing I have to say in the following pages should be taken to mean that I think an open, tolerant or merciful society can dispense with criticism, sometimes of the most persistent and uncompromising kind. But criticism has its dangers too. It can become carping—a willingness to criticise everything willy-nilly. It may descend into the worship of change for its own sake. It may mistake particular ailment for general disease.

This has indeed happened in whole areas of our modern intellectual activity. A chorus of complaint has been orchestrated in many of our universities and polytechnics, and its baleful melody has been repeatedly heard on television too. Rootless and faddishly inclined sociologists and educationalists have been particularly active in the denigration of all things British or, indeed, Western. Our society is corrupt; our economy is predatory; our institutions are moribund; our civilisation is doomed. Our women-folk are downtrodden. The world, or at least our part of it, is universal woe. Such is the spirit of 'criticism'.

It is noticeable, indeed, that with the unanswerable empirics of socialist tyranny now on display in almost half the world, the bulk of so-called radical analysis has moved away from previously central issues like free enterprise versus state planning towards questions such as the arms race and the relations between the sexes or between different races. These issues have the immense advantage that one-sided pronouncements on them cannot be clobbered by intractable evidence such as food-shortages and the wholesale stifling of dissident activity.

Sometimes the critical excesses *vis-à-vis* our society *are* still combined with the most uncritical adulation of one-party despotisms in exotic parts, though paradise has a disconcerting tendency to be on the move—Russia, China, Cuba, Tanzania are among the far-off places which have at times been acclaimed as its resting-place. Sometimes, and probably more typically, all self-styled Marxist societies are rejected. But perhaps precisely that is the point. Indeed, one might hypothesise that the intensity of the criticism of what is here and now may be a rising function of millennarian doubts.

Amid the confusing welter of contemporary intellectual life, in which for better or worse Marxism has been so notable, perhaps one line, at least, of clear tendency is increasingly apparent: the emergence of a purely critical neo-Marxism, one with little or no eschatological pretentions. Marxism is a classic case of a degenerating paradigm in Popper's sense, albeit till now absorbing with impressive ingenuity obstacle after intellectual obstacle to its continuing claim to reasonableness or relevance.[2] However, it may well be that the adjustments are now pressing painfully on the very margins of possibility. The Marxian tunnel of history is collapsing, or at least there is little or no light of salvation discernible at its far end. Perhaps the noisy and vulgar reverberations of neo-Marxism today are the panic of a perceived ensuing end, a realisation that women, blacks, students and Third World peasantries are no more willing or equipped to act out the set-pieces of the fantasy than the proletariat it was intended for. As the veils of credulity slip and the slum bureaucracies of Soviet Europe and the gangsterdoms of Africa are seen for what they really are, what is left for the credo but despair and hatred?

Certainly, something of this sad sort must lie behind the extraordinary flood of self-hatred and condemnation now apparent at so many levels of our society. At any rate, nowhere are the voices of hyper-criticism and self-abasement more persistent and strident that in writings on 'racism'. This grating neologism perhaps eclipses, in the mythology of outrage, even its partner in unmelody—'sexism'. To read much of the literature in the area is to enter a world of relentless intellectual breast-beating and teeth-gnashing, where guilt-ridden or hate-enflamed ideologues try to press on us the view that our society is a kind of proto-Nazism, determined or at any rate structured in all its aspects to humiliate, exploit and frustrate the lives of our now very large non-white minority. What is surprising, especially in view of the continuing intellectual distinction in some fields of the educated classes in this country, is the lack of apparent will and determination to rebut these grotesque charges, and to develop a more sophisticated and less corrupted theoretical socio-economy of race.

The question arises whether one kind of social system is inherently more or less inclined to racial prejudice than another. To take the most horrendous example of ethnic prejudice in human history, namely German National Socialism, one might propose that the socialist case is not promising. It is true that, by stipulative wriggling, socialists may refuse to accept that any regime as foul as Hitler's could be 'socialist'. Indeed, this is a game they are also inclined to play in the face of Soviet crimes of various, and continuing kinds. The Soviets have murdered far more people in their seventy-odd years than the Nazis were able to do in their mere twelve; and though the racial record of the Soviet Union has nothing to compare with the mind-numbing horrors of the Holocaust, it is still appalling, with whole nations obliterated or deported, and a record of anti-semitism that British 'anti-Zionists' could aspire to only in their most malignant dreams. It is actually time to ignore those whose normative pre-emption of 'socialism' permits them to exclude from claim to that title any regime which commits monstrous acts.

We might also usefully invoke Marx's two classical criteria of capitalism: private property in the means of production and money wages realised through market forces. It is notable that neither Nazi Germany nor contemporary South Africa meets the second of these criteria. Clause IV socialism was on Hitler's order book had Germany won the war,³ and though this is not remotely the case with South Africa, it is notable that, contrary to the mythology of neo-Marxism, it is the operations of the state, not the workings of capitalist markets, which tend to express, compound and institutionalise racial hatred. The contemporary cases of Britain and the United States, where the state has sought to intervene *in favour* of racial minorities, are historically exceptional. It was an aspiring socialist state which engineered Nazism, not German capitalism. The most that could be said of South Africa is that certain capitalist forces sustain apartheid. Its origin is the swollen state apparatus which is a creature of poor white Boer politics.⁴

Nor, it seems, is the apparatus of 'anti-racist' intervention in British society as felicitous as it is often claimed—and sometimes intended—to be. The writings of George Gilder and Thomas Sowell on the American pattern of intervention are convincing and carry a sombre warning for us in Britain.⁵ Those non-whites who plug their lives into the normal workings of a capitalist economy, those who make their own way in job or business markets, those who buy their own housing—they are the fortunate ones. For the case against socialism, defined as the substitution of publicly provided resources for privately generated ones, is as strong intra-nationally as internationally. It is the apparatus of welfarism in the United States that tends to make a large portion of the black American population into a helpless group of dependants. Just as earlier black gains at the turn of the century were effected by the *normal* operations of developing capitalism and were reversed by *political* intervention in favour of poor white racism, so current welfare policies do not free but perpetuate the bondage of the large group of American blacks who fall within their compass.⁶

Things look no more helpful in the British case. In the last ten years the weirdest and most extreme politicisation of local government has occurred in many parts of Britain, again tending to generate not the independence of inner-city populations but growing paralysis and dependence on the part of the very populations, often in large measure non-white, which the policies purport to help.

The thesis that the poorest regions of our depressed inner cities can spend their way out of distress by pumping in funds raised in more prosperous areas, and that this is *a fortiori* what is needed for non-whites because of the 'racism' of the white British is very doubtful. Jon Davies has shown that even in inner-city areas it is both feasible and desirable for the population of relative newcomers to buy their *own* houses and establish an independent pattern of business and employment.[7] A convincing case could indeed be made for the thesis that both the international evidence and *a priori* economic reflection suggest that it is on the whole state interventions—whether evil or in intention benign—which tend to persecute or inhibit people on racial grounds and that, as Milton Friedman contends, advanced capitalist economies are based on impersonal markets which are functionally indifferent to the race, gender or religion of economic agents.[8]

If this thesis is correct it would not follow from the demonstration that British society is deeply racially prejudiced that the best way to deal with such prejudice is via an extension of state powers. But *is* British society 'racist', as so many critics claim? What is racial prejudice and what causes it? The unfortunate truth is that these questions of nature, extent and origin tend to be no more helpfully discussed in most of the literature than questions of therapy and amelioration.

No-one would sensibly deny that many people in our society are prejudiced against others of different race. Some white people hate blacks and Asians and vice versa. No-one knows how much prejudice there is or how intense it is. It would be very difficult to measure. The tendency of the literature is to represent such prejudice as extreme. Should we not at least consider the possibility that many people, perhaps even a majority of the populations concerned, are *mildly* prejudiced, or, to put it in less exciting language, have certain cultural preferences about food, clothes, marriage, religion and so on? Perhaps (and has anyone done the counting?) a majority of whites, blacks and Asians are in favour of intra-racial marriage, for example. If this is so, what is so appalling about it? The idea that people could live without racial sentiment, without a sense of history or continuity or identity is an obvious nonsense.

Both justice and mercy require that we resist and reject racial prejudice in all its manifestations. However, it is painstaking and fine analysis that is required, not the bandying about of coarse and voracious categories of goodies and baddies. We need to recognise what is morally repugnant and what acceptable in relations between the races. Preference is not prejudice, whether it be exercised by recently arrived cultures and minorities or by the indigenous majority. To refer again to the crucial issue of marriage, I hold that to prefer one's children (without benefit, in an open society, of legal regulation of such preferences) to marry people of the same race as oneself is an acceptable preference, as much for native Anglo-Saxons surely, as for Jewish, brown or black minorities. The right to exercise this preference seems to me every bit as important as the right of people of different races to inter-marry without being persecuted or harassed.

We should recognise the limits of moral improvement. The desire to widen the range of individual discretion can conflict with respect for cultures. We can accede to the right of Hindu citizens of Britain to marry Christians, Moslems or atheists. This acceptance, however, carries with it the further acceptance of possible cultural violation and broken hearts. This side of the grave, at any rate, there is no perfection, nor shall all tears be dried. Honest supporters of the liberal order must conclude that some of the principles they hold most dear may be at war with each other.

If triumphalism in an optimistic form is to be rejected, should we not reject its pessimistic equivalents also? The hate-relations industry and Mr Enoch Powell seem to agree about one thing—the inability of the white British to absorb large numbers of non-whites. I disagree. There was, in my view, nothing inevitable about the horrible social conflagrations in some inner cities in the last half-decade. The etiology of such troubles is doubtless complex. It is certainly not a question purely of race. In Birmingham a *white* man has been charged with the murder of Asian shopkeepers. Nor are the upheavals mechanically related to unemployment. In the case of the policeman murdered in Tottenham, two of the persons charged are below employment age and the third has a job. To argue that a person of one race might have killed people of a second race out of resentments caused by the prejudice of members of a third, or to argue that A who is not unemployed, might have murdered B because C *is* unemployed, is to engage in rather remote-control notions of causality.

Crime, petty and random *and* large-scale and planned, had something to do with these frightful events. So too did material distress, inadequate family life—how else could young people be roaming the streets out of control?—and in all probability inadequate schooling. But so also, I will suggest, though there is no way of proving it, did the insistent and repetitive liturgy of anti-British 'anti-racism', especially the sustained campaign against the police. Indeed the pathological hatred of the white British which is now more or less standard in the case of many publicly funded bodies may well have been the true dynamic of these grisly happenings.[9]

All the same is it not the truth that Britain has absorbed several million non-whites with—until recently—remarkably little trouble? Would not Enoch Powell's lurid prophecies of the late 1960s have been effectively falsified already in the absence of this virulent ideology of hatred? With inexorable monotony the National Front continues to forfeit its electoral deposits. The people in Britain, most of them at least, white, black or brown, do not want totalitarian politics of any persuasion. And we have done better in some respects than France in the area of race relations. For all the French's famed indifference to questions of colour, inter-racial murder is a commonplace thing in contemporary France.

No-one doubts that in Britain Asians are sometimes terrorised by louts. Most dwellers in big cities will have seen examples of this. Nor are the police everything they should be. They contain at least their share of uneducated bigots. Doubtless, too, some employers are prejudiced. But how one characterises a society or age is bound to be affected by where one looks. Twenty years ago most economic historians thought of the British 1930s as a period of economic failure. They were looking at the unemployment. Now that they have looked at the rising living standards of the period they have reached rather different conclusions.[10] If there really were all the obstacles which the critics claim, how could Asian immigrants have penetrated the professions and all levels of business as successfully as manifestly they have? Are the black doctors, bus conductors, students, and schoolteachers I meet really weighed down by an intolerable burden of prejudice from me and my like? They are more cheerful and polite than we deserve, if that is indeed the case.

In fact such contradictions abound. Take the question of immigration control of non-whites. First, it is absurd to deny that an established community has the right to define and defend its essential identity. At present, that essential identity includes whiteness, though this may not be the case in centuries to come. If a majority of the citizens of a Caribbean island preferred immigrant citizens to be of the same race and general culture as themselves, let us say black and English-speaking, in what sense could measures to enact these preferences properly be called 'racist'? Just as serious, however, is the prudential fault in the case. The very people who seethe about racial prejudice in Britain are those who also denounce immigration laws as racist. They seem not to notice the contradiction. It is very like the central oddity in the Marxist sociology of education. Those who proclaim most noisily that the education system 'reproduces' the capitalist class-structure are also loudest in their opposition to education cuts. In both cases, however, the hated policy would seem eminently desirable. If life in Britain means endless misery for non-whites, then common decency suggests a policy of rather tight control of non-white immigration.

In fact there is another contradiction. The notion that black or brown people would *want* to come to a country which daily assaults their humanity is an insult to their intelligence. But they do want to come. They wish to do so, indeed, in rather unmanageable numbers. The logic of the situation is inescapable. Whatever the difficulties they anticipate, would-be immigrants regard the net tally of costs and benefits as positive.

Most striking of all is the way in which the evil of racial prejudice has come to occupy a central, almost a reflex and stylised place in contemporary moral concerns. It is treated as if it were a sin apart. It is not. Like envy, greed or violence, it ranges from the mild to the murderous. Our follies are heterogeneous. It does no service to the cause of moral improvement to deal with one of them as if it were some special wickedness, outranking all other versions of human unwisdom. Indeed there is no evil inherent in the awareness of race as such. It is when that awareness takes the form of intolerance or envy or hatred that it becomes unacceptable.

The argument that our society is deeply racist is sometimes expressed in the most pernicious and extreme forms. Liberals are held to be worse than the National Front.[11] Liberal society is held to be more intolerable for non-whites than apartheid South Africa.[12] Such opinions are either vulgar and ignorant or dishonest. How can the (anyway unproven) prejudices of the well intentioned be held worse than malignant hatred? How can a society which by law and administration has sought to diminish the effects of discrimination on minorities be counted more odious than a regime which by law oppresses a majority?

The fact is that such questions concern only details. The larger and more urgent question concerns the *nature* of this strange addiction to gloom and flagellation. Why should those who will tell us fiercely at one moment that no one culture can be counted 'better' than another feel so compelled at another instance to apologise so profoundly for the shortcomings of their own? The logical confusion is obvious enough, but what is its provenance?

The sociological study and the politics of race in Britain have been appropriated by an irresponsible cult of criticism which is now wildly out of control. It is by a paradox fitting to such excess that the anti-racist movement is itself so racist. Hatred of the white races is not a justifiable attitude. Nor, indeed, is it us but the Americans who bear the worst burden of hatred directed at the most materially successful civilisation in history. But there is another, far less known hatred at work. It is a hatred and contempt for *black* people, who now constitute a principal element in the group which Marxian socialism has always most despised: the urban working class. How can this be, how can such a staggering reversal have occurred? To explain this, something of a diversion is required.

The late and never to be enough lamented Arthur Koestler maintained that owing to a mal-integration between the old (primitive) and new (complex) parts of the human brain we are psychologically disjointed creatures. We manifest radical paranoia which expresses itself in pathological self- and own-group fascination, combined with rejection and loathing of others, especially alien groups.[13] This observation seems to hold for many countries of widely varying type: it is true for many African countries; true in the Middle East; brutally true in many Communist countries;[14] true in Northern Ireland. The neo-Marxists, of course, are assiduous in their attempts to link all this racial disaffection with capitalism; the truth, however, is that such hatreds look like historical hangovers in capitalist contexts, and while nothing reduces to economics save only economic phenomena themselves, capitalist economies do seem very successful at impersonalising economic transactions.

The paranoia, however, is probably only to be disguised and diverted, not eradicated, and George Orwell was one of the first writers to observe that a sophisticated version or rather, inversion, of this trait of in-group love and out-group hate, is very characteristic of twentieth-century socialist intellectuals in free societies like Britain. It is a mania which has grown to fantastic proportions in recent years. Many of the ordinary and uncorrupted people of Britain of all races are now the victims of this mushrooming nonsense. When mastery of English is the employment currency of Britain only a disposition to interfere with the prospects of others would lead anyone to propose compulsory courses in Asian languages. Even when cultural perspectives are not 'widened' in error, as when steel-band music (from Trinidad) was taught for its 'black' relevance to pupils whose parents came mostly from Jamaica, the old socialist desire to push others around, to decide what is good for them, is often quite apparent.

Nor does anti-racism escape—indeed it compounds—the prejudice it so noisily pretends to disdain. The surface pronouncements are trivial and shifting. There has been a torrent of literature dealing with the nature, effects and incidence of racial prejudice; but underneath there is an abiding contempt for non-whites, one wound inextricably into the pattern of hatred for, or self-hatred by, whites themselves. Such a complex is hard to unravel; but what but contempt for non-whites could lead to the now common view that only whites are racist? It is another way of saying that non-whites are stupid. In any case, it is an arrant lie.

The endless agitation about South Africa is an international version of this attitude. People feel, quite rightly, that white people should not have created a monstrosity like apartheid but, quite wrongly, at the same time, that the black gangsters who run most of Africa are not culpable in the same way for the many foul deeds done in their countries.

One might use another of Koestler's ideas in this regard. He held that the Marxist intellectuals of the 1940s and early 1950s manifested a 'controlled schizophrenia', whereby ordinary moral categories were applied to most issues but a special class of items were accorded privileged status. Any class would, in principle, do, but in this case the class just happened to be Marxism and the Soviet Union. Horrors like the Stalin trials, the Nazi–Soviet Pact, the deportations, etc., were exonerated as 'historical necessity'.

Is not a controlled distortion being operated when 'police brutality' is an unproblematic category of actions, and 'mugging' by young black males is held to be problematic, a 'racist' construction? Obviously the examples could be multiplied, but the fact is that the race relations industry processes its raw facts through very differentiated grids, depending on whether the result is to be endorsed (racist teachers) or rejected (the effects on educability of the one-parent family).

We now have millions of non-white citizens. It cannot be politically healthy that so much of the literature on race relations in Britain is distorted in a way not much removed from systematic lying. The real racism is to assume that a dictator can be exonerated if he is a black man. The real bigotry is to excuse a black young person for mugging because he is a black from Brixton. And, as with most folly, it is the poor and the weak of all races who must pay.

There are certain useful truths to be gleaned from the initial notion that social contexts in some degree form man and that different contexts form him differently. But the partial explanation of this or that act in terms of the context from which it emerged is not a justification. Nothing is more integral to the *trahison des clercs* than the false notion that 'tout comprendre c'est tout pardonner'. Quite rightly, we do not forgive the small group of white proletarians who join the National Front. Why, then, should we forgive the tiny handful of young blacks who decide that mugging is not a mug's game? It is one thing to agree that social structure A is more favourable to virtue than social structure B. It is quite another to argue that to belong to B is to be free, *ipso facto*, from moral constraints. And, above all, one might inquire: just who do these atheistical Marxists think they are that they can tell devout Jamaican Protestants that their children cannot know right from wrong?

The origin of these confused attitudes is obviously complex. In part it is a question of the decline in religious values. While the main version of the search for a secular religious substitute, namely socialism, has now been discredited, its eschatological residua, the quests for sexual or racial liberation, continue to supply convenient banners of moral indignation.

In part the anti-racist crusade is also a legacy of Empire. It reflects a one-sided, indeed on balance a wrong evaluation of imperial history. It was George Orwell who noted forty years ago that large sections of the world had got worse since the demise of British power, a then-unpopular opinion. He could voice it today with much more confidence. It is part of the price of a free society that it must endure distorted criticism. Given the abundant evidence of the tragic consequences which can stem from the false diagnosis of present ills, the defenders of freedom have both the right and the duty to point out that our society has been the first one in history even to admit the evils of racial prejudice, much less seek to redress him.

Notes

1. W. W. Rostow, *How it all Began* (McGraw-Hill, New York, 1975). D. J. O'Keeffe, 'The Paradox of Culture: Higher Education as Ideology' in *Higher Education Review* (August 1983).
2. A brilliantly succinct account of Sir Karl Popper's theory of degenerating paradigms is given by Mark Blaug in his essay on human capital theory. See M. Blaug, 'The Empirical Status of Human Capital Theory' in *Journal of Economic Literature*, p.839 (1974).
3. There seems to be little doubt that Nazism was a Marxist heresy. The socialism of *Mein Kampf* is unmistakable.
4. It seems very probable that the potential of the state, any state, is asymmetrical *vis-à-vis* good and evil, the former being very difficult and the second distressingly easy to achieve.
See P. Johnson, *History of the Modern World*, Weidenfeld 1983.
5. G. Gilder, *Wealth and Poverty* (Basic Books, New York, 1980): T. Sowell, *Race and Economics* (Longman, London, 1975).
6. Gilder, *op.cit.*
7. J. Davies, *Asian Housing in Britain*, Research Report No.6 (Social Affairs Unit, 1985).
8. M. Friedman, 'Capitalism and the Jews' in *Encounter* (June 1984).
9. David Dale says of the Institute of Race Relations that it has a hatred of England bordering on 'clinical paranoia'. D. Dale, 'The New Ideology of Race' in *The Salisbury Review*, p.21 (Oct. 1985).
10. Indeed the conclusion that living standards rose in the inter-war period is now a commonplace outside the ranks of the TUC. See A. J. P. Taylor, *English History 1914–1945* (Penguin, Harmondsworth, 1970).
11. I have heard this said by a sociologist at a departmental staff-meeting.
12. I have heard this, too, at the same meeting.
13. A. Koestler, *The Act of Creation* (Hutchinson, London, 1964).
14. T. Garton-Ash, 'Culture and Anarchy' in *The Spectator* (26 Oct. 1985), p.14.
15. G. Orwell, 'Notes on Nationalism' in *Polemic*, No.1 (Oct. 1945).

Index

Aberdeen University 123
abolition movement, the 72
academic education, traditional 166
   values, traditional 163
'access' 6, 44
   equality of 146
   theory, the 46, 48
   to education and jobs 59
Africa 63
African churches 183
   languages, the dictionaries of 103
   Organisations, The Committee of 89
   spiritual churches 183
Africanisation, the policy of 87
Africans, the 35, 49, 87
   in Britain 87
Afro-Caribbean 20, 22, 35, 49
   people 18, 107
   the interests of the 121
   underachievement of British 20
Afro-West Indian Council of Churches 174–6
Aldred, Pastor Joseph 171–2
Aludura church, the 183
   custom of Tabora, the 183
American blacks, the bondage of 188
   Civil War, the 62
   pattern of intervention 188
   War of Independence 61
Amin, Idi 76, 87
   rule of 22, 76
Amsterdam, the University of 32
Anand, Mulk Raj 69

Anglican churches, white 184
Anglicans 170
'anglocentric' curriculum 127–9
Anglo- or Euro-centric view 142
   -Saxon 54
apartheid 175, 178, 188, 194
Aquinas, Thomas 72
Arab learning 67
Arabia, culture of 134
Arabian culture 134
Arabs 63
Archelaus 157
Archer, John 66
Armstrong, William H. 109
Arnold, Matthew 141
Arohan 70
Ashanti from Ghana 179
Asia, the Chinese in South 48
Asian bourgeoisie 122
   children, performance of 46
   communities, the 121
   community, the 49
   culture 87
   economic success 46
   history 63
   immigrants 143
   language, compulsory courses in 194
   people 18, 107
Asians 19, 35, 87
   British 22, 87
   progress of East African 46
   school performances of 138

'assimilation' 147
Augustine, Saint 53
Auschwitz 7, 76
  horrors of 74–5, 77
  propagandist elements of 78
  teaching pack on 7, 78, 80
Austen, Jane 8
Avon 4
Azadi (Freedom) 70

Bagdad 67
Barbadians 169
Barber, Francis 65
Battersea 66
BBC television 97, 101
behaviourism 161
Bennett, John 100, 102
Berkshire 22, 37
  Education Committee 34
  Royal County of 142
Beswick, Esmé 177
bias, intentional and involuntary 60
Birmingham 169
black activists in Britain 183
  American population, the 188
  Anglican churches 184
  aspirations 86
  bourgeoisie 122
  church movement 174–5, 178
  churches 177
  Christian, the 176
  community, internal problems of the 138
  communities, the 35
  consciousness 169, 173
  definitions of 6, 34–5, 49–51
  disparaging connotations of 103
  experience, the 109
  failures 19
  GIs 66
  history, seminars on 173
  intelligentsia, the 45
  mayor, Britain's first 66
  militant pamphlets 181
  movement, the 177, 180
  people, contempt for 193
  people, prejudice against 103
  politics 174
  politicians 175
  power movement 52
  power politics 169
  pupil performance 45
  pupil's self-esteem 46
  racism 54
  ruling classes 71
  separatism 174
  state schools, separate 50
  struggle 90
  struggle in Britain 83
  trade union activists 85
  unity 90
  –white relations, the history of 91
Black African campaigns 39
  American campaigns 39
  and Ethnic Women's Forum, the 176
  Britons 169
  Church Movement, the 183
  Movement, left-wing 171
  Movement, Pentecostalists and the 169
  Panther heroes 86
  Pastors' Conference for Racial Awareness 177
  People's Freedom Movement 89
  Power Movement 169
  Power, the fashion for 170
  Unity and Freedom Party 123
  Workers' Co-ordinating Committee 123
blacks, discrimination against 45
 -only meetings 175
  police, attitudes to 59
Blyton, Enid 8, 10, 110
Boateng, Paul 174, 180–1
Bodley Head, the 108
Boer politics, white 188
Boltwood, Bishop 179
Boltwood's Chapel 180
'Bolshevik' 51
'bourgeoisie', the 169
Brabantio 114

Index   199

Bradford 12, the 76
  persecutions in 145
Bradford's United Black Youth League
  89
Brazil 64
Brent 37
Brentano 163
Brighton Conference Centre 171
  Convention, the 172
  the Mayor of 172
Bristol, persecutions in 145
  riot in 72
Britain, Africans in 169
  culture of 134
  history of 134
  multi-racial 55
  political culture of 128
  pre-war 65
  racism and black resistance in 122
  racism in 137
  structures of power in 34
  values of 7
Britain's black population 121
  colonial past 84
  culture 141
  ethnic minorities 121
  future of freedom in 81
  institutions and customs 137
  racial problems 123
British, anti- 191
  Association for the Advancement of
    Science 8
  Association, the 119
  Association's sociology section 118
  blockade, the 65
  citizenship 140
  Council of Churches 175-7, 183
  culture 18, 130-1, 138, 140
  culture, attack on 38
  culture, denigration of 37
  culture, racism in 119
  culture, the teaching of 133
  democracy 73
  denigration of all things 186
  guilt 137, 142
  history 142

history, biased account of 38
history, distortions of 6-7
identity, nature of 51
imperialists, the 68
labour movement 62
politics, mainstream of 124
power, demise of 195
ruling class, the 67
rural workers 67
society, attack on 37
society, conflict in 39
society, ethnic minorities in 124
society, Marxist perspective on 120
society, values of 83
whites, stereotyping of 7
woollen workers 67
working class, the 123
Britten, Benjamin 134
Brixton 195
  Black Youth In Crisis Outreach
    Workshop 177
  Council of Churches 177
  riot in 72
Brixton's New Testament Assembly
  177
Brooks, Reverend Ira 175-7
Brunning, Robert 108
Bunche, Dr Ralph 15
Burton, Sir Richard 134
Bustamente, Alexander 66
Butt, Ronald 7

Cagle, J. C. 172
Cairo 67
Calvin, followers of 53
Capey, Arthur 8, 106
capitalism 24, 62, 69, 80, 88, 187-8
capitalist, anti- 63
  class, the 192
  economy 188
  markets 188
  social system 25
capitalists, British 67-8
  exploitation by Indians 69
Caribbean, the 169-70
Carr, E. H. 60

Casey, John 118
caste system, the 128
Catholics, Roman 99, 170
Cay, The 109–10
censorship 7–8
Centre for Urban Education Studies (CUES) 97
Children's Crusade, the 64
Rights Workshop 8, 108–10
China 103, 134, 186
Chinese 35, 104
Charlie and the Chocolate Factory 110
Chowdry, Mr Yunus 85
Christ 144
Christendom, culture of 133
Christian guerrilla fighters, non- 183
misionaries 70
religion, the 130
Christianity 128, 133, 143–4, 179
Christians, unfriendliness of white 170
Church Community Project, the 176
of England, the 179, 183
of God of Prophecy 171–3
of the Lord (Aludura) 181
of Social Action 184
Churchill, Winston 70
civil order, obedience to a 129
war 111, 176
Civil Rights legislation in the USA, the 1964 15
Service, the 37
class conflict, promoting 80
differences, regional and 140
middle 107
struggle, the 63, 122
the white working 174
traitors 85
CND, the 160
Coard, Bernard 24, 45, 67
Coleman, Martin 176
Colonial Freedom, the Movement for 62
colonialism, anti- 114
Britain's record of 79
colonies, restoring independence to 71

Committee of Inquiry, the 137
Commons, select committees of the House of 44
Commonwealth history 62
settlers from the new 139
Communist culture 132
Community Relations Commission 123
relations councils 44
relations personnel 59
Relations Unit, the 175
Roots Trust, the 176
Service 176
Conrad, Joseph 114
Consequentialism 158–61
Conservative Party, racism in the 106
Cox, Caroline 7, 74
CRE (*see* Racial)
Creole 27
Crusoe's man Friday 113
Cuba 186
Culloden, survivors of 64
cultural differences 20
imperialism 178
pluralism 144
relativism 9, 25–8, 127, 132–3, 135
Curzon, Lady 69
Cypriots 35

Dale, David 7, 167
Damascus 67
Dance, E. H. 60
Davies, Jon 189
Davis, Angela 86
Defoe, Daniel 113
Delhi 68
democratic principles, a threat to 146
process, threat to the 2
society, destruction of the 37
democracy, liberal 10
the values of a pluralistic 146
Depression of the 1930s, the 66
Deptford Fire, the 76
DES, the 145
Descartes 159
Diego 65

Index

discrimination against non-whites 19
  effects of 192
  elimination of 15
  negative 16
  positive 5, 16, 84–5, 93
  positive or negative 25
discriminatory practices 21, 34
Dissolution, the 99
Djilas, Milovan 43
Doctor Dolittle 110
Dorsey, Thomas 172
Dragon's Teeth 97
Drake, Francis 65
Dundee 66
Dutch Reformed Church in South Africa 72

economic exploitation 84
  historians 191
education, advocates of multicultural 10
  anti-racist 1, 10, 90, 92, 160–7
  attack on 33
  in London, multi-cultural 97
  inspectors, multi-ethnic 59
  Marxist sociology of 192
  multi-cultural 45–7, 108, 127, 141
  or indoctrination 75
  political 146
  programme, BBC's multi-ethnic 100
  religious 143
  traditional 165
Education Act, the 1944 143
  Authority, the Inner London (*see* ILEA)
  Committee, Berkshire 17
  for Equality (EE) 17
  the Advisory Committee for Multi-Cultural 17
educational opportunity, access to 45
  philosophy 9
  validity of school policies 4
Edward III 99
Egypt, dead culture of 134
Eldridge, Professor John 118
empirical evidence, neglect of 35

Enclosure Acts 67
England, the law of 130
English Channel, the 64
  culture 134
equal opportunity 25
equality 23
  of opportunity 5, 15, 140, 147
  racial 53
Equiano 65
Erskine 177–8
establishment sentiments, anti- 9
ethnic and cultural differences 37
  minorities 19, 35–6, 120–21, 141
  minorities, economic advancement of 93
  minority, the 181
  minority communities, the 54
  minority, cultural identities of the 139
  minority cultures, the 140
  minority groups 80, 146
  minority problems 138
Eurocentric bias 38
Eurocentrism 63
European history, importance of 142
Evans, I. O. 67
exploitation, forces of 85
extermination, mass 74
extremism, counter- 32
  the rise of 32

Falklands War 75–6
family, one-parent 195
  values, the influence of 47
fanaticism 51, 154
Fanon, Frantz 86
Fereira, Michael 76
Fire, the Great 100
Flew, Professor Antony 5, 15, 118
France, 64–5, 134, 191
free opinion, threat to 2
  society, price of a 196
  speech 44
freedom, attack on 8
  defenders of 196
  inconvenience of 145

of inquiry 26
of speech 26, 128
of writing 26
price of 81
Friedman, Milton 189

Gandhi 71
Gandhi, Mrs 69
Garvey, Marcus 176
GCHQ 7
    trade union issue 77
genetic differences 29
genocide in modern world 78
    policy of 74
Georgia Tom 172
German National Socialism 187
Germany, culture of 134
    National Socialist 78
    Nazi 188
Ghana 181
Gibson, Dr Ashton 174–5
Gilder, George 188
GLC 155, 180
    anti-racists 82
    feminism 176
    Women's Committee 176
Goebbels, Dr 72
Gospel Music, Father of American 172
    Music in Britain 176
government, politicisation of local 188
Grant, Bernie 93
Greece 35, 64, 131, 134, 161
Gregory 64
Grenada 24
group conflict, inter- 80
Guardian, The 72
Gulag Archipelago, labour camps at the 78
Gwynne, Jessica 167

Hackney Black People's Defence Organisation 89
Hall, Linda 7, 97
Hall, Professor Stuart 83
Hampshire, Stuart 157

Hamlyn, D. W. 168
Handsworth, riot in 72
Harding, D. W. 114
Harlem 20
Hastie, Tom 5–6, 59
Hausa 104
Health Service, National 44
    Indian doctors in the 248–9
Henry VIII 99
heroin-addiction, growth of 50
Herrenvolk 62
heterosexism 162
history, ethnic prejudice in human 187
    importance of British and European 142
    Marxist view of 55, 91
    race and propaganda 59
    revolution in the teaching of 59
    rewriting 43
Hitler 61, 77, 187–8
Holland, culture of 134
holocaust, the 75, 77–8
    concept of the 74
    horrors of the 187
Holy Land, the 64
Honey, John 31
Honeyford case, the 82
    multi-cultural views of 118
    Ray 6, 8, 16, 43, 62, 82, 119, 167
How Racism Came to Britain 6, 7, 62, 67, 69, 70, 72, 92
Huckleberry Finn 8, 110–13, 119, 177
Hull University 64
human rights, denial of 76
humanity, crimes against 78
Huxley, Aldous 59, 161

Ibos from Biafra 179
immigrant groups 24
    pressure groups 59
    worker, the 88
immigrants, Asian 143, 191
    British treatment of 73
    Chinese 36

non-white 18–19
immigration, coloured 142
  control of non-whites 191
  history of 93
  laws 192
  non-white 192
  peaks for the Germans 36
    for the Irish 36
    for the Italians 36
    for the Russians 36
  the traumas of 170
  to Britain, history of 89, 147
imperialism, the evils of 62
Incas, the religion of the 128
India 68
  British control of 68
  British ruling class in 69
  Indian cottage industry 67
  culture 134
  independence 69
Indianisation, policy of 70–71
India's struggle for independence 70
Inquisition, the New 117
integration, slow process of 141
intelligentsia, fear among the 107
ILEA (Inner London Education Authority) 1, 17, 24, 34–5, 37, 80, 83, 97, 142, 149, 177
  anti-racists, the 84
  anti-racist strategies 3
  anti-sexist strategies 3
  documents 23, 25
  the Learning Resources Branch of 7, 74
  left-wing complexion of 77
IRA, actions of the 76
  bombers 172
Ireland 64
Irish, the 19, 35
IRR (*see* Race Relations)
Islam 144
  culture of 133
Islamic architecture, the glories of 66
Islington, persecutions in 145
Italy 64
  American 5th Army in 66

Jamaica 66, 194
Jamaican culture 82
Jamaicans 169
Jamshedpur 69
Japan, culture of 134
  customs of ancient 128
Jeffcoate, Robert 141, 161
Jensen 22
Jewish people, extermination of 74
Jews, the 35
  treatment of 78
Johnson, Dr 65
Jonson, Ben 158
Judaeo-Christian values 128
Judaism 128
  culture of 133
judgementalism, the crime of 82
justice, mandates of 16
  rules of 16
  social 45, 59
  system of criminal 16

Kalhana 68
Kant 160–1
Kelly, Jimmy 76
Kenyan Asians, expulsion of 87
Kenyatta, Jomo 87, 176
Kerridge, Roy 10, 169
Kierkegaard 156–7
King, Martin Luther 53, 176
Kipling, Rudyard 134
Klein, Gillian 115–16
Koestler, Arthur 193–4
Koran, the 67

Labour Party, black sections in the 50, 86
  militancy within the 85
  corridors of power 124
labour, migrant 88
Lancashire cotton workers 62
language, race and colour 97
  state-controlled 43
Lashley 45
law courts, the 44

LEA (Local Education Authority) 1, 23, 76, 140, 143
 advisors 4
 Birmingham 1
 Bradford 1
 Brent 1
 Coventry 1
 Newcastle 1
 Reading 1
Leavis, F. R. 110, 113, 164
Left, the white 176
left-wing phraseology 176
Leninist organisations 88
 tradition 89
Levy, David J. 8, 117
Lewis, Primila 69
Liberation 164
Little Black Sambo Stories 108
Little, Professor Alan 48
Livingstone, Ken 176
London University Institute of Education 32, 38
Losoko of Lagos, King 63
Lucknow University 68
Luther, followers of 53

Macbeth 158
MacIntyre, Duncan 61
McDonald, Mr Trevor 85
Mahomet 67
Majumdar, Professor D. N. 68
Manchester 169
Manchester Guardian 106
Marathas, the 68
Marco Polo, the story of 66
Marks, John 5, 6, 32
Marlow 114
Marten and Carter 67
Marx 187
Marxism 85, 169, 171, 185
 neo- 10, 186, 188
Marxist activists, effort of 124
 beliefs 39
 groups 183
 history 120
 -inspired ideology 8

 intellectuals 194
 left, the 90
 -Leninist tactic 39, 80
 monstrosity, neo- 23
 societies 186
 view of history 55
Marxists 89
 atheistical 195
 neo- 193
 revolutionary 33
Mbenzi tribe, the 71
Mediterranean, the 64
Meredith, Burgess 66
Methodist feeling, anti- 174
Methodists 170
Michael X 86–7
Middle East, the 76, 193
Miles, Robert 121–2
Militant Tendency 124
Moghul emperors, the 68
Mohammedan rule 67
Moore, Professor Robert 118–20, 122–3
moral concerns, contemporary 192
 development 163
 education 163, 164
 philosophy, tradition of 156
 relativism 133–44
 training, the traditional basis of 155
 understanding 159
morality 133, 156, 158, 165
Morell, Frances 149
Moroccans 35
Mortimer, Dr 47–8
Mount Zion Spiritual Baptist Church 179–80
mugging by young black males 194–5
Muhammed Ali 86
Mullard, Professor Chris 6, 32, 35, 37–8, 45, 49, 150
multi-cultural 9
 curriculum 4, 134
 education 129
Multi-Cultural Centre, Bristol's Horfield 4
multi-culturalism 3, 82, 142–3, 147

obstacle to 140
opposition to 82
multi-culturalist 128
  lobby, the 141
multi-culturalists, the 84–5, 129
multi-faith syllabus 144
-racial Brent 181
murder, institutionalised mass 78
  inter-racial 191
  of Asian shopkeepers
  of Tottenham policeman 190
Murray, Dr 47
music, steel-band (from Trinidad) 194
Muslim military prowess 67
  seamanship 67
  universities 67

Naipaul, V. S. 54
Napoleon 64
NATFHE 150
National Child Development Study (NCDS) 19
  Children's Bureau (NCB) 19
  Front, the 52, 174, 191–2, 195
  Health Service (see Health Service)
Nazi 158
  activities 76
  culture 132
  discussion on neo- 75
  domination 71
  extermination programme 77
  neo-52
  oppression, neo- 79
  propaganda 61
  regime 76–7
  –Soviet pact, the 78, 194
Nazis 73, 187
Nazism 188
  proto- 187
negroes and the Left, coalition of 169
Nesbit, Robert 53
Newham 8, the 76
Newsam, Peter 80
Newsam's Law 59
New Testament Church of God 173, 175, 181

Testament, 'racism' in the 114
Newton, Huey 86
New World negroes, original tribes of all 179
Nigeria 179, 183
Nigerians 181
Nixon, Jon 1, 149
Nkrumah 176
Nobel Prizewinners, America's 21
Noël, Father 179
Noël, Mother 180, 184
North Africa 64
  Muslims of 64
  American Indians 69
Northern Ireland 193
Nyere, Julius 86

Oakeshott, Michael 162
O'Keeffe, Dennis 10, 185
Okeley, William 64
Oldman, David 118
Omai from Tahiti 65
Open University, the 29
opportunity, differences in 24
  inequality of 28
Orwell, George 1, 7, 9, 193, 195
Othello 114, 132

Pakistan 49
  culture of modern 133
  the new 70
Pakistani shopkeepers, willingness of 50
Palestine, the culture of early 131
Palmer, Frank 1, 149
Parekh, Professor Bikhu 64
Patrick, Saint 64
Peace Studies 164
Peach, Blair 76
Pearce, Simon 9, 136
peasant share croppers, exploitation of 70
Penguin Education 16
Pentecostal churches 169, 171, 177, 179, 180–1
  fellowship 170

Pentecostalists 171, 174, 177
  and the Black Movement 10
  Caribbean 183
  English 171
Persia, culture of 134
Peterkin, Pastor 176
Phizacklea, Annie 121–2
Pheonix, MBE, Sybil 174
Pitt, Lord 85, 87
Plato 156–7
PLO, the 76
'pluralism' 146–7
Pluto Press, the 122
police attitudes to blacks 59
  'brutality' 194
  campaign against the 39, 191
  indifference 7
political activism 124, 158
  agitation 1, 6, 38
  campaigns, left-wing 18
  censorship 76
  conspiracy 3
  education 145–7
  movements 32
  philosophy 130
  revolution 2, 8
  prisoners 86
politics, ethnic 32
  street 52
polygamy 128
Polynesia, the morality of 128
Positive self-images 166
Positivism 161
Powell, Enoch 190–1
prejudice of white landlords 169
'proletariat', the 169
propaganda 7
Prophet 45
protest marches 170
Protestant 107
Protestants, Jamaican 195
Pudd'n'head Wilson 116

Queensland Figaro 65

Racial Action Adjustment Society, The 89

Discrimination, The Co-ordinating
  Committee against 89
Equality, Commission for (CRE)
  15, 18–19, 21, 23, 49, 169
racial awareness movement 169
  conflict 33
  discrimination 1, 25, 36, 48, 151
  harmony 85, 120
  hatred, institutionalised 188
intimidation 151
  liberation, quest for 195
  marriage, intra- 189
  Marxism 170
  mischief 82
  prejudice 54, 65, 90, 151, 162–3,
    189, 192, 194, 196
  politicians, the 171
  politics 169, 174
  strife 73, 141
  tensions, heightening of 6, 33, 79,
    120, 122
  victimisation 1, 155, 162
  violence in London in 1958 38
race and racism, obsessions with 28
  -awareness training 1, 45–6, 84,
    151, 152, 154
  industry's policies 59
  industry's published material 61
  lobby, devotees of the 49
Race Relations Act, the 1976 5, 15
  Relations Board, the 123
  Relations, Institute of (IRR) 6–7,
    61–4, 67, 70, 72, 79, 82–3, 90,
    120
  Relations, Marxist-dominated
    Institute of 38
  Relations Policy and Practice Unit
    32
race relations 91
  relations doctrine 44, 55
  relations, free speech on 147
  relations in Britain 193, 195
  relations industry 6, 16, 54, 59–60,
    62, 65, 67, 71, 73, 93, 195
  relations lobby 5, 44, 51, 54
  relations, Marxist militants of 22
  relations, propagandist, the 50

relations rhetoric 50
relations, the literature of 45
relations, threat to good 52
relations, vested interests in 20
races, relations between the 190
racism and black resistance 123
   and capitalism in Britain 38
   anti- 29, 32, 84, 117, 124, 145, 149, 151, 154–6, 164, 166–7, 191, 194
   -awareness 1, 4, 45, 106, 151, 163
   contemporary issues of 78
   definitions of 33–4
   doctrine of anti- 51
   doctrine of benign 53
   elimination of 110
   in children's books 8
   in employment practices 36
   in English studies, anti- 106
   in local government, anti- 120
   institutionalised 1, 6, 22, 37, 82, 84, 90, 93, 137, 146
   malign 53
   Marxist version of anti- 120
   moral argument against 151
   non- 154
   neo-Marxist conception of 29
   of Britain, endemic 150
   of the white British 189
   overt and covert 178
   perception of 152
   repudiation of 28
   scientific 118
   the ideology of anti- 121
   the institutionalisation of 122
   the mythology of British 185
   the wrongness of 160
   theory and practice of 147
   true sense of 23
   weapon of 88
   white 18–19
   writings on 187
   unconscious 1, 7, 84, 97, 151–2
   unintentional 1, 145, 151, 152
racist academics, anti- 124
   attitudes, anti- 162
   campaigns, anti- 38
   crusade, anti- 195
   curriculum, anti- 4, 151
   discourse, anti- 153
   doctrine, anti- 2, 137
   education, anti- 5, 160, 167
   elect, anti- 82
   fiction, anti- 164
   genocide 78
   images in children's books 108
   intervention, anti- 188
   literature, purges of 119
   material 8
   mentality 154
   movement, the anti- 32, 193
   network, anti- 83
   philosophy, the anti- 145
   policies, anti- 3
   position, the anti- 33, 38
   proposals, anti- 4
   rhetoric, anti- 6, 43
   struggle, the anti- 122
   teachers 195
   the anti- 161
   writing, anti- 178
Racist Group, the Sheffield anti- 150
   White British Society 25
racists, the activities of the anti- 121
   agenda of the anti- 33
   anti- 8, 34, 37, 47, 85, 114, 119
   non- 3
   publications of the anti- 38
Rastafarianism, fashion for 170
Rebellion, the 1745 64
Reformation, the 53
   the Counter- 51
religion, freedom of 128
religious, education 143–4
   faith, decline of 10
   values, the decline in 195
respect for persons 155
revolution 176
   not education 32, 38
revolutionary cause, black service to the 85
Richard III 61
riot in Brixton 121
   in Tottenham 121, 150

208   *Index*

    in Handsworth 121
riots, inner-city 120
    racial 72
Roach, Colin 76
Rome 64, 131, 134
Rose, Professor Steven 29
Russell, Bertrand 156, 166
Russia 64, 186
Rutter, Professor 47

Saint Gallen University 100
Saklatvala, Shapurji 66
Salisbury Review, The 8, 118
Sartre, J. P. 160–61
Savery, Jonathan 4
Sawyer, Tom 113
school curriculum, revolution in the 45
Scottish coalmines, serfdom in 64
science, natural 117
Science, the British Association for the Advancement of 117
scientists, natural 118
Scruton, Roger 8–9, 118, 127, 167
SDP, the 4
Seale, Bobby 86
Searle, Chris 164
Secrets Act, Official 76
semite, anti- 160
Semitism, anti- 74, 161, 187
sexual liberation, quest for 195
Shakespeare 8, 114, 132, 158
Sharp, Granville 65
Shreir, Sally 43
Sikhs 23
Singh, Charanjit 4
Sivanandan, Dr Ambalvaner 7, 82–93, 120–22
slave market, Roman 64
    markets, East African 63
    trade, the 92, 142
    trade, the African 68
    trade, the Atlantic 63–4, 98
    trade, prohibition of the 38
    traders 72
slavery 63, 92

    Christian movement's opposition to 65
    in the British Empire 65
    movement in Britain, anti- 65
    rationalisation of 53
slaves, the European 64
social conflict 37
    engineering 9, 142
    justice and equality 146
    system, the 23
    tension 7, 80
    unrest 8
socialism 195
    case against 188
    Marxian 193
Socialism, realities of 81
Socialist Methodists 174
socialist tyranny 186
Socialist Workers' Party, the 122
Socialists, the International 122
Sociology of Knowledge, the 162
Sofer, Anne 4
Solomon, Job ben 65
Sounder 109, 110
South Africa 188
    agitation about 194
    apartheid 53, 55, 192
Soviet camps 77
    crime 187
    Europe, slum bureaucracies of 186–7
    prisons 78
    -style liquidation 77
    tyranny 43
    Union, Marxism and the 194
    Union, racial record of the 187
Sowell Thomas 20, 24, 28, 32–4, 37, 48, 55, 89, 188
Spain 64, 134
Spectator, The 118
Spinoza 130, 156–7
Stalin trials, the 194
Standard English 27
Stepney, Bishop of 8
Stereotypes 62, 63, 177
Stone, Maureen 45

Index

Strathclyde 117
  conference, the 118
Syrian government, excesses of the 76
Swahili 104
Swann, Lord 136-9, 141-7
  Committee, the 45, 47, 50
  Report, the 2, 9, 48, 136

Tanzania 186
Tanzanian economy, the 86
Tata family, the 69
Taylor, Theodore 109
teacher training 145, 147
Terrorism Act, Prevention of 76
TES, the (*Times Educational Supplement*) 3-4, 54, 64, 108, 118-9, 150, 154
Times Higher Education Supplement 105, 118
Tin-Tin 119
Thatcher, Mrs Margaret 73, 106, 173, 177
Third World, the 65, 92
  Lobby, the 143
  peasantries 186
tolerance, promotion of 9
threat to 2
totalitarian politics 191
  temptation 147
Toxteth, riot in 72
trade union legislation 76-7
tribe-spotting 179
Trinidadians 169
Trotskyite left, the 124
truth, the pursuit of 166
Tudor military *coup d'état* 61
  propaganda 61
Turkish 35
Turnbull, Colin 27
Twain, Mark 110, 112-13

Uganda 50, 87
  refugees from 22
UK, education in the 7
Unconscious, the 153
Uncle Tom's Cabin 111, 116

unemployment 190-91
  youth 19
unequal relations 34
unions, trade 44
United Nations, the 90
Urdu 27
USA, the 20-21, 36, 48, 64, 110, 185, 188
USSR, extermination programmes in the 77
USSR's role in National Socialist Germany 78
utilitarianism 158

value judgements 25-6
  philosophy of 26
Vietnam 49
Vietnamese 35
Vincent de Paul, Saint 64

Waldorf, Stephen 77
Wallace, John H. 110-14
Waltham Forest, persecutions in 145
Weil, Simone 156, 165
Welfare Party line 178, 181
West African 'Spiritual Church' 181
  Africans 183
  Bengal Marxist government 70
  Indian 19
  Indian children, academic performance of 82
  Indian Christians 50
  Indian churches 184
  Indian failure 47, 170
  Indian family life 48
  Indian newspapers 177
  Indian organisations 47, 89
  Indian Pentecostalists, political attitudes of 173
  Indian pupils 51
  Indian underachievement 137
  Indians 35, 174-5
  Indians, black 36
  Indians, British 87, 169-70
  Indians, school performance of 138
  Indies Federation 21

Western civilisation 136
　European societies 62
'White', favourable connotations of 103
White, Mr and Mrs 76
white prejudice 138
　races, hatred of the 193
Whiggism, trans-Atlantic version of 185
Wight, Isle of 64
Wilberforce 38
Willesden, New Testament Church of God at 175
Winch, Peter 168
Wise, Valerie 176
Wittgenstein, Ludwig 156–8
Wood, the Right Reverend Wilfrid 183

Woodruff 45
World Council of Churches 176, 180, 182–3
　Studies 164
　War I, 102
　War II, 71, 78
Wyndham, John 113

Yoruba language 182
　tribe, pagan rituals of the 179
Young World Books 164

Zinkin, Taya 106
Zionist conventions 179
Zionists, the 181
　British anti- 187
　generation of 78
Zwingli, followers of 53